A New Psychotherapy
for Traditional Men

Gary R. Brooks

A New Psychotherapy for Traditional Men

Jossey-Bass Publishers
San Francisco

Copyright © 1998 Gary R. Brooks

Jossey-Bass books and products are available through most bookstores. To contact Jossey-Bass directly, call (888) 378-2537, fax to (800) 605-2665, or visit our website at www.josseybass.com.

Substantial discounts on bulk quantities of Jossey-Bass books are available to corporations, professional associations, and other organizations. For details and discount information, contact the special sales department at Jossey-Bass.

For sales outside the United States, please contact your local Simon & Schuster International Office.

TCF Manufactured in the United States of America on Lyons Falls Turin Book. This paper is acid-free and 100 percent totally chlorine-free.

Library of Congress Cataloging-in-Publication Data

Brooks, Gary R., date.
    A new psychotherapy for traditional men / Gary R. Brooks. — 1st ed.
        p.   cm.
    Includes bibliographical references and index.
    ISBN 0-7879-4123-9 (acid-free)
    1. Men—Mental health.   2. Individuality.   3. Psychotherapy.
4. Identification (Psychology).   5. Emotions.   6. Interpersonal
relations.   I. Title.
RC451.4.M45B76   1998
616.89'14'081—dc21   97-45455

HB Printing   10 9 8 7 6 5 4 3 2 1   FIRST EDITION

Contents

For Alan Johnson, who was taken away much too soon,
for Roy Scrivner, who helped make it okay
for men to love one another,
and for Gordon, a brother who has always been there.

Introduction

There have been many defining moments in my erratic development as a psychotherapist, but none more compelling than the moment I realized that Leon,[1] a huge and very unhappy Vietnam combat veteran, intended to throw me through the wall of the group therapy room. After heaving one chair to his left, he launched a second chair to his right with a sudden kick from one of his powerful legs. As he advanced toward me, I realized that in Leon's mind, I had come to represent everything he had been fighting against. "You all taught me how to kill! I'm fuckin' good at that! I don't wanna kill anymore! I wanna build. I wanna be productive. I don't want to destroy any more! When are you all gonna teach me how to be a goddamn man?!"

Not a complete fool, I could see that I had been a bit too aggressive in helping Leon get in touch with his anger and rage. (The Gestalt "uncovering" techniques that had seemed so impressive in graduate school seemed pretty problematic here.) Even though almost all my mental energy was committed to finding a safe way out of my immediate dilemma and defusing this explosive situation, at some level I was also making new realizations. Number one—never underestimate the degree of frustration and rage in many men's lives. Number two—don't assume that all men can moderate this

1. All names have been changed to protect clients' privacy.

rage once it has been aroused. Number three—I will be of minimal therapeutic value to any man who sees me as one of the enemy.

Even today, I'm not completely sure what prevented further escalation of that intense moment. My astonishment and obvious fear must have signaled to Leon that I intended to back off and leave him alone. In some way, however, he also seemed terrified at the sudden appearance of his destructive potential. He stood over me for several moments, continuing to rant, not really seeing me and not really addressing me but nevertheless needing to give voice to his considerable frustration and pain.

Then, Scotty, an African American Vietnam veteran, took charge of the situation. With great calm and purpose, Scotty moved about the room to restore order. He replaced overturned chairs and directed bewildered group members back to their seats, all the while speaking quietly to Leon with a hypnotically calming tone. Scotty may not have gone to graduate school in psychology, but he knew intuitively that it would help if Leon saw him as belonging to the same army and as fighting the same battle. At that moment, Scotty realized, far better than I did, that in spite of Leon's enormous capacity for destruction, he desperately wanted to find the right path. He wanted to fulfill the dictates of manhood and become a proud and productive man.

For the past ten years, I have fervently studied manhood and masculinity, perhaps because I wanted to learn all I could about Leon and men like him. In this endeavor, I've discovered that Leon is definitely not one-of-a-kind. Something is quite amiss in the lives of almost all contemporary men. I've found few men who have illustrated the problems as dramatically as Leon, but I've also encountered no man who has completely figured things out.

We live in a time when it is very difficult to nail down a simple definition of masculinity, to know which of many conflicting paths to follow, and to feel ultimate comfort and security with oneself as a man. My reading tells me that it was never an easy task to define manhood. But today, matters are more complex because there are no more frontiers, no damsels in distress, no tolerance for heavy-handed sexual styles, fewer "manly" jobs, and less acceptance of the homophobia and gay bashing that used to allow men a measure of crude reassurance. So, in part, this book is about the difficulties of modern manhood.

The contemporary crisis of masculinity is problematic enough, but for psychotherapists, the challenges are greater yet. Most men, by virtue of their (our)[2] internalized ideas of manliness, have major impediments in resolving this crisis. Trained to suppress emotional distress, to prefer action to reflection, to avoid subtle signals of interpersonal conflict, to experience shame at any hint of failure, and to resist asking for help, most men seemed destined to do all the wrong things to quiet internal affective distress. So this book is also about the multiple self-defeating techniques that men adopt to avoid therapists' offices and examination of their inner life.

In an ideal world, the mental health community would recognize the pain and confusion of contemporary men and would accommodate to the many maladaptive ways in which men deny or avoid their pain. This recognition would help the mental health community become acutely aware of the "maleness" of men's problematic behaviors. It would lead to the creation of gender-sensitive therapy interventions that are compatible with men's avoidant and resistant style.

But this simply has not taken place. Even in a profession that has been dominated by men and by androcentric perspectives, a field that has recently been challenged to acknowledge the unique perspectives of women, there has been no appreciable recognition of the special perspectives of traditional men. There has been little

2. Because I believe that almost all men share a number of core issues, I try, whenever feasible, to include myself as part of the population being described. Therefore, even when I refer to men as "they" or "them," the reader should not assume that I am excluding myself.

effort to create therapy approaches that are geared toward men's perspectives. This book attempts to redress that oversight.

Over the past two decades, I have been a fortunate listener to the stories of a wide range of troubled men. Like many therapists, I have heard about the common struggles of relatively successful men who have encountered disappointments or discovered areas of unfulfillment. I've met with corporate men, professional men, managers, and entrepreneurs. Many of these men have recognized the need to change and have shown willingness to seek help. But I have also been lucky enough to witness the struggles of a different population of men, men more like Leon.

Because of both my personal background (blue-collar) and my primary professional work setting (a Veterans Affairs, or VA, hospital), I've had the rich opportunity to experience the world through the experiential lens of working-class men, military veterans, homeless and estranged men, substance abusers, violent men, and men accused of sexual misconduct. These men, closely attached to traditional definitions of masculinity, have felt the world turn upside down. Many have spent their lives pursuing a masculine ideal that has continually eluded them. Others believe that they have met the standard, only to find it shifting and the world demanding something more or something different. Many are angry and bitter; almost all are confused.

Regardless of their affective state, their resistance is manifest. They are not about to consider psychotherapy as a possible solution to their problems. Instead of viewing the therapist's office as a place of understanding and compassion, these men see it as a place to experience hostile rejection, shame, and alienation.

When I first began working with traditional men, I felt it urgent that they follow my directives and change themselves. I expected them to gain a quick appreciation of introspection, tenderness, sensitivity, and personal vulnerability. When these men resisted, I tried harder. They were unimpressed. Frustrated and discouraged, I began to listen rather than to preach. Intrigued by what I was hearing, I embarked on a project to begin recording and cataloging their concerns.

This new listening posture changed everything. Although somewhat perplexed by my ignorance, these men generally were quite receptive to questions like "What is a man supposed to be?" Most of them enthusiastically approached the project of educating me about the inner workings of traditional men's lives. (They assumed that as a professional I had lived a life free from problems even remotely like theirs.) The more they talked, the more *we* learned. As I listened to them, I became much better at accessing the core elements of my own traditional masculine socialization. Therapy shifted dramatically; whereas it had begun as a tedious process of hammering deviant men into more socially acceptable people, it turned into an exhilarating process of jointly discovering common problems rooted in rigid cultural expectations.

Ultimately, I discovered how to help and how not to be viewed as the enemy. When we talked about our culture and about the stresses of masculinity, I found myself joining these men in a way never before possible. I was behind the lines with them, struggling against a common opponent.

This way of relating to male clients should not be seen as an excuse for abandoning appropriate clinical responsibility or for allowing men to behave inappropriately in the world. Nevertheless, in my view this approach is the key to successful work with traditional men. Thus, another reason I have written this book is to convey the benefits of this way of viewing male clients.

This shift in perspective makes a phenomenal difference in my work with traditional men. The approach alone, however, will not help men adjust to the sweeping transformation in their lives. Insight and contextual awareness are critical steps, but cannot, by themselves, produce all the needed changes. Over the past several years, I've scoured the new men's studies literature, consulted with colleagues, and experimented with new behaviors in my own life to discover creative ways to translate my ideas into changes in men's lives. I've found that these new perspectives almost invariably generate major affective benefits; men are enormously relieved to realize that their problems are not unique and not totally the result of their personal failings. They are invigorated to discover connections with other men and they enthusiastically embrace mutual support and a joint commitment to change.

But their enthusiasm is not enough. They must channel it into cognitive, behavioral, and relationship changes that match the practical and political realities for men *and* women. Unless careful planning goes into psychotherapy, men's zeal can be dampened by disappointment and frustration. Without an appreciation of women's perspectives, men's increased connection can become a powerful force of political backlash and a retreat into misogyny. Psychotherapy with traditional men needs to be integrated with contextual awareness, forming a strategic plan to help men join with women to shape lives that empower each other. A desire to communicate this vital point is another important reason that I have written this book.

I have come to believe that psychotherapy with traditional men is much more complicated than simply adding a few new techniques to one's therapy repertoire. Much as feminist therapy requires a fundamental change in one's ideas about the roots of women's problems and the processes of psychotherapy, a perspective on traditional men also requires that we therapists consider the many ways in which we interact with client problems. We cannot be apolitical; if we are not part of the solution, we are part of the problem. We are agents of a gendered culture and *must* be gender-aware therapists. To accomplish this, we probably will need to change ourselves, to reconsider our previous comfort with a very solid barrier between clients and therapists, and to rethink any ideas about a rigid boundary between therapy and the larger culture. We will need to consider the intersection between psychotherapy and social action as we endeavor to create new social contexts and environments. This is a final reason I have chosen to write this book—I'd like see psychotherapists become part of the effort to create a better world for women and men.

In the following chapters, I present a comprehensive plan for intervening effectively with traditional men. In Chapter One I review the most relevant aspects of the contemporary crisis of masculinity, and in Chapter Two I examine the primary causes of men's resistance to psychotherapy. In Chapter Three I identify what are, in my opinion, the core elements of all psychotherapy interventions for traditional men. Chapters Four and Five highlight the benefits and pitfalls of group and relational therapies. In Chapter Six, I give special attention to the issue of therapist gender, suggesting ways to maximize the benefits inherent in various pairings of therapists and clients. Finally, in Chapter Seven, I outline a framework for future change that should allow men and women, both as clients and therapists, to challenge the most constraining features of gendered culture and to realize more fully their human potential.

Acknowledgments

Because I've been writing this book for more than six years, there have been moments when I have wondered if I would ever complete it. Once again, Alan Rinzler, that tyrant in sheep's clothing, has insisted that I focus my energies and get the job done. For that, I am very grateful.

I'm also very thankful for a number of professional colleagues who continue to support and critique my work, stimulate my thinking, teach me stuff I really need to know, and provide a national friendship network I desperately need: Ron Levant, Louise Silverstein, Glenn Good, Don-David Lusterman, Roy Scrivner, Lenore Walker, Lucia Gilbert, Roberta Nutt, Mike Gottlieb, Neil Massoth, Phyllis Frank, Bob Brannon, and Mike Andronico.

At home, I've been fortunate to have several very special psychologist friends who have been a welcome refuge from an environment increasingly unfriendly to psychologists. I'm very grateful to John Cooney, Betty Clark, and David Rudd for being such good pals.

I'm fortunate to have had several bosses who have been appreciative of my efforts. Special thanks are extended to Jason Worchel, Jack Burke, and Joanne Malina.

I also appreciate the work of several others who have given me especially useful insights into the interplay between gender and psychotherapy: Laura Brown, Beth Erickson, Murray Scher, Dorothy Cantor, Judith Jordan, Robert Pasick, Bill Pollack, Kenneth Solomon, and Robert Silverberg.

Over the past twenty-five years I have been very lucky to have worked with a number of traditional men who were willing to expose their inner pain. Their anguish is deserving of greater compassion from both the mental health community and the public at large. Thank you, George, Jesse, Billy, Buck, Ron, Harry, Norman, and Jim. I consider you to be brothers and friends. Thanks to you I have become a better therapist and person.

My mom, who has always been a major supporter, is now receiving support herself from her new husband, Allen Marshall. Allen, thanks for all you do. Once again, I'm deeply grateful for the love and support of my wife, Patti, and my daughters, Ashley and Allison.

1

The Contemporary Crisis
of Masculinity
Why Men Need Psychotherapy

There is great concern about the state of modern manhood. Whether one studies the popular culture or the professional literature, the signs of alarm are very much the same. In February 1994, *Time* magazine ran a cover story entitled "Are Men Really That Bad?" The title alone suggests that the prestige of masculinity is in steep decline. Mainstream films, from *Thelma and Louise* to *Waiting to Exhale* and *First Wives' Club,* speak forcefully about women's frustrations with men. Humorous attacks on men's foibles are the staple of television programs such as *Home Improvement* and *Men Behaving Badly,* as well as Rob Becker's hit stage production *Return of the Cave Man.* John Gray (1992) has sold millions of books by suggesting that men are from a different planet, and many others have struck it rich by suggesting new ways for women to avoid problematic men (Stephenson, 1991; Norwood, 1985).

In another vein, Robert Bly has become a national cult figure with his mythopoetic men's retreats, his lectures about how "female energy" endangers manhood, and his call for increased attention to "the male mode of feeling." In the past few years the Promise Keepers, a socially conservative group of Christian men, have attracted an enormous following by calling for men to reclaim their traditional role as family leaders.

In the professional literature, psychologist Ronald Levant has argued that "American manhood is in crisis" and that the "traditional code of masculinity [is] in a state of collapse" (1994, p. 1). According to psychiatrist William Betcher and psychologist William Pollack, "We live in a time of fallen heroes. The monuments built of men, by men and for men have tumbled. Men have not just been brought to earth, their strengths put in perspective by their flaws. . . . The empire seems to be crumbling" (1993, p. 1).

In brief, we are at a critical historical juncture. Even though many men remain relatively complacent with traditional formulas, increasingly large segments of the culture have become outspoken in their criticism of traditional masculinity in general, and the behavior of certain men in particular. Many critics have suggested that the long-standing pattern of celebrating male heroes be supplemented with greater attention to problematic male behavior. Louise Silverstein and I have suggested that this problematic behavior be conceptualized as the "dark side of masculinity" (Brooks & Silverstein, 1995).

THE DARK SIDE OF MASCULINITY

Inspired by women's rights advocates, the larger culture has taken a firm stand against the worst excesses of patriarchal, chauvinistic, and misogynistic male behavior: violence, coercive sexual conduct, and irresponsibility in society and in relationships. For a fuller examination of this dark side of masculinity, I briefly review several of these phenomena.

Violence

Although there has been considerable controversy about whether the O. J. Simpson murder trial focused enough on the issue of domestic violence, it is clear that the trial brought this issue into the public eye more than ever before. This is appropriate, as men's violence against women has been overlooked for far too long.

According to Michelle Harway and Marsai Hansen (1993), several studies have indicated that one in every six wives has been hit by her husband at some point in the marriage. Despite the enormous difficulty in obtaining accurate data, most studies suggest that between one-fifth to two-thirds of men are violent in dating relationships (Straus & Gelles, 1990). The former U.S. Surgeon General identified domestic violence as the number one health problem for women in the United States.

Rape and Sexual Assault

It seems even more difficult to give accurate figures about the prevalence of rape and sexual assault. If one accounts, however, for most research about the number of women raped in their lifetime, one can put the low figure at one in twenty women and the high figure at nearly one in two. Most women are raped by intimate partners or men they know. Many men have a minimal understanding of the problem's scope. For example, almost no college men would describe themselves as "rapists," but some research shows that one-third of the college men sampled engaged in sexual contact unwanted by the woman partner, and one-fifth attempted "unwanted intercourse" (Ward, Chapman, Cohn, & Williams, 1991).

Sexual Harassment

The confirmation hearings of Supreme Court nominee Clarence Thomas moved the topic of sexual harassment into a central, and controversial, position in the national limelight. Once considered relatively rare and often excused by men as harmless fun, sexual harassment is now recognized as a serious problem, both in terms of frequency and negative consequences. For example, large-scale surveys indicate that one in two women will be sexually harassed at some point in their working lives.

Strong federal statutes and "zero tolerance" policies against sexual harassment have been implemented. Although some have complained that federal laws are an overreaction, researchers and activists counter that sexual harassment is similar to rape and sexual assault. They situate sexual harassment along a continuum of male sexual aggression and other male efforts to control women's behavior. Supporting this claim, researchers have found that sexual harassment rates are highest in work environments in which women have traditionally been underrepresented.

In *Ground Zero: The Gender Wars in the Military*, Linda Bird Francke (1997) notes that the military is rife with sexual harassment, denigration of women, and "shared male delight in publicly exhibiting the collective libido."

Male Sexual Misconduct as a Group Norm

Over the past decade, numerous high-profile men have been charged with gross sexual misconduct. Politicians (Gary Hart, Bob Packwood, Bill Clinton, Clarence Thomas, Dick Morris), entertainers (Woody Allen, Pee Wee Herman, Hugh Grant, Marv Albert), sports stars (Mike Tyson, Wilt Chamberlain), and even a televangelist (Jimmy Swaggart) have all faced public condemnation for their alleged sexual behavior. When their sexual misconduct has been exposed, these men are usually condemned as morally or psychologically flawed; few pay appreciable attention to the many ways in which they are just behaving according to dominant norms of male sexuality. Alan Gross and Bernie Zilbergeld have written extensively about how the most dominant messages that young men hear about sex celebrate promiscuity (Gross, 1978; Zilbergeld, 1992). Ron Levant and I have written about how young men hear repeatedly that nonrelational sexuality (sex without emotional attachment) is superior (Levant & Brooks, 1997).

Not only the "social construction" of men's sexuality but also the disruptive influence of many male environments has recently come into question. Peggy Reeves Sanday (1990) has written about how college fraternities encourage sexual aggression against women. Michael Messner (1992) and Donald Sabo and R. Runfola (1980) have argued similarly that organized sports environments sexualize violence and encourage aggression against women.

Substance Abuse

Alcohol abuse has long been one of the most difficult public health problems, as alcohol abusers occupy up to one-half of all hospital beds at any given time (Robertson, 1988). They attempt suicide at rates seventy-five to three hundred times those of nonabusers (Berglund, 1984). Alcohol, of course plays a major role in many automobile accidents, physical health problems, incidents of violence, and absenteeism in the workplace.

Alcohol abuse is largely a "male" problem. Estimates vary widely, but all experts acknowledge the dominance of men in the alcoholic population, with most suggesting a ratio of four or five male alcoholics to every woman alcoholic (Grant, Harford, Hasin, Chou, & Pickering, 1992). One in fifty women will become an alcoholic, whereas one in ten men will (Heilman, 1973). Drug addiction is even more of a "male" problem, as more than 85 percent of drug abusers are men (Stephenson, 1991).

Masculinity and substance abuse seem to go hand in hand. In reviewing the literature on gender and substance abuse, Ron Levant (1994) identifies several precursors of substance abuse in traditional male socialization: encouragement to take risks and flout authority, pressure to achieve, low tolerance of dependent behavior, and preference for emotional numbing as a coping style.

High-Risk Behavior

It isn't difficult to make the association between masculinity and high-risk behavior; when one pictures a high-risk activity—hang gliding, cliff diving, high-speed driving, rock climbing, or snowboarding—one pictures a male participant. For example, most contestants in ESPN's *Extreme Games* are young men.

The data support this gender stereotype, as high-risk and antisocial behaviors are far more common among young men than among young women. For example, Harris, Blum, and Resnick

(1991) show that adolescent males are much more likely to injure themselves in automobile or motorcycle accidents, diving injuries, or sports-related activities. Men are six to ten times more likely to carry a gun, be arrested for drunken driving, get into a barroom brawl, or join a violent gang (Brooks & Silverstein, 1995). Men also are four times more likely to commit suicide.

Absent Fathers

Whereas fathers of the late nineteenth and early twentieth centuries were integrally involved with their children's lives, the shift from a rural to an industrialized culture has made such involvement difficult. Emotionally uninvolved and physically absent fathers are another aspect of the dark side of masculinity. Over the past decade, a number of family researchers have suggested that men, on average, have very little to do with their children. In the late 1980s, Michael Lamb (1987), a leading expert on fathering, estimated that fathers spend only twelve minutes per day with their young children. Although other researchers have suggested that fathers' time with their children may be increasing somewhat, most acknowledge that the increase is minimal. Moreover, fathers continue to display a preference for younger children and for their sons, too often neglecting their daughters and their older sons.

Another dark aspect of fathering has been that of fathers' financial absence. Although courts award child support to more than 90 percent of all custodial mothers, only about half of them ever receive any financial help from their children's fathers (Okin, 1989).

Homelessness and Vagrancy

Some men, finding themselves completely unable to fulfill the dominant male imperatives of being the breadwinner and the family leader, give up and drop out, sometimes even to the point of becoming homeless and disenfranchised vagrants. Department of Justice figures indicate that seven of every eight vagrants are men (Brooks & Silverstein, 1995). Once they drop out, these men pose a significant challenge to mainstream culture, only infrequently reintegrating. Compassion is in short supply, although lately there has been a more empathic approach to this population, with terms such as *homelessness* replacing the older pejoratives *bum* and *tramp*. Unfortunately, according to Marin (1991), this new spirit of compassion is usually reserved for the "innocent victims," that is, women and children. By and large, homeless men continue to be viewed as asocial misfits and antisocial bums.

Inadequate Partners

More and more women have become outspoken in their criticism of many men's functioning in relationships. A decade ago, Shere Hite published *Women and Love* (1987), a stinging indictment of men's low level of emotional functioning. Hite reported that 98 percent of the women she surveyed were dissatisfied with the amount of verbal closeness and emotional intimacy they received from their male partners. Two years later, Arlie Hochschild's *The Second Shift* (1989) gave voice to another growing dissatisfaction—working women's rage at the slow pace at which men were assuming responsibility for household labor. The essence of Hochschild's message was that although a great many women have taken on enormous new responsibilities in the working world, very few men have assumed more than token responsibilities in terms of domestic chores. The dominant message of these and many subsequent books has been clear and emphatic: women, who have been doing the bulk of the tedious labor in the home *and* the great majority of the emotional work in relationships, are getting fed up. It's time for men to get with the program.

Responses to the Problems

It is difficult to know exactly how to respond to this depressingly broad litany of grievances against contemporary men. One response is to deny the problems and to blame matters on women and on a radical feminism that demeans men and exalts women. In *Backlash: The Undeclared War Against American Women* (1991), Susan Faludi eloquently describes this problematic response.

Another response is what Louise Silverstein and I have called the "aberrant male theory" (Brooks & Silverstein, 1995). This approach attempts to contain the problems by pinning them on a small number of pathological or aberrant men who are qualitatively different from the vast majority of good men.

A third response, illustrated by the recent books of William Bennett (1995) and Robert Bork (1996), acknowledges the problems but places the blame on a culturewide moral decay and a deviation from traditional values.

Finally, there are those who take an "essentialist" position. In other words, the problems are an inevitable outgrowth of biological differences between the genders (Goldberg, 1973), the way the brain is wired (LeVay, 1993), or evolutionary history (Buss, 1994).

In my opinion, these responses to the contemporary crisis of masculinity are not only inaccurate but also potentially injurious, as they work against any efforts people make to improve the situation. I believe that most modern men are in some degree of emotional distress because the definition of masculinity is changing. Some men seem to be doing pretty well as "masters of the universe," in the words of Tom Wolfe (1988). These men may continue to do well, may never encounter serious problems with traditional male role expectations, and may never enter a therapist's office. But, in my experience, these men are very rare.

Some men are accepting change, as they see how it can be beneficial to reject the more confining aspects of their male heritage. For example, some men have embraced the reality of dual-career marriages (Gilbert, 1993) and have experimented with new types of marital relationships. Some have attached themselves to the recent role of "new father," subsuming some aspects of their career to the needs of their children. Some men have joined feminist causes, and others have sought opportunities for deeper connection with other men through wilderness retreats and men's groups.

Although some men are accommodating more effectively than others, I believe that almost all men are having some measure of difficulty living out the traditional male life script. Most are in the midst of a comprehensive "gender role journey" (O'Neil & Carroll, 1988), an effort to move from anachronistic, rigid models of manhood to those that are more creative, flexible, and adaptive to the demands of modern life.

THE CRISIS OF MASCULINITY

Most men's studies writers agree that the sweeping changes in manhood are a direct outgrowth of two related forces—the women's movement and the upheaval in the connection between men and their work.

Changes in Women's Roles

Over the past thirty years, the contemporary women's movement has turned men's lives upside down. Not all women, of course, view themselves as part of the women's movement. Even fewer consider themselves "feminists." Among men, a minuscule minority would report themselves to be part of the women's movement. Yet the women's movement has had an enormous impact on their lives all the same.

Traditional patriarchal wisdom and power have been challenged in a fundamental way. Feminism has demanded a voice for women's experience and a realignment of traditional power arrangements between the genders. Women are far less likely to subordinate their emotional needs to those of men and family, and they no longer unthinkingly accept the role of emotional supporter and nurturer of the men in their lives. All women have stood to benefit, being increasingly able to determine the course of their own lives, in terms of both economic self-sufficiency and control over their reproductive choices. All women stand to gain from the demand that women be free from threats of physical abuse, sexually harassing work environments, and sexually coercive dating relationships.

Changes in the Workplace

But it's not just the direct assault of the women's movement that has put men's lives in disarray. Enormous changes have been under way in the most cherished bastion of masculinity—the workplace. For centuries, men have held almost exclusive dominion over the world of work (outside the home). When not off fighting wars, men ran the farms, factories, foundries, and corporations. That simply is not the case any longer, as a vast majority of women have entered the workforce and now earn a substantial portion of total family income (U.S. Bureau of Labor Statistics, 1991). Nearly six of every ten married women now earn an income (Gilbert, 1993, p. 262). Only 10 percent of American families now fit the traditional model of having a wage-earning husband and a homemaker wife (Gilbert, 1993).

As a result, the male "good provider" role (Bernard, 1981) has less prominence than ever. Many men resent the loss of their exclusive breadwinner role; others feel humiliated and ashamed to be violating a vow they once made to themselves: "No wife of mine will ever have to work!"

To make matters even more difficult for traditional men, the workplace itself is changing. Once, men could affirm masculinity through physical exertion, displays of strength, stamina and endurance, as well as occasional acts of courage or bravado. Whether sweating in the steel mill or repressing their fear on the "high steel" of skyscraper construction or in the mine shaft, men relied on work to help them feel "manly."

But in the latter half of the twentieth century, the economic system of the United States has shifted dramatically from manufacturing (for example, steel and plastics) to service (for example, information processing and public service). With this shift in the nature of work, greater emphasis has been placed on interpersonal skills and "the values espoused by the new male—cooperation, self-expression, and sensitivity" (Brod, 1989, p. 277). Clearly, the contemporary climate has presented radically new expectations for most traditional men.

Some men support and applaud these changes. Most men, however, have far more complex and troubled reactions. Nearly all are in a state of disequilibrium; many are bitter, angry, hurt, or resentful. Although they may not voice it clearly, many men wonder, "What the hell is going on? What do they expect from us?" Most feel that something is very wrong; they think, "I wasn't raised for this!" And they are right—they weren't. Let's review how they (we) were taught to be men.

The Traditional Male Role

Although masculinity has only recently become an object of scholarly study, there have been some pretty strong expectations of men for a long time. Tom Wolfe (1988) described the world of the early Mercury astronauts as one preoccupied with determining which men had "the right stuff." Fasteau (1974) characterized the male machine (that is, the ideal man) as "different from other beings— women, children, and men who don't measure up" (p. 29). Within Judeo-Christian theology, in which God is considered all-knowing and all-powerful, it is believed that God created *man* in his own image. (It wasn't until later that God supposedly fashioned Eve from Adam's rib.)

Aside from relatively minor variations in history and in certain cultures, there has been a well-established, uniform conceptualization of masculinity. In fact, there has been so much consensus that, until recently, "masculinity" has never received much scholarly attention. Much as fish don't realize the existence of water, men haven't really reflected much on what makes a man be a man. This has changed, however, as women have begun paying great attention to the critical role of gender in their lives. Much as feminism and women's studies have moved gender into a central place, a newly emerging field of men's studies has begun examining men's lives.

In the past two decades, considerable progress has been made in identifying and quantifying the traditional male gender role. Despite occasional differences in methodology and terminology, men's studies writers have shown great consistency in defining traditional masculinity.

Deborah David and Robert Brannon (1976) presented one of the earliest yet most enduring categorizations of the male role. According to this formulation, men are expected to adhere closely to four principal behavioral tenets:

The sturdy oak—men should be emotionally stoic and deny vulnerability.

The big wheel—men should be preoccupied with work, status, achievement, and success.

Give 'em hell—men should be forceful and interpersonally aggressive.

No sissy stuff—men should reject everything associated with femininity.

In 1982, psychologist Jim O'Neil described "the masculine mystique," which he felt programmed men toward restrictive emotionality; health care problems; obsessions with achievement and success; restricted forms of sexual behavior and expressions of affection; socialized concerns for power, competition, and control; and homophobia.

Jim Doyle (1995) has identified five primary "elements" of the male role: the antifeminine element, the success element, the aggressive element, the sexual element, and the self-reliant element.

Ron Levant (1994) described seven male role norms. These include avoidance of femininity, restricted emotionality, nonrelational attitudes toward sex, pursuit of achievement and status, self-reliance, strength and aggression, and homophobia.

MAJOR THEMES IN MEN'S LIVES

It's fairly basic knowledge among therapists that you cannot really expect to make a difference in clients' lives (or even be taken seriously) unless you know what makes them tick. That is, you must be keenly aware of the most salient themes in their lives. As a psychologist with a special interest in men's studies, I have intimately observed men as they react to the contemporary crisis of masculinity. As I noted before, my therapy practice has afforded me access to the private worlds of many troubled men.

One aspect of my experience has astonished me. Despite the enormous variations in their life circumstances, virtually every one of these men is struggling to make sense of what it means to be a man. This struggle is not always apparent, but by paying attention the clinician can uncover several poignant themes in men's lives. Over the past twenty years, as I have worked with men, some variant of these themes has always emerged. More important, whenever I explore them with men, I uncover a wealth of useful therapeutic material. More important still, when the environment is companionable and accepting, I have rarely seen a man describe his feelings about these issues in a dispassionate manner. Men feel very strongly about such issues, but usually do not have easy access to that passion. If traditional men are lectured to or told how they think or feel, they will argue. If they sense disapproval or condescension, they will resist. If they are approached with empathic curiosity, however, they will tell their stories with great urgency and enthusiasm.

In the following sections I identify the themes I've found to be most poignant for traditional men and provide a brief introduction to some of the men themselves.

Work

Butch, a forty-two-year-old unemployed construction worker has been a difficult guy to engage in my VA therapy group. There is no doubt that he is unhappy with his life situation, but when it comes to expressing his concerns, he seems lost. Equally unsure of what to do, I notice that he has come to group on returning from occupational therapy and has placed an unfinished jewelry box under his chair. I comment, "Looks like you're working on a project."

Surprised and somewhat embarrassed, he replies, "Oh, that. It's just a little something I'm working on for the missus."

At first I buy his dismissive tone, but something about his response provokes curiosity. I ask him to tell me about the project. He begins tentatively but picks up steam as he describes his work on the jewelry box.

"You know, I really don't understand it, but when I'm working on this box, I feel better than I do any other time. It just may be that it distracts me from my troubles, but I don't think it's just that. I just love the smell of the wood. I love the way it feels when I sand it smooth. I guess it just feels really good to be accomplishing something again."

Butch's simple statement seems to hit a respondent chord, as all other group members quickly echo his sentiments. Nothing feels better than working on a job; nothing feels worse than idleness.

Fortunately, at the time of that discussion with Butch, I hadn't yet read the men's studies literature about the centrality of men's work to their overall sense of well-being. As a result, I wasn't tempted to interpret or prematurely analyze Butch's disclosure. Instead, I just listened. I thought about my own sense of pride when working. I marveled at how this theme resonated among the other men and created a special sense of closeness and interconnection.

Later, as I explored the men's studies literature, I discovered that researchers had expressed similar ideas repeatedly. David and Brannon had noted how "the big wheel" dimension of masculinity emphasizes the importance men place on work and occupational success. Sociologist Jesse Bernard (1981) described the good provider role as the key element of most men's identity. Donald Bell (1982) noted that in Western society, a man's sense of self is derived mainly from his daily labor. To men, the question "What do you do?" is synonymous with "Who are you?"

All men's studies writers emphasize the importance of the work role, but in my experience, few give enough attention to social class differences. For professional, academic, and executive men, status and abstract symbols of success are critical (Thompson & Pleck, 1987). Traditional blue-collar men, however, have a more basic relationship with work. For them, work provides the *daily* opportunity to demonstrate masculinity in the form of physical strength, toughness, and the creation of a tangible product. In my view, this greater need for concrete affirmation of virility through work makes working-class males more vulnerable to the psychological losses stemming from unemployment, disability, and retirement.

Violence

Several of the group members have a history of violence but have refused to say much about their violent side. I decide to tell them my "Get off my bumper!" story. I describe the situation in which I left home for work on an otherwise uneventful morning. Not unusually stressed, I glanced into my rearview mirror to note a pickup truck right on my rear bumper. Annoyed, I turned a corner, only to find him right there again. By this time, I was really pissed and decided on the classic bumper-clearing strategy—I slammed on my brakes. It had the desired effect; stunned, he was forced to screech to a halt. But he then sped up to get back on my bumper, making all sorts of obscene gestures and seeming to mouth a ton of violent threats. I became really furious myself and gave him the one-finger salute.

At that point in the story, I stop, noting that the group is quite attuned to the mood; they are worked up and ready to go to battle. I ask them, "Why do I do this stupid shit? I'm a married man with a family to care for. This guy could have a gun and could kill me. Am I crazy, or what?"

With great relish, the group explains my behavior to me. "Hey Doc, you ain't so strange. You're just defending your turf. You can't have some guy pushin' you around or you'll be everybody's patsy someday."

We spend the remainder of the group time dissecting the situation and the multiple messages men receive about violence. Bill talks about growing up next door to the town bully, who pushed his face in the snow on a daily basis. Neil describes how surviving in the ghetto meant being willing to fight and not being seen as a "punk." Many group members remember a scene in which their fathers smacked them around when they came home crying after being beaten up. No group member seems to have much good to say about reacting nonviolently to provocation.

To the traditional man, violence is what Marc Fasteau (1975) has called the "crucible of manhood." In the area of violence, more than in any other, the respective genders are exposed to vastly different messages. Unlike young women, young men are taught that violence is a basic element in their nature and a mechanism for establishing masculinity. Failure to succeed in the frequently violent male rites of passage exposes young men to being denigrated as a "sissy," "wimp," or "little girl." Throughout their lives, men are exposed to mixed messages about violence. Although naked displays of violence are usually abhorred, violence is sanctioned in organized sports, the military, and law enforcement. In corporate America, violent impulses may be displaced through the "hostile takeover."

In the world of underclass men, the situation is especially problematic. Psychologist Janis Sanchez-Hucles (1997) has described the subculture of poverty and its continual exposure to unpredictable violence as disposing young men to the psychic numbing of posttraumatic stress disorder (PTSD), relationship problems, and a perpetuated legacy of violence. Additionally, she notes, the proliferation of youth gangs in urban environments only further promotes violence. Sadly, most young men come to feel they have no alternative but to embrace the belief that "sometimes you have to fight when you're a man."

Women

Perry, a retired real estate salesman, has been unusually quiet and withdrawn for the entire group session. When challenged by a younger member, Perry reluctantly admits that he's become very uncomfortable with the recent tone of the group, ever since the female psychology student joined as a student therapist. "Look, I'm as liberated as the next guy, but I just don't like it when a sweet young girl like Melissa [Melissa is thirty-two] is exposed to the stuff that goes on in here, especially the type of language that you guys use. For me, gutter talk isn't appropriate around women." Several guys react angrily to Perry's statement, but a few sheepishly apologize for their ungentlemanly behavior. Unable to resist the opening, I encourage the men to share their positions on this issue, as well as a range of internalized expectations about women.

In discussions, no topic enlivens men's interactions as much as the role of women in their lives. Men are socialized to hold a variety of conflicting images of women, and they spend their lives struggling to develop mature relationships with women in a patriarchal culture that promotes chivalry and misogyny. In *The Psychology of Women*, Juanita Williams (1977) describes the limited roles patriarchal cultures ascribe to women: "necessary evil," "mystery," "temptress-seductress," and "earth mother." This earth mother image acknowledges men's early dependence on women, as well as the lifelong appeal of "feminine" nurturance. Developmental theorists Nancy Chodorow (1978) and Carol Gilligan (1982) have pointed out how this pursuit of exaggerated "masculine" independence causes men to repress the "feminine" in themselves and to reject their dependency needs.

As suggested by Williams's description of the temptress-seductress role, sexuality is a particularly problematic area for men. In *The Centerfold Syndrome* (Brooks, 1995a), I have described a pattern of relationship difficulties that result from normative male socialization and from the social construction of heterosexual men's sexuality. The glorification of women as sex objects and as trophies that men win through competition denigrates women. It also creates many substantial problems for men. First, it teaches men to be voyeurs and visually obsessed sex addicts who crave validation from attractive women. Second, because men see themselves as sexual pursuers and women as the gatekeepers of sexual activity, men end up elevating women to a position of power over them. Finally, men learn to be sexual in such conflictual ways that they ultimately become unable to distinguish their need for intimacy from their need for sex.

Other Men

Tommy, Emmit, and Peter had been together in their therapy group for several weeks and had seemed especially attuned to one another's moods. Midway through a particularly downbeat session, Peter notes that Tommy seems really "bummed-out." Tommy starts to speak but is quickly overcome with emotion and hesitates. Only after Peter pushes him to continue does Tommy relate his painful story.

Several years before, as his dad was dying from cancer, Tommy had promised his dad that he would care for Artie, his mentally retarded younger brother. Of late, Artie has developed major conduct problems, and Tommy's promise to his father has become nearly impossible to fulfill. Making matters worse, Tommy, who has struggled to overcome a war-related kidney injury, has lost his job. With great anguish he describes his decision to have Artie placed in a residential treatment facility. Although Peter tries to comfort him, Tommy cannot forgive himself for failing in his duty to protect his brother.

Stimulated by Tommy's guilty revelation, Emmit begins to relate a similar story. As the oldest male in a fatherless ghetto home, Emmit, even though he was only ten himself, had felt responsible for finding food for his four younger sisters and newborn brother. With a mixture of pride and shame, he describes his late-night trips to grocery store trash bins to salvage discarded and rotting food. Like Tommy, he becomes choked up as he confesses his failure. Despite his constant efforts to keep his family intact, his younger siblings were removed from the home by the state.

Peter, obviously moved by the suffering of his friends, tries to find comforting words but is overcome by his own memories of failures.

"You know," he says, "when I was in 'Nam, I knew how to look after my guys. I knew what to do. I could watch out for them and protect them. Hell, there were times when I saw my guys under fire and I never thought twice about getting them out, no matter what the cost. But even then it doesn't always work. . . . Sometimes shit happens that you can't control . . . no matter what you do." Peter stops as he stumbles upon an especially painful memory.

This session and the several that follow it help Tommy, Emmit, and Peter become even more closely connected by their shared sense of masculine duty and their sense of past and current failures. Yet they also seem reluctant to acknowledge their connection. When Tommy fails to return from a weekend pass, Emmit and Peter are oddly cool and reserved.

Two years later, I again encounter Peter, who tells me that he's heard Tommy is gravely ill in a local hospital. I ask if he intends to visit.

He looks at me strangely, then looks away shaking his head slowly. "No, I don't think I can handle that . . . too much for me."

There are many inconsistencies in the way men relate with other men. As can be seen from the stories of Tommy, Emmit, and Peter, men are capable of such intense loyalty and commitment that they will lay down their lives for one another. Yet, when it comes to the complicated business of being emotionally intimate and revealing weakness and vulnerability, many men freeze.

Sociologist Peter Nardi (1992) has pointed out that, despite common myths about the superiority of male friendships and the "petty jealousies" that divide women, men have far fewer close friendships with other men than women do with other women. Many men find buddies for "guy" activities like poker, fishing, or drinking, but most men lose the type of close friendship they had during childhood and adolescence.

Together, competition and homophobia produce considerable problems for men in their relationships with other men (Brooks, 1995a; Pittman, 1993; Solomon, 1982b). Because men are raised to believe that masculinity is not innate but needs to be "proven," men tend to structure interactions with other men as challenges and contests. Intimacy between men is difficult, partially because it requires the admission of vulnerability, which risks the loss of the competitive edge. Additionally, because men so frequently connect intimacy with sexuality, strong emotional feelings for another man provoke an intense fear of homosexuality. Ubiquitous homophobia allows men to have buddies for hunting, sports, and drinking but few or no intimate male friends with whom they can share their deepest fears and anxieties.

Fatherhood

It starts with a simple question: "Did your dad love you?" Immediately, the group becomes intellectual and analytical. Several demand clarification, wanting to know if I mean whether he loved privately or whether he displayed it. Some differentiate between love and respect or pride. I soon notice that Jim is hanging his head and wringing his hands. When I ask him about his thoughts, he blurts out, "No, the son of a bitch never said a goddamn good thing about me! I did everything I could possibly do—all-state baseball, honor roll, and a distinguished graduate of the police academy. The day I heard that he died, I felt really empty. Why was it so hard for him to say one damn nice thing about me?"

Most men have very strong feelings about their fathers. Many feel a mixture of admiration and love. Many others feel bitterness and resentment or remote detachment. Few report a lifelong intimate and supportive relationship with their fathers, but most have spent their lives yearning for it. For men, one of the most promising developments of the past two decades has been the emergence of what Joseph Pleck (1987a) refers to as the "new father" model. In contrast to the more traditional ideas of a father as a distant breadwinner and moral overseer, this new father is expected to be present at his children's birth, more involved with them as infants, more participative in the day-to-day work of child care, and as involved with his daughters as with his sons. Despite these newly appearing patterns, the older and more restricted traditional fathering ideals prevail, especially in many working-class and ethnic minority environments.

Many factors contribute to the persistence of traditional fathering models. Joseph Pleck (1993) argues that most social institutions (for example, schools, corporations, and churches) subtly discourage fathers' involvement with children. Ron Levant (1990) has written extensively about the fathering "skill deficits" common to most traditional men. James Balswick (1988) has drawn attention to how male "emotional inexpressiveness" hampers men's ability to function fully as fathers. Additionally, because young women generally baby-sit, it has been uncommon for young men to have much exposure to nurturing roles. Finally, because most traditional fathers are fearful of producing "soft" sons, they commonly forgo sensitivity and compassion to emphasize emotional stoicism, interpersonal toughness, and competitive accomplishments.

Men and Health

The group is shocked to learn that Jeff has missed group because of emergency hospitalization. Everyone knows he is overweight and has been complaining of periodic "spells," but no one has thought of him as particularly sick. Later, Jeff's wife reveals that six months earlier, Jeff was found to have extremely high blood sugar levels. He was advised to lose at least fifty to sixty pounds, quit drinking beer, change to a low-fat diet, and start a walking program.

For quite some time the group complains about the sorry state of the medical profession, before beginning to tell comical stories about Jeff's stubbornness and unwillingness to comply with the doctor's orders. Leo admits that he is avoiding a recommended prostate exam, cracking up the group with, "It'll be a cold day in hell when I let some crackpot go deep-sea diving in my backside. Hell, last time I gave in to my wife's threats and went in for one of those things, I think he scratched my tonsils." All agree that each will probably outlive every "moneygrubbing" doctor.

The average life span of a man is eight years shorter than that of a woman. Although there have been attempts to explain shorter male lives from a biological perspective, most observers agree with gerontologist Royda Crose (1997) that the male gender role has many toxic components. Several of these are worthy of note.

Despite the common belief that women are the usual targets of violence, men are actually four times more likely to be homicide victims and one and a half times more likely to be assaulted. Because men are taught to deny their vulnerability, they are less likely to perform routine preventive health behaviors. Male discomfort with the passivity and dependence of the sick role causes them to ignore warning signs of illness and to avoid bed rest when ill (Harrison, Chin, & Ficcarrotto, 1989). Masculinity is often associated with inattention to diet and consumption of high-fat foods, as parodied in Bruce Feirstein's book *Real Men Don't Eat Quiche* (1982). Finally, the male tendency to seek "heroic" role models glamorizes high-risk behaviors such as high-speed driving, sports excesses, and alcohol consumption contests. Many observers concur with the assertion by Harrison, Chin, and Ficcarrotto (1989) that "the male sex-role may be hazardous to your health."

The Importance of the Themes

These six dominant themes in men's lives—violence, work, women, other men, fathering, and health—seem to comprise the central content of successful psychotherapy with traditional men. In fact, regardless of a man's current emotional status, I cannot imagine an unproductive discussion with him about any of these six topics. Deeply appreciating these dominant themes—the *content* of the traditional male role—is a critical first step in understanding traditional men. An additional step is appreciating the *process* of male socialization, that is, how these themes are hammered into young men's heads (and bodies).

THE TRAUMATIC PROCESSES OF MALE SOCIALIZATION: MAKING BOYS INTO MEN

I have just finished a painful workout at the Racquet Club and can't wait for a long shower and lengthy soak in the hot tub. I am amused and touched to come upon Bruce, a surgery resident and one of my racquetball partners, who is entertaining his five-year-old son. The son is thrilled to be with his dad and to have a chance to play (even though the racquet is nearly as big as he is). After I shower, I run into them again. They have finished their game and the son is ecstatic that he won one point from his dad in the third game. Bruce turned to his son and says, "I let you have that one." Stunned by this, I give Bruce a reproachful look. He responds, "Hey, nothing comes easy in life! When I was his age, my dad had me jump down to him from the mantle over our fireplace. Just as I leaped, he moved out the way. As I lay on the floor, he said, 'Let that be a lesson to you. Don't ever trust anybody in this world!'"

Because all people have experienced (and continue to experience on a daily basis) some degree of gender role socialization, the *content* of the role expectations should sound familiar. Less recognized, however, are differences in the *process* of socialization, qualitative differences in how boys and girls are trained in their gender scripts. To appreciate this subtle difference, we must first consider the nature of patriarchy and its differential valuing of women and men.

In patriarchal culture, masculinity is more valued than femininity. In the most extreme patriarchal cultures, the birth of a male child stimulates celebration; the birth of a female child stimulates disappointment or even, in some horrible scenarios, infanticide. In a patriarchal environment, masculinity comes with certain entitlements or privileges, as men as a group are overvalued, whereas women as a group are devalued. However, all men do not benefit equally from male entitlement. Some men reap considerable privilege from their masculine status, but many others receive minimal benefit or are penalized for not being "manly enough."

This "manly enough" issue is at the heart of the problem. In a wide-ranging study of cultures around the world, anthropologist David Gilmore (1990) found that masculinity is almost universally an "achieved status." That is, manhood is not granted automatically to boys as they age but must be achieved through vigorous "rites of passage" that are often terrifying and dangerous. Gilmore's central thesis—that manhood ideology makes most men feel enormously insecure and threatened—has major significance here.

For American men, manhood is never guaranteed; for men to feel secure about their worthiness, they must prove it over and over. Throughout childhood, boys are taught to reject anything that makes them appear weak or feminine, while they struggle constantly to achieve status within the community of men. Fighting, playing sports, being sexually active, taking risks, and using alcohol are commonly seen as signifying virility. Passivity, aesthetic interests, celibacy, caution, and alcohol abstinence are commonly viewed as embarrassing or shameful.

In this hierarchical value system, boys are encouraged to compare themselves with each other, always wondering if they measure up. As a result, they are prone to feeling envious of more "manly" peers and fearful of being surpassed by other boys. In this system, even the most hard-won sense of masculinity is jeopardized by the slightest brush with role failure or weakness.

In addition to these competitive pressures, boys also encounter the inflexibility of masculine role mandates. Developmental researchers have validated this, finding that role deviations in boys generate more severe sanctions than those of girls do (O'Leary & Donahue, 1978). Young girls who experiment with male behaviors are likely to be encouraged, ignored, or mildly rebuked. However, young boys who experiment with behaviors that are even remotely "feminine" are subject to harsh negative responses. Fathers, in particular, are more likely to enforce narrow gender role expectations for boys.

It can be argued that the entire process of transforming boys into men systematically deprives young men access to the full range of human potential, particularly in the area of emotional expressiveness. In his recent book about men and depression, Terrance Real (1997) describes how the traditional rearing of boys produces "the loss of the relational." Young men, expected to disavow anything considered feminine, learn to reject most forms of emotional expressiveness and vulnerability. Ultimately, Real argues, this detachment from self and others produces covert depression and a number of falsely empowering activities, including substance abuse and violence.

For many men, anger becomes the only form of emotional expression. Don Long, a developer of men's antiviolence and anger management programs, has elaborated on this destructive feature of men's socialization regarding negative affective states. In his therapy programs, he targets the "male emotional funnel system," whereby a broad range of negative emotions—fear, disappointment, hurt, jealousy, or guilt—become channeled into anger (Long, 1987). A primary task of these programs has been to help men examine their rage, identifying and experiencing the broad range of emotions formerly disguised as anger. To accomplish this, men usually need to become aware of early socialization messages that equated anger with strength and power and that linked other emotions with weakness and vulnerability.

Another men's studies researcher, David Lisak, has suggested that "empathy deficits" also provide a clue to men's propensity to experience anger and rage (Lisak, 1997). Lisak theorizes that male socialization makes the experience of emotional vulnerability so terrifying that young men feel intense distress when witnessing it in others. To cope with that distress, men learn to convert it into anger or aggressive action. In his extensive research with sexually aggressive men, Lisak found that the harsh shaming and self-denigrating common in male socialization set the stage for men to have deficient capacities for intimacy and empathy (for both themselves and others).

SIGNS OF MEN'S PSYCHIC DISTRESS

Earlier in this chapter, I detailed a range of ways in which the "dark side" of masculinity creates major problems for others. Before leaving this matter, I want to emphasize that the traditionally rigid standards of masculinity are a very bad deal for men, as well. The less obvious dark side of masculinity is the way in which contemporary men are subject to feeling immense distress and psychic pain.

Anger, Bitterness, and Frustration

The most obvious element of men's affective distress is their anger, bitterness, and frustration. To illustrate the intensity of their distress, I'd like to return briefly to Leon, the man I described at the opening of this book. Leon, as you may recall, was a working-class man who had been drafted to serve in Vietnam. Despite his honorable service there, he had been almost completely unable to find a job after his weight problems forced him to take a premature military discharge. What I did not disclose earlier but what is relevant is Leon's status as an African American man, because exposure to racial prejudice adds another layer to his bitterness. "When are you all gonna teach me how to be a goddamn man?!" With these eloquent words, Leon reveals both his intense rage and the bewilderment and hopelessness lying just beneath it.

In many ways, traditional men in general, and working-class men in particular, seem to be continually susceptible to the powerful and potentially destructive emotions of anger, bitterness, and frustration. Some of this is a direct outgrowth of the way most boys are raised and socialized regarding emotional expression. Some is an outgrowth of the way men have responded to changing gender politics. A remaining portion of this seems related to men's heightened sense of occupational insecurity, felt most intensely by working-class men.

Anger at Women

It seems that it has always been common for men to express anger and hostility toward women. From the simple No Girls Allowed sentiments of childhood to the supposedly sophisticated opinions of intellectuals ("Regard the society of women as a necessary unpleasantness of social life and avoid it as much as possible."—Leo Tolstoy, quoted in Doyle, 1995, p. 135), misogyny has long been an integral aspect of patriarchal culture. This is not a simple phenomenon, as almost all men love individual women and many men feel very positively toward women as a group. Over the past several decades, however, as women have begun to make inroads in environments formerly dominated by men, a new strain of misogyny has appeared.

As early as midcentury, sociologist Mirra Komorovsky (1940, 1976) studied unemployed men and found a "perceived loss of status following unemployment." According to her, these men displayed increased "toughness," overemphasized male authority, and were oversensitive to the slightest threats to status. She said of any such man, "Incidents which would have passed unnoticed now arouse his anger" (1976, p. 27).

Over the past three decades, women have entered the workforce in unprecedented numbers. Currently, less than 20 percent of all men are exclusive breadwinners, with the percentage even lower among working-class families (Gilbert, 1985). This new development has hardly gone unnoticed by traditional men, who likely represent a sizable portion of the antifeminist audiences of Rush Limbaugh and Phyllis Schaffly. In the early 1990s, Susan Faludi

(1991) documented reactionary trends in the media, fashion industry, and public and private sectors that have added further fuel to traditional men's "backlash" against women.

Not surprisingly, much of this culturewide dissatisfaction with women's new roles surfaces in many working-class marriages. In their volume about the interaction of gender and stress, Rosalind Barnett and Grace Baruch (1987) note that this shift in the division of labor has had a pronounced effect on the level of psychological distress in marriages. "Marital strain appears to be the cost, at the least the short-term cost, of current social redefinitions of family roles" (p. 140).

Because hostility toward women is so deeply embedded in the fabric of traditional men's lives, it must be discussed in therapy. This isn't difficult, however, as I have generally found that all-male groups will enthusiastically embrace the topic with even the slightest provocation. Even men who profess nothing but the highest regard for women will commonly shift from an egalitarian posture to a much more skeptical one when they enter a safe, all-male environment.

The Emotional Distress of the Underclass

Most recent writing about men has focused substantially on the political benefits of patriarchal manhood: entitlement, power, and privilege. This is appropriate because men, as a group, have considerable power in the public realm. But one of the striking revelations of men's studies research has been that most men feel quite powerless in their private lives. Michael Kimmel (1994) has referred to this as "a paradox in men's lives, a paradox in which men have all the power yet do not feel powerful" (p. 135).

This situation is even more complex for underclass or marginalized men. The notion of patriarchal privilege is far more applicable to white, heterosexual men of the middle and upper classes than it is for working-class men. Although patriarchy does provide even them with a sense of privilege over children and women, this is counterbalanced by deep shame about their inadequacy in relation to other men.

In the 1970s, Richard Sennett and Jonathan Cobb (1973) wrote eloquently about "the hidden injuries of class." Lillian Rubin (1976), in an examination of the stresses of life in working-class families, argued that the American myth of equal access to the rewards of competitive culture sets the stage for a "devastating self-image." Rubin found that working-class men "tend to deal with this injury to personal dignity by containing their anger and pain. . . . Often, however, it's not enough; it doesn't work. Some find the respite they need in angry explosions, some in deep withdrawals. Again and again, the men and women I met recall parents, especially fathers, who were taciturn and unresponsive" (p. 36).

Psychologist Richard Majors and sociologist Janet Billson, in their examination of class injury to African American men (Majors & Billson, 1992), have described the mechanism of "cool pose," which is a survival strategy involving exaggerated postures of anger and hostility. These authors' ideas echo those of anthropologist Elliot Liebow (1980), who found lower-class African American men to be deeply troubled but likely to conceal these feelings behind a fictional presentation of themselves as "hypermasculine supermen." Lee Rainwater put the class issue in perspective with his statement that "the identity problems of lower class persons make the soul searching of middle class adolescents and adults seem rather like a kind of conspicuous consumption of psychic riches" (quoted in Pleck & Pleck, 1980, p. 376).

Even military service, which has historically offered underclass men vocational alternatives, has become a source of resentment. The inequities of the Vietnam era draft and the culturewide animosity that the war generated have left many veterans feeling unhappy and grossly unappreciated.

Guilt and Shame

Although anger is the most obvious emotion we see in contemporary men, the majority experience many other forms of psychic distress. Perhaps because women have been taught to take excessive responsibility for the well-being of loved ones, we are more likely to associate guilt and shame with women. Depression, which is far more common among women, is typically viewed as a product of women's tendency to *internalize* blame, whereas aggression and acting out are thought to result from men's tendency to *externalize* these uncomfortable feelings.

The available works about therapy with men tend to focus more on men's anger and grief than they do on shame and guilt. It is not that men don't have considerable difficulty with shame and guilt. Rather, these feelings are so painful that men will do almost anything to avoid dealing with them directly. Rarely have I seen men spontaneously acknowledge more than the most superficial sense of guilt. Men's socialization encourages them to inflate their self-worth and adopt a veneer of arrogant self-confidence. Because any form of criticism can be viewed as an affront to a man's need to be a total success, men tend to be hypersensitive and overreactive. Guilt and shame are typically hidden behind walls of denial, blame, or a substance-induced emotional numbness. However, gentle probing frequently uncovers an abundance of deeply painful guilty feelings that have been assiduously pushed out of awareness.

There are multiple reasons that men are prone to feel guilty. The masculine code emphasizes competition, performance, and success at all cost. In this hierarchical worldview, only "winners" are entitled to feel satisfied. Yet most men are destined to be "losers." They are taught to be good providers and heroic protectors of women and children. If they fail, they are prone to feel emotional devastation. Psychologist Joe Pleck (1987b) has described "breadwinner suicides" as an extreme outgrowth of chronic unemployment. In his studies of the impact of the Great Depression on families, psychiatrist Nathan Ackerman (1967) reported that male breadwinners experiencing the economic dislocations of the mining industry felt "profound humiliation" (p. 126).

Failures at being "protectors" are no less devastating for men. Most commonly this appears as survivor guilt among men exposed to the trauma of military combat. It has been incredibly painful for me to hear Vietnam veterans describe their inability to forgive themselves for not fulfilling promises to protect comrades. Guilt is also an issue for many men with high-risk jobs that expose them to violence; firemen, policemen, and emergency medical technicians continually witness suffering and death that they are helpless to prevent. Inner-city youth are increasingly exposed to guns, violence, and death. More than 50 percent of young urban children have witnessed a shooting (Sanchez-Hucles, 1997).

In the area of rape and domestic violence, guilt and shame are especially central to the therapy process. Guilt (or a lack thereof) is most likely to be an issue for a rapist or batterer, but many other men are also prone to experience major distress in this area. When domestic violence has occurred, male family members who were not directly involved commonly experience intense guilt, because they blame themselves for failing to protect their loved one.

Grief

Grief is a healthy response to the inevitable losses one encounters throughout the life cycle. Sadly, male socialization significantly impedes men's ability to experience the restorative benefits of this basic human emotion. The "sturdy oak" tenet of masculinity prescribes that men adopt a "stiff upper lip" when faced with death or loss. Often, men feel the need to be emotionally strong and stoic and to serve as an example of emotional strength for the "weaker" ones. Many men inhibit their grief so severely that they never experience the raw pain of their losses. Others, perhaps the fortunate ones, stumble upon their grief years later and are amazed to discover the intensity of their pain, as well as the liberating effects of catharsis.

There are a number of significant life events that require a man to grieve. Developmental theorists Nancy Chodorow (1978) and Carol Gilligan (1982) emphasize that young boys feel the need to define themselves with clear acts of intrapsychic and interpersonal separation from their mothers. The cost of this exaggerated emphasis on nonrelatedness is a lifelong sense of grief about losing the warmth and nurturance that would otherwise have been possible (Terrance Real's aforementioned "loss of the relational"). Maturing men, of course, push this grief far from awareness. If pressed to remember their separations from mother, they would describe the process as a necessary, natural event that makes them proud. Such is the strength of the injunction against being a sissy or a "mama's boy."

Further contributing to a man's grief at losing his mother's nurturance is the extreme difficulty he has in finding nurturing older males. The loss of "male mothers" is a primary theme in the work of poet Robert Bly (1990), who sees grief as endemic in modern men. Bly theorizes that sociocultural changes have prevented men from maintaining close relationships with their fathers and with a community of male mentors. Therefore, according to Meth and Pasick (1990), Bly suggests that "grief, rather than anger is the doorway to men's feelings" (p. 163).

The limitations of the traditional father role may also be replete with precursors to male grief. The "distant breadwinner" fathering role demands that men subordinate family experiences to the needs of the workplace. Whether physically unavailable to witness their children's milestone events or emotionally detached from family life, traditional men frequently are estranged from loved ones. As they struggle to meet the demands of the masculine role, many men experience a lack of familial connectedness and a profound sense of interpersonal loss. Particularly vivid may be the experiences of men undergoing divorce (Myers, 1989). The typical divorce pattern— the father leaves the home while the mother retains custody of the children—usually creates major financial burdens for women and separation trauma for men.

Anxiety: Pressures of the Boy Culture and Male Chorus

Keith is an eighth grader who has been referred to me for counseling, which is part of the protocol for violating the school's code of conduct. Keith and a senior, Marvin, had a fight in the school gym. Fighting is old news for Marvin, a well-known school tough guy, but it is a first-time event for Keith. In fact, up until now, Keith's disciplinary record has been spotless.

In my office, as Keith recounts the story, I have a hard time picturing Keith as a street fighter. He is tall and very slender, somewhat like the stereotyped gangly and awkward nerd. Quiet and soft-spoken, he is apparently embarrassed by his situation. I ask him to describe what happened. He is reticent to answer, but for an instant I think I detect a slightly sheepish grin. After taking a moment to organize his thoughts, he begins to describe the events.

Keith and his friends had been playing basketball when they were challenged to a game by Marvin and his gang, "The Warriors." Feeling that they had little choice, Keith and his buddies agreed to play. On one of the very first possessions, Marvin drove into the lane to try a layup over Keith. In going up to block the shot, Keith clumsily threw an elbow into Marvin's chest, knocking him off-balance and sending him crashing to the floor. Stunned, Marvin was unable to get up for several seconds. For different reasons, all the other youths were equally stunned as the play halted and silence replaced the usual din of voices. No one could comprehend the sight—Marvin on the floor, writhing in pain after a blow that Keith delivered.

Suddenly, Keith's friends began gleefully whooping, "Way to go, Keith!! Big-time block, dude!" High fives and celebrations just infuriated Marvin and his buddies. Everyone looked at Marvin to see what he'd do. On cue, Marvin stood and pointed his finger at Keith, saying, "I'm gonna kick your ass, you string-bean punk!"

Keith seems lost in the memory of the event and pauses in his telling of the story, but I persuade him to continue. He explains that he really wanted nothing but to get out of the gym. He certainly wanted no part of a fight, but the pressure was overwhelming. He knew he should walk away but also realized that the verbal abuse would be unbearable. Finally, as Marvin got more and more in his face and continued to taunt him, Keith pushed Marvin away. The fight was on. They wrestled for several minutes before a teacher finally interceded.

Keith's dilemma is one that I believe to be universal among traditional males. He was caught squarely in a precarious clash between cultural standards, a classic double bind or no-win situation. Keith, like most males in the culture, had learned the standard lessons about mature social conduct, good citizenship, and personal responsibility. Fighting is inappropriate, adults had said, and he should just say no to those who tried to provoke him into a fight. Yet, at the same time, Keith was quite aware of the other, more private lessons he had incorporated from the world of "real men." According to those lessons, he had no alternative but to fight, regardless of the risk to health or civic reputation. By "backing down," he would expose himself to ridicule, humiliation, and further abuse from young men buying into traditional male ideas about manhood and violence.

This clash between public and private standards of conduct, between "real men" and "sissies," generates enormous anxiety in many men and is central to their distress. It is therefore a pivotal element in any effort to provide realistic help. In his study of working-class boys in the public school system, sociologist Andrew Tolson (1977) described the male peer group as an informal culture that interacts with, and sometimes counteracts, the formal culture of the school. Interestingly, he noted that both the school and the peer group emphasized male competition and hierarchy but that only the peer group endorsed fighting. According to Tolson, fighting was the common outgrowth of extreme competitiveness and the best alternative for young men who envisioned that they would not be able to compete on the career ladder.

Many others have noted the critical mediating role of the adolescent male peer group. Jerome Bernstein (1987), a Jungian analyst, described the male group as "the single most powerful source of rites of passage in the psyche of man" (p. 139). Historian Anthony Rotundo (1993) has described the evolution of "boy culture" in early nineteenth-century America, a historical development in which all-male groups were the principal socializing influence for young men. Not expected to work in the family, these boys were allowed to spend considerable time together without adult supervision.

In reviewing these writings about traditional adolescent male socialization, we can begin to appreciate Keith's dilemma. Young men may have every intention of behaving appropriately, but to which master must they be loyal? Even when they wish to become "good citizens," they are simultaneously pulled in other directions.

As noted earlier, anthropologist David Gilmore has documented that most cultures teach young men the overriding importance of earning acceptance into the male world. The social psychological research on male and female groups conducted by Elizabeth Aries supports these observations. Aries found that when men gather, they are intensely competitive and preoccupied with hierarchy to the point that all of the men she studied were continually concerned about "how they stood in relation to each other" (1976, p. 13).

Psychiatrist Frank Pittman (1990) has taken this notion a step further with his description of the "male chorus." This term refers to a group of men in a man's life. It is more than just a real-world male group among whom a young man must navigate; it is also an internalized variant of male judgmental pressure. For Pittman, this "invisible chorus that haunts men's lives" is composed of all a guy's comrades, rivals, buddies, bosses, male ancestors, cultural heroes, and especially his father. These internalized images push a man to "sacrifice more and more of his humanity for the sake of his masculinity" (p. 42).

Loneliness: Men's Emotional Isolation from Other Men

Marty was unusually quiet for an entire group session and then did not come to the next session. Two weeks before, he had been very different. Glenn, a fairly new group member, had been especially depressed about an imminent divorce. Marty, who had gone through a painful divorce himself five years earlier, was closely attuned to Glenn's distress and had provided encouragement and compassionate support.

In the week of his silence, Marty had rebuffed inquiries about his welfare, suggesting that he just needed a little time and space to process a few things. When he failed to appear for the next session, group members became concerned and asked me to contact him. When I did, I was greeted coolly with an unconvincing excuse that some job conflicts had come up and that he would need to withdraw from group for an indefinite period. Because we had an agreement that group members would always attend their "farewell" session, I insisted that Marty attend group one more time.

In the farewell meeting, Marty is again dismissive of others, simply claiming that he is busy and preoccupied. After thirty minutes of dull and avoidant conversation, with little input from Marty, Jim explodes angrily.

JIM: Okay, I've had about enough of this. We're all pretending nothing's going on, but something isn't right! What gives, Marty? And don't give me that bullshit that you're just busy. Something ain't right with you.

Marty starts to respond quickly, but stops, exhales loudly, and slumps back into his chair. For the next several minutes, he remains quiet, seeming to struggle with what to say. Tears start flowing down his cheeks. Finally, he tries to describe his feelings.

MARTY: Yeah, you're right, asshole, things really suck right now. It started a few weeks ago when we were talking about Glenn's divorce. I thought I'd been doing okay with my own, but somehow everything got really stirred up again. I've never gotten over losing Carrie, and I've really been missing my kids. Last week just before group was the worst. . . . I'd gotten my pistol out and laid it on the table. I started drinking, trying to get up the nerve to. . . . Well, I couldn't . . . but I sure as hell didn't feel like I could face you guys.

GLENN: Marty, shit, I had no idea you were that upset. . . . I feel really bad.

JIM: Yeah, and I'm pissed off. . . . What's the deal? Here you are helping us, we're all there for each other . . . and then you get ready to eat metal and suddenly we don't matter. . . . That really sucks!

GARY: Marty, I wonder if you could tell us why you felt the need to keep us this to yourself.

Again, Marty is quiet for several moments, trying to find words.

MARTY: You know, I've been wondering about that. Christ, I definitely needed help, but I couldn't bring myself to talk to anybody. In a way, I guess I felt ashamed. . . . I wasn't sure how you all might react. . . .

JIM: Marty, that's nuts, man. You know better than that. . . . We've all been there.

MARTY (an embarrassed smile on his face): Yeah, that's true. . . . I just don't know what it is.

GARY: Marty, it's not easy to let yourself care, to get close, to reach out to other men. Sometimes it seems better to wall ourselves off than to feel vulnerable. These guys will support you if you let them. . . . Think about it.

Although they all are nodding in assent, all the group members allow Marty some emotional space. At the end of the group meeting, however, Jim walks toward Marty and embraces him. For several minutes, Marty sobs. Wordlessly, they part. Marty allows several others to embrace him, as well.

Most traditional men spend their lives in marked emotional isolation. They suffer alone, steadfastly hiding their inner turmoil from other men. Many traditional men are able to find a degree of intimacy with a woman, but even then, they can only do so with considerable difficulty. Even though they doggedly resist it, men desperately need the companionship of other men.

The irony of men's emotional isolation is that, as noted earlier, it flies in the face of conventional wisdom about the superiority of male friendship over female friendship. For years, we have been told that women are backbiting, catty, and disloyal, whereas men have lifelong relationships of deepest devotion, as did Butch Cassidy and the Sundance Kid or Don Quixote and Sancho Panza. The reality turns out to be more like that portrayed in the movie *Stand by Me*, whereby aging men long for the intimacy they enjoyed with adolescent male buddies.

Men's studies literature and research into gender patterns of friendship have revealed that although men and women report similar amounts of time spent in same-sex relationships, the time they spend together is qualitatively different. Sharon Brehm (1985) found that men tend to have friendships characterized by shared activities (for example, hunting, fixing a car, playing cards), whereas women are more likely to have friendships characterized by interpersonal intimacy and discussion of feelings. Paul Wright (1982) described this difference as men's preference for "side-by-side" relationships and women's preference for "face-to-face" relationships. Many researchers have documented that traditional, role-oriented males are less likely to discuss personal problems openly with other men—even those they identify as best friends (Dosser, Balswick, & Halverson, 1986).

Overdependence on Women

In the group described above, we saw how Marty and Glenn were devastated when they lost their relationships with female partners. This scenario has a familiar ring; in many tragic stories, men who are unable to face life alone kill themselves or their estranged partners. Once again, contrary to conventional wisdom, a traditional man does not cope very well without a woman in his life. Married men are less stressed and more emotionally satisfied than single men. Divorced men have much greater difficulty than divorced women adjusting to the loss of a partner's emotional presence.

Michael McGill (1985), who researched the intimate relationships of more than one thousand men, found that most men disclose the intimate details of their lives to only one special woman. Few men, however, were found to have anything remotely similar with another man. As a result, almost all men become highly dependent upon a woman to provide the intimacy and support that is so integral to their emotional well-being.

Joseph Pleck (1980) has carefully analyzed the complex nature of men's ambivalent relationships with women and has made an exceedingly important observation. Men, he notes, ascribe to women "expressive" power and "masculinity-validating" power. *Expressive power* refers to a pattern in traditional male-female relationships in which men learn to experience their emotions vicariously through women or rely on women to facilitate emotional expressiveness. Many men depend on women to help them express their emotions, indeed to express their emotions for them. "At an ultimate level, many men are unable to feel emotionally alive except through relationships with women" (p. 421).

Masculinity-validating power refers to the traditional pattern in which men rely on women to attest to a man's masculine worth—to appreciate, or validate, his performance as a provider, protector, or sexual gratifier. "In traditional masculinity, to experience oneself as masculine requires that women play their prescribed role of doing the things that make men feel masculine" (Pleck, 1980, p. 421).

The research of Jeanne Tschann (1988) provides another perspective on men's overdependence on women. In her study of interpersonal self-disclosure, Tschann found some interesting differences. Consistent with past research, she found that men were much less likely than women to reveal personal information to a same-gender friend. Of additional relevance, however, was her discovery that for men, marriage made a critical difference. Women, regardless of marital status, were fairly open with their women friends. Men, on the other hand, disclosed even less personal information to their closest male friends if they were married. The implication is clear—men tend to meet their intimacy needs with their spouses and they become complacent about their male friendships.

In this chapter, I've tried to illuminate the many ways in which contemporary men struggle with what it means to be a man. I've elaborated on how the dark side of masculinity harms women, children, and the larger culture. Additionally, however, I've attempted to show that the traditional social construction of masculinity and the unforgiving processes of shaping boys into men create a less visible dimension of this dark side—it can devastate men's lives. From the earliest moments when male children are deprived of emotional tenderness and physical comforting, through the adolescent years when they are subjected to vicious hazing from older and more powerful males, to their middle-aged years when they anxiously compare themselves to unrealistic standards of male success, until their final years when many men first confront their relational losses, traditional men also suffer from the dark side of masculinity.

In Chapter Two I turn to the next part of the problem—why so many men adamantly resist seeking the help they desperately need.

2

Why Traditional Men Hate Psychotherapy

More and more men are finding their way into therapists' offices. Although researchers report that women seeking psychotherapy still outnumber men two to one (Vessey & Howard, 1993), many observers are impressed with the increasing numbers of men seeking treatment. Are we witnessing a radical shift in men's attitudes? Could it be that hordes of men have become so weary of masculine role burdens that they are searching for any available means of help?

For the most part, I don't think so. Yes, some men are fed up with the most stultifying aspects of traditional masculinity and are willingly seeking help through psychotherapy. But they are the exceptions. Traditional men hate psychotherapy and will do most anything to avoid a therapist's office. Murray Scher (1990) has long held that men enter therapy only when they are desperate: "The man who comes into the consulting room is usually there because he believes there is no alternative. Very few men come for therapy because they subscribe to its life-enhancing qualities. Even if they did they would likely not see it as something for them anyway. Men are in therapy because something, internal or external, has driven them to it" (p. 323).

Many factors drive men into therapy—for example, unhappy spouses, disappointed bosses, admonishing physicians, mandating courts, failing bodies, or uncooperative sexual organs. Because the impetus to begin therapy can come from many sources, we should not assume that a man's presence in the therapy room is an unqualified indication that he wants to change. We must be aware that there are enormous differences between those few men who willingly seek therapy and those who enter therapy through coercion. In fact, I believe that men's aversion to therapy is so powerful that it's wise to assume that most male clients, at some level, don't want to be there. Furthermore, when they are there, most men have great difficulty conforming to the role of the "ideal" therapy client.

Resistance is a major problem that therapists face in clients, of course, but it doesn't always take the same form or spring from the same sources. In this chapter I focus on four causes of traditional men's resistance to psychotherapy: (1) the stereotypes of psychotherapy (how therapy is portrayed by the culture), (2) the social construction of masculinity (how men are conditioned by the culture), (3) problems of political power and triangulation, and (4) the way therapists treat traditional men.

STEREOTYPES OF PSYCHOTHERAPY

We live in a "gendered" culture. That is, dominant cultural institutions (families, schools, workplaces, and churches) teach individuals to behave either as "women" or "men," to adopt communication styles consistent with this difference, and to participate in relationships according to prescribed gender rules. Interestingly, the dominant cultural institutions themselves are "gendered," in that they also have differential meanings to women and men. For example, for many centuries, the workplace has been a "manly" environment, whereas the family has been seen as a "feminine" environment. Psychotherapy, a relatively recent institution, is curious from a gender perspective. Many have noted that this institution has been designed and conducted primarily by men but directed primarily toward women.

Through television, cinema, theater, and print media, our culture has not been particularly kind in its public portrayals of psychotherapy. This shouldn't be too surprising, given the prominent stigma attached to anything associated with mental illness. But the problem seems larger, as nearly all depictions of psychotherapy have been devoid of positive images. In the melodramatic films of the 1930s, 1940s, and 1950s, therapy was seen as an arcane and mysterious process conducted by aloof, omniscient, and somewhat eccentric Freudian analysts. In films such as *All About Eve*, therapy clients were portrayed as grossly disturbed and in need of extensive professional help.

In the past few decades, psychotherapy has become more integrated into the cultural mainstream, but the public images of therapists and clients are not faring much better. Grossly deranged therapy clients have been replaced by more ineffectual and neurotic variants. In Charles Schulz's *Peanuts*, we find Lucy administering five-cent psychiatric help to a hapless Charlie Brown. Woody Allen has elevated haplessness to new heights, personifying the unmanly man addicted to therapy without hope of termination. In *What About Bob*, Bill Murray played the therapy client from hell who actually seemed sympathetic when juxtaposed against an even less attractive figure—the snobbish and egocentric therapist played by Richard Dreyfuss. Bob Newhart's psychology office was populated by a regular stream of wimps, losers, and social misfits. The insecure and ineffectual psychologist played by Bob Newhart did little to elevate popular regard for the field of therapy or the competence of therapists. Newhart's successors have been no better. The cartoon *Dr. Katz, Professional Therapist* is comically conflicted and indecisive. To the traditional man, Kelsey Grammar and David Hyde Pierce of *Frasier* are classic effete snobs and "weenies." Women therapists (Barbara Streisand in *The Prince of Tides* and Lena Olin in *Mr. Jones*) are sometimes presented as more competent, but they can't seem to keep from falling in love with their male clients.

These negative stereotypes are especially problematic for traditional men, because they already have been shaped to avoid the behavior of the ideal therapy client. What follows is a dramatic illustration of this mismatch.

Typical Psychotherapy Demands	Masculinity Demands
Disclosing private experience	Hiding private experience
Relinquishing control	Maintaining control
Nonsexual intimacy	Sexualizing of intimacy
Showing weakness	Showing strength
Experiencing shame	Expressing pride
Acting vulnerable	Acting invincible
Seeking help	Being self-reliant
Expressing feelings	Being stoic
Being introspective	Taking action
Addressing relationship conflict	Avoiding conflict
Confronting pain	Denying pain
Acknowledging failure	Endlessly persisting
Admitting ignorance	Feigning omniscience

This list obviously oversimplifies matters, in that psychotherapy is far more complex than the list reveals. At times, therapy calls for characteristics and behaviors from both lists. The point, however, is that most traditionally socialized men, already averse to psychotherapy, only feel more resistant when they hear these simplistic and negative images of psychotherapy and psychotherapy clients.

THE SOCIAL CONSTRUCTION
OF MASCULINITY

Many men's studies writers have commented on the poor match between traditional masculine socialization and the demands of the psychotherapy relationship. In this section I examine more closely some of the principal areas of conflict.

Competition and Hierarchy

Men are raised to think hierarchically. From the time they are young, their fathers, coaches, teachers, and peers stress the need to compete with others and to establish a place in the pecking order. Much as top-ten football teams vie for higher national rankings, men are encouraged to think of themselves as locked in a struggle with other males to reach the higher rungs of competitive ladders. This process promotes continual envy of men who occupy higher rungs and constant fear of ambitious men on the rungs below. Christopher McLean (1996, p. 20) expresses this well: "All the institutions within which men lead their lives are implicitly or explicitly hierarchical. . . . They all encourage striving for success, which may involve stepping on the shoulders of one's friends and associates. The struggle and the structure tend to become all-absorbing, and men are encouraged to regard all other parts of life as secondary. Men's working lives are a permanent battlefield, with countless casualties, whose failure only serves to increase the prestige of those who succeed. . . . Most men's lives are ruled . . . by the inner knowledge of having failed as a man, and the fear of being discovered."

The pressures of this hierarchical mind-set create multiple impediments for men who might benefit from therapy. To those who view the world as a competitive environment in which many people seek rewards that are in short supply, therapy seems an annoying distraction. Just as a pit stop causes a race car driver to lose precious laps, therapy takes time that could be used to perpetuate one's competitive advantage. Furthermore, there is no guarantee that therapy will enhance performance in any appreciable way. At times, intensely competitive men will seek technical assistance or "coaching" to upgrade performance but never to take a substantive look at their lifestyles or value systems. Sports psychologists and corporate psychologists are generally called in to make men better competitors, not to make them more fully functioning human beings.

Excessive emphasis on competitive drive can also create problems when men actually do enter psychotherapy. Many writers have documented the tendency for men to compete with their therapist, fight for control of the therapy hour, or spar over the accuracy of diagnostic formulations.

It has never been completely clear to me exactly how Jack ended up in my therapy office. A successful attorney who previously sought consultation on forensic evaluations, Jack called me saying that if I were going to be in my office that evening, he would like to "drop by to go over a few things." Because we've always handled consultation referrals over the phone, I wondered if perhaps Jack had something more personal in mind.

Accustomed to Jack's typical arrogance and smug self-confidence, I had trouble picturing him showing a more vulnerable side. I need not have worried. When he arrives, Jack is obviously ill at ease, talking more and speaking more loudly than usual (which is somewhat difficult, as his overbearing style almost always borders on the obnoxious). He paces about my office area, seeming to disapprove of its size and frugality (or is that my imagination?).

After several minutes, he finally sits, but barely—he perches on the edge of the seat with his feet under him. Mostly, he rambles and boasts—about his reputation in the legal community, about his ability to generate huge fees, about the prestige of the schools his kids attend, and about the Jaguar his wife drives. He then shifts to quizzing me about the stresses of my professional life, making cryptic references to the demands of working like a dog to make a decent living in a "crappy one-horse town run by ignorant yahoos." Seeing my opening, I query, "I guess life can get a bit overwhelming at times?"

Jack pauses only an instant before smiling sarcastically and replying, "Whoa, Doc, take it easy. You figuring I need some heavy-duty psychoanalyzing? Maybe some of that hocus-pocus talk radio garbage?" Seeming to recognize my surprise, Jack tries to take the edge off. "Hey, look. I know you head doctors are expected to sniff out personal problems, but things are terrific in my life. Sure, everybody has to take his turn swallowing crap, but I'm doing fine. God knows Linda is always bitchin' me out about some imagined crime, but I sure don't need a head shrinking right now."

Although I am tempted to push a little harder, I back off and let Jack resume his evasive harangue. Seeming to sense that he is on the brink of a more substantive revelation, Jack stands to calculate his best escape. "Look, it couldn't hurt to discuss a couple of things, but I've got a very big trial next week. Why don't I call you when it's over?"

As it turns out, it will be several years before I talk to Jack again.

Competence and Vulnerability: The Difficulty of Seeking Help

For most men, masculinity is all about displaying competence and fearlessness. But this is a difficult posture to maintain. "Men not only fear, they are scared that others may discover their fear. Thus men learn to hide behind a precarious posture, an air of cool confidence, a stance of toughness and self-reliance. The lessons in self-reliance begin early and last for most of a man's life. . . . Most men come to believe that other men actually do not have fears. For these men who have fears—the vast majority of men, that is—a cover is necessary; an image of self-reliance becomes a kind of ruse to hide behind" (Doyle, 1995, p. 195).

Traditional men like to see themselves as problem solvers, as people who fix things that are broken, as sources of wisdom and sage advice. Built into this worldview is a powerful aversion to anything that even remotely suggests failure or incompetence. Therefore, men have enormous difficulty with the simple phrase "I need help." By now, most everyone is familiar with the popular parodies of men who refuse to ask for directions when traveling or who never look at the directions when assembling a new product.

Developmental researchers have shown that young boys, far more than young girls, are taught task persistence. That is, they learn not to give up or ask for assistance (Lips, 1989). Angry protests of "I want to do it myself," sometimes considered discourteous in girls, are a welcome sign of independent spirit in boys. This pattern can have many advantages for boys but can become burdensome when it reaches the absurd "rugged individualist" levels that often develop for men. Many become so attached to self-reliance that they interpret any input, even friendly advice or constructive criticism, as an assault on their competence. These men often seem to need, above all else, to prove that their way is right (even if it does not show positive results). With this mind-set, it isn't surprising that traditional men feel insulted and rebel at any suggestion of psychotherapy.

I have seen Chuck and Claire for two sessions but have not yet developed a good feel for Chuck. Claire is working full time and does the bulk of the domestic labor. Chuck also works, but he does little around the house except "man's" work—mowing, painting, and plumbing. Because it is winter, Chuck now does little after work except to watch football games and go hunting. Although I appreciate Claire's position about the unjust distribution of labor, I want to make a connection with Chuck before beginning to initiate marital labor negotiations. I soon find my opening.

After weeks of procrastination, Chuck finally agreed with Claire that he would remove the old sofa from the garage. He wasn't sure how he'd accomplish it, but he figured he'd somehow stuff it into their minivan. When he arrived home from work, he was surprised to learn that Claire had called their neighbor to borrow a pickup truck. He expressed his annoyance, but Claire responded, "No, it's really okay. Bill said he'd love to volunteer the truck. In fact, he said he'd come over and help you move it." Chuck became furious. "Oh, that's just great. Who asked you to do that?" A heated twenty-minute argument ensued but never really resolved their dispute. Claire remained astonished at Chuck's pigheadedness; Chuck remained angry at Claire's infringement of his self-reliance (to say nothing about his imagined indebtedness to a guy he wanted nothing to do with).

At first blush, it is difficult to ignore the obvious wisdom of Claire's position or to feel much empathy for Chuck's apparent indolence. But I think I have a sense of his distress.

"Chuck, you seem like a guy who tries to do his part. But from Claire's position, this looks totally lazy. I think there's more to it than just that. Can we try to help Claire understand your position?"

"Yeah sure, Doc," responds Chuck, "but I'm not sure I understand it myself."

Over the next two sessions, we work to explicate the factors involved in Chuck's anger about Claire's intervention and his passive-aggressive resistance to her efforts. Chuck acknowledges a sizable "macho" need to take care of matters himself, to resist asking for help whenever possible. He recalls being taunted by his father whenever his strength, stamina, or cleverness didn't measure up to those of his older brothers. He also discusses his feelings about his neighbor Bill, who fancies himself an expert on all matters, particularly the home and garden. Because Bill "knows everything about everything" and loves to display his superior knowledge, naturally he'd love to "assist." In reality, he'd subject Chuck to several hours of instruction and only semisubtle put-downs. (In a later session, Chuck admits that he stubbornly resisted the therapy appointments, assuming that any male therapist would be very much like Bill—smug, superior, and condescending.)

Finally, Chuck and Claire uncover a larger pattern, a tug-of-war over leadership of domestic chores. Chuck feels that Claire is always looking for tasks for him to do and that she expects immediate compliance. Although he usually intends to do the "more reasonable" ones eventually, leaving the rest undone (who needs an immaculate garage?), he resents her "bossing him around."

Over the next several sessions, we continue to explore the particular and gender-based causes of Claire and Chuck's struggles.

Chuck recognizes the self-defeating nature of his behavior and agrees that the best strategy to avoid nagging is to follow through on promises. However, both agree that they need to divide tasks equitably and negotiate timetables openly.

Interpersonal Control, Power, and Dominance

Murray Scher (1990) has noted that the two primary foci of masculinity are "to be unlike women and to be in control" (p. 322). As much as men are expected to maintain constant mastery over their environments and themselves, they also expect themselves to maintain masculinity through power, influence, and ascendancy over others. Jim O'Neil (1982) has described "control over women" as an especially critical aspect of traditional masculinity. Young men are typically reinforced for appearing active, forceful, and powerful; for imitating the brutish displays of televised wrestlers; or for humiliating weaker boys through "in your face" taunting.

These power and control issues become especially relevant when considered in the context of psychotherapy. Because they associate therapy with weakness and powerlessness, men like Jack avidly avoid it unless they are coerced by a boss, wife, family member, or the court system. In this situation of coercion, a man's feelings of being in the "one-down" position are intensified; his presence in the therapy office becomes a testament to his loss of control. It isn't surprising, then, that so many traditional men will do whatever they can to escape therapy. If they cannot avoid it, they often become passive-aggressive or manipulative, hoping to use therapy to align with the therapist to help them restore their position of dominance.

Many men feel a need to perpetuate what psychologist Lucia Gilbert and Murray Scher have called "entitlement and patriarchal privilege" (Gilbert & Scher, 1987). Feminist writers have been correct to point out that, in terms of power, masculinity has many advantages. Recently, however, greater recognition has been given to many men's deficient sense of personal power. At some level, most traditional men see their worth as closely tied to their power and relationship leverage. The thinking goes like this: "She loves me because I am powerful. If I lose that power, or even if she acquires comparable power, I will become unlovable. She will lose respect for me." It is critical that we appreciate this dynamic, because it commonly causes men to go to great lengths to avoid a one-down position.

For the first few sessions, therapy has gone well with Luis and Maria, a middle-aged Mexican American couple. Luis, a Vietnam combat veteran, frequently has such severe PTSD symptoms that he has difficulty holding jobs. To help allay family financial problems, Maria has taken a clerical position at a local law firm. Although Maria's employment hasn't become an overt issue in therapy, Luis has become irritable and unusually reactive ever since Maria received her first paycheck. The matter comes to a head when Mary confronts Luis about his recent moodiness. Luis immediately responds, "Why don't you just get a divorce?" Maria is shocked but also irritated by his petulant response.

I turn to Luis to explore the roots of his irritation. He provides an odd but helpful statement: "Look, with her hanging around with all those guys in neckties, it's just a matter of time before she starts getting very impressed with herself. I'd rather get it over with now."

For Luis, the matter is simple—a man's relationship security is rooted in his ability to perform and to control his partner. Without that control, he is likely to be replaced by an economically higher-functioning man.

Fortunately, support from the therapist helps Luis give voice to his fears, even though he senses that this disclosure will make him appear even more insecure and weak. He is convinced that "real men" don't have doubts and insecurities and has resisted therapy out of a belief that therapy will reinforce his sense of personal weakness and loss of control. He is pleasantly surprised by the experience.

Once he admits his fears, he is stunned by Maria's response; she just stares incredulously at him. Then to his amazement, she bursts

into laughter. "You nut, sometimes you blow me away with your silli-
ness. You're my lover. I'm crazy about you, and I couldn't care less
about some tie-wearing jerk!"

Luis beams. For the remainder of the session, Maria playfully
strokes Luis's arm and shoulder, to his considerable pleasure. The
issue, of course, isn't completely resolved. Luis is repeatedly subject
to periods of insecurity, and Maria, at times, is highly impatient with
Luis and disappointed about their economic hardship.

What is critically important, however, is that each has been able
to provide insight to the other about their gender-based perspectives
on power, dominance, and "success." Luis has gained much more
realistic information about what Maria considers important. Although
she values economic security, she also values his emotional support
and cooperation. Partnership, not domination, is most valuable to her.

Inexpressiveness and the Devaluation of Emotion

Traditional men's difficulties with emotional expressiveness are
among the most noted of all their problems. Some researchers, in
fact, have labeled most men as emotionally incompetent or emotionally constipated. For example, Deborah David and Robert
Brannon (1976) identified a cardinal component of traditional masculinity as "no sissy stuff," or men's need to avoid the "feminine"
disposition toward emotional sensitivity. Restrictive emotionality
is a critical component of Jim O'Neil's Gender Role Conflict Scale
(O'Neil, Good, & Holmes, 1995). Jack Balswick (1988) has written extensively about the problems created by the "inexpressive
male." Ron Levant considers "alexithymia" (the inability to access,
label, and express feelings) to be at the core of most men's gender
role strain.

> I believe that a mild form of alexithymia is very wide-
> spread among adult men and that it results from the male
> socialization ordeal, which requires boys to restrict the
> expression of their vulnerable and caring emotions and
> to be emotionally stoic. . . . As a result . . . men are often

genuinely unaware of their emotions. Lacking this emotional awareness, when asked to identify their feelings,
they tend to rely on their cognition and try to logically
deduce how they should feel. They cannot do what is automatic for most women—simply sense inwardly, feel the
feeling, and let the verbal description come to mind
[1995, p. 239].

When we appreciate the enormous problems men have with intense emotions, we aren't surprised to see how uninterested and at
times even frightened they are to enter psychotherapy. Above all
else, therapy has been portrayed as a medium for people to "get in
touch with their feelings."

But it's more than just a matter of awkwardness with emotional
expression that hampers men. Men also have a low opinion of affective experience in general. Deborah Tannen, for one, has amply
demonstrated that women and men have radically different positions
on interpersonal communication, both in their preferred style and
in their overall objectives. In her psycholinguistic research, Tannen
(1990) found that women's interpersonal communications typically
emphasize understanding and supporting others, giving praise, validating experience, and forming a connection. Men, on the other
hand, are more likely to emphasize giving advice, sharing information, impressing others with accomplishments, and issuing challenges. For women, psychotherapy can become a welcome place to
establish emotional connections with another, to validate personal
experience, and to discuss previously hidden emotional distress. Men
commonly emphasize that interpersonal encounters should have a
purpose and produce tangible outcomes, so they are likely to demean
therapy as a waste of time or as "emotional masturbation."

The session with Paul has been going very badly. I know his arrogance and bluster are a cover for his extreme discomfort, but I am
trying to find a direct way to provoke his interest in therapy. We talk
about his wife's impatience, his declining work performance, and the

reappearance of tension headaches. But my efforts are to no avail as he continues to put up a front.

Frustrated by his defensiveness and hurt by his insults, I unwisely react with a direct assault on his resistance; I challenge him to pay attention to the warning signs and to start airing his suppressed feelings. His response awakens me to the great gap in the value he and I place on therapy: "Doc, I guess it comes down to this. All this therapy is fine for some people, but it isn't for me. If I spend several hundred dollars, I expect to have something like a new stereo to show for it. I don't have time for chitchat or feel-good jargon. If you can show me how these conversations are going to pay my bills or get my job done, I might consider it. Otherwise, I'll stick to something that works."

Flabbergasted and, I must admit, very annoyed, I respond with an intellectual defense of therapy and a terse dismissal of the prospects for effective therapy with him. Not surprisingly, he leaves feeling justified in his contempt for therapy and therapists.

Although we never encounter each other again, I will never forget the interaction and have profited greatly from our unpleasant exchange. As I've become more appreciative of men's resistance, I've become more forgiving, less reactive, and, I think, far more creative in my response to this common attitude toward therapy. (This is elaborated in Chapter Three.)

Intimacy and Sexuality

In light of the way most men have been socialized regarding intimacy, it would be hard to design an interpersonal context more problematic for men than individual psychotherapy. Women and men are very different in the degree to which they have intimacy in relationships. Research shows that although both genders report that they have ample close friendships, the nature of these friendships are qualitatively different. As would be expected from women's preferred face-to-face relationship style, they place much greater emphasis on intimacy than do men in their side-by-side relationships.

Julia Wood (1994, p. 185) summarizes the gender differences as follows: "First, communication is central to women friends, while activities are the primary focus of men's friendships. Second, talk between women friends tends to be expressive and disclosive, focusing on details of personal lives, people, relationships, and feelings; talk in men's friendships generally revolves around less personal topics such as sports, events, money, music, and politics. Third, in general, men assume a friendship's value and seldom discuss it, while women are likely to talk about the dynamics of their relationship."

In brief, women are simply more comfortable than men with emotional intimacy—they place greater value on it and have many more intimate friendships. One aspect of this gender difference is that men tend to have difficulty distinguishing their emotional intimacy needs from their sexual needs—a critical component of what I have called the Centerfold Syndrome. Our culture teaches young men to objectify women's bodies, fixate on visual stimulation, compete with other men using women's bodies as symbolic trophies, depend on women's sexual validation, and substitute sexual intimacy for true emotional intimacy. Traditional sexual scripts call for young men to function sexually without any sense of emotional closeness *and* to associate all feelings of emotional closeness with sexuality. "As young men are learning to wall themselves off from too much emotional intimacy in sex, . . . they also are taught to sexualize all feelings of emotional and physical closeness. As a result they cannot experience nonsexual intimacy. . . . More often than not, this blurring of sexual needs and intimacy needs will create significant relationship constraints" (Brooks, 1995a, pp. 10–11).

We see, then, that the intimacy demanded in psychotherapy is particularly difficult for men. With female therapists, heterosexual men have great difficulty controlling fears of engulfment and a tendency to sexualize the relationship. With male therapists, men are subject to homophobic panic whenever they experience affection or emotional intimacy.

David is an especially attractive client. Bright, articulate, and successful, he has come to me for help with a failed engagement. A stylish financial analyst in his early thirties with expensive tastes, he has dated a series of very attractive young women. Fearing that he is getting too old for the "dating game," he wants to settle into one relationship. He became very enamored of his fiancée, Chris, but backed out a few months before the scheduled marriage. He wants to continue seeing Chris, but she has insisted that he get into therapy to "make up his damn mind."

Before coming to see me, David originally saw a younger woman therapist but discontinued their work after three sessions. When asked about it, he says he was uncomfortable with some suggestive comments that she made and was afraid that a sexual element was creeping into the picture. Although I encourage him to try to work through this with her, he insists on seeing a male therapist.

Our therapy seems to go very well, as David is unusually insightful and open to self-examination. He realizes that he wasn't really very interested in marrying Chris but feared "becoming a lonely old bachelor." He also identifies a number of other relationship issues that he wants to explore.

Then, two months into the therapy, he stops coming. I call him, but he doesn't return the calls.

More than a year later, David finally calls me back. He is engaged once more and wants to clarify his thinking again. Eventually, of course, we turn to the issues of his earlier termination. At first, David is uncharacteristically evasive, offering a series of weak explanations. Unconvinced, I ask him pointedly if there is any relationship between his two premature terminations. He immediately dismisses this as foolish but is strangely tentative. I gently probe a bit more until he finally acknowledges some very unsettling confusion.

"Well, I guess I might as well level with you. Man, this is really hard. Yeah, I started having some very bizarre feelings. Look, I know you're a happily married guy, and . . . shit, this is too weird. . . . I guess I started to wonder about . . . well, hell, I might as well say it. I wondered if there was some sort of sexual thing going on. . . . Then I started wondering if I was queer myself. . . . Damn, the whole thing got too strange and I decided to drop the whole matter."

David's confrontation with his homophobia is especially helpful to the therapy process. Over the next several sessions, he realizes that although he is heterosexual, affectionate feelings and even an occasional sexual fantasy are not atypical or abnormal. In fact, confronting these issues opens major inroads for an intense exploration of his homophobia, as well as his long-standing confusion between intimacy and sexuality.

POLITICAL POWER AND TRIANGULATIONS

No one likes being teamed up against. Family systems therapists have long recognized the serious problems created by "triangulations," that is, the uniting of one or more family members (or subsystems) against a single family member. Murray Bowen (1978), a prominent psychiatrist and family therapist closely identified with triangulation theory, considered triangles to be the natural or inevitable reaction of people under stress. "A two-person emotional system is unstable in that it forms itself into a three-person system or triangle under stress. A system larger than three persons becomes a series of interlocking triangles. . . . As tension mounts in a two-person system, it is usual for one to be more comfortable than the other, and for the uncomfortable one to 'triangle in' a third person by telling the second person a story about the triangled one. This relieves the tension between the first two, and shifts the tension between the second and third" (p. 478).

Of particular interest here is the family systems idea that triangulations need not be strictly limited to alliances between persons; social institutions are commonly included in triangulations. Bowenians are especially cautious that a therapist (or a therapist's agency) not be triangulated by a distressed couple (that is, drawn into taking one party's side against the other). Structural family therapist Salvador Minuchin (1974) has written extensively about the ways in which physical problems (diabetes, asthma, anorexia) in one family member can provoke triangulations among parents, children, and health care institutions. Similarly, school phobia can be viewed as a problem that triangulates families and schools.

For some, the institution of psychotherapy has had an inglorious history in terms of triangulation. Phyllis Chesler's *Women and Madness* (1972) spearheaded a feminist outcry against many mental health and psychotherapy practices that oppressed women. A major thrust of the critique was that psychotherapy was commonly conducted as part of an insidious form of triangulation between the male-dominated culture at large and the male-dominated field of mental health in an attempt to silence women's voices. "It is obvious that a predominantly female psychiatric population in America has been diagnosed, psychoanalyzed, researched and hospitalized by a predominantly male professional population. Despite individual differences among clinicians, most have been steeped, professionally and culturally, in both contemporary and traditional patriarchal ideologies. . . . The *institution* [italics hers] of psychotherapy can also be viewed as a form of social and political control" (p. 105).

Over the past three decades, there has been considerable attention to the ways in which sexist psychotherapy practices have harmed women. In a seminal 1970s study, Inge Broverman and her colleagues documented a "therapeutic double standard" in terms of clinicians' attitudes toward "healthy" women and men (Broverman, Broverman, Clarkson, Rosencrantz, & Vogel, 1970). After analyzing clinician ratings, the researchers demonstrated that in the minds of most clinicians, "healthy" women were thought to differ from healthy men by being more submissive, less independent, less adventurous, more easily influenced, less aggressive, less competitive, more excitable in minor crises, more capable of having their feelings hurt, more emotional, more preoccupied with their appearance, and less objective.

In response to feminist critiques of sexist psychotherapy practices, a specially appointed task force of the American Psychological Association criticized therapy practices that fostered traditional
sex roles, promoted bias in expectations of women, used sexist psychoanalytic concepts, and allowed women to be viewed as sex objects
(Task Force on Sex-Bias and Sex-Role Stereotyping in Psychotherapeutic Practice, 1978). Additionally, many feminist activists have
offered major critiques of assessment practices in general, and of the
American Psychiatric Association's official diagnostic system—the
Diagnostic and Statistical Manual of Mental Disorders—in particular.
Over the past twenty years, continual controversy has resulted in
the elimination of certain "official" diagnoses shown to be particularly damaging to women (such as masochism or self-defeating personality disorder, hysterical personality disorder, and late luteal
phase disorder) and in challenges to others that have remained
(such as histrionic personality disorder and premenstrual dysphoric
disorder).

As women's political clout and relationship leverage have increased, the mental health field has become far more attentive to
sexist therapy practices that harm women. At the same time, however, a new problem has emerged. In many ways, women and men
have shifted in their relationship to the mental health field, with
women and therapists commonly aligning, leaving men on the outside. This should not be interpreted as a statement that patriarchal
alliances against women have been eliminated or that the alliances
against men are as hazardous as the earlier ones against women. Nevertheless, many mental health practitioners have begun to argue that
far greater attention needs to be paid to the special problems of men.

Warren Farrell, author of *Why Men Are the Way They Are*
(1987) and *The Myth of Male Power* (1993), has been a leading
voice in charges that "male bashing" has become a common cultural practice. In 1992, Kevin Kelley and Alex Hall edited a special
issue of the *Journal of Mental Health Counseling* that argued that the
mental health community should become much more sensitive to
the needs of men:

Societal expectations and norms have changed as much for men over the past three decades as they have for women. There is not, however, an extensive literature that discusses how these changes are manifested in mental health counseling for men. Most deliberate education of mental health counselors regarding gender focuses on the concerns of women. It is our contention that men's issues are not well understood either by men themselves or by most mental health counselors. When men's issues are addressed in the counseling literature, it is too often in the context of treatment of the relatively few men who batter, abuse, and victimize others. Mental health counselors must raise their awareness of men's issues before they can be genuinely helpful to men working on gender issues in counseling [p. 255].

This is a delicate issue that can be misinterpreted easily. I have considerable difficulty with some of the more extreme claims that men are the victims of male bashing and that feminists are the villains. After all, for many decades, the mental health community has been dominated by men. Even though there has been some feminist resistance to paying greater attention to men's issues, most feminists have been highly supportive of this new focus. In my opinion, the struggle is not against feminism but against complacency and ignorance.

Women's studies has led the way in showing that gender experience is a critical component of client problems. Just as we have begun to extricate these issues for women, we need to accelerate our study of how these issues harm men. One significant way is that many men now view therapy as "women's work." Whether resisting their partner's overtures to join therapy or participating and feeling teamed up against, men deprive themselves of the benefits of therapy. Women have come to embrace therapy as a source of aid and comfort, and thus have been far more likely than men to seek psychotherapy for themselves and their children. In family therapy literature, there has been abundant attention paid to the "missing father" and ways of involving him with the therapy project. Television talk shows, whose audience is primarily women, are rife with mental health themes. Popular psychology books are purchased largely by women. More and more, psychotherapy and its offshoot industries of self-help and self-improvement have become the domain of women. As a result, a curious new form of triangulation has emerged; the mental health field's former alliance with men has been paralleled by a new alliance between the field and women. Women have become enamored of psychotherapy; men have remained skeptical.

In the past, this difference in the two genders' appreciation of psychotherapy has caused the bulk of therapy work to take place between women and therapists. But lately, a shift has taken place. More and more, an unhappy woman will force her male partner to see a therapist, threatening to leave unless the man gets help. In this way, the alliance between an individual woman and a therapist has sometimes taken a new, uneasy form, posing a threat to the man, who often believes himself to be opposed by this woman-therapist team.

Terry, a thirty-one-year-old house painter, has called asking for the earliest possible appointment—preferably that night. He arrives twenty minutes early and takes the first opportunity to identify the problem. "I'm emotionally abusive," he says.

I am struck by his definitive identification of the problem and by his enthusiasm for treatment, but I certainly want a bit more background information.

"Could you help me understand why you consider yourself to be emotionally abusive?" I ask.

Puzzled by my denseness, Terry searches for the right explanation. "It's mostly that I put my own needs before those of others and I tend to shut people out."

Because this seems promising, if vague, I push for more details. "Tell me more."

Terry bristles and snaps, "That's the best I can do!"

This seems a curious reaction, so I continue to ask for clarification.

"Okay, Debbie, my wife, has filed for a divorce and has told me to pack my stuff. She says she's sick of my shit. I mean, she hates the way I treat her. She said there's no way she'll consider staying with me unless I get help with my emotional abuse. Look, that's the best I can do. You need to take over from here."

I try but never get very far. After two desultory sessions, Terry moves back home and cancels his next appointment.

As we can see, Terry came into therapy under coercion. Debbie had made it clear that she would not stay in the marriage unless he agreed to see a therapist. In his mind, he was on the outside of a powerful triangle with Debbie and me aligned against him (even though I had never spoken to her). In response, he went through the motions but never considered therapy anything but a penance or punishment for poorly understood transgressions. Unfortunately, I was never able to change that situation—to convince Terry I could see the world from his perspective and to "sell" him on the potential benefits of therapy.

In later chapters I describe this process of establishing a shared worldview as a critical component of psychotherapy for traditional men. For now, I depict a more successful version of that process, which occurred when I saw Nat, a man in a nearly identical situation.

GARY: Nat, I can see that you have some very mixed feelings about coming here. Also, I know that I'm asking a tough question when I ask what your wife expects from you in here. Apparently, because she calls you neglectful, she's unhappy about something. If it's okay with you, I'll call her sometime to get more information. But for now, let's talk about how things are going for you.

NAT: I'm fine. I just want to get on with my life.

GARY: Looks like there are some frustrating aspects to it.

NAT: Shit! [He looks away, shaking his head.] You don't know the fucking half of it!

GARY: You might be surprised. I've talked with lots of frustrated guys. Life ain't so easy these days. Too much work for too little return. Too many expectations and damn little appreciation. And far too few pleasures and gratifications. Sometimes life sucks for a guy. Makes you wonder just what the hell they expect from us.

NAT: Now you're talking. Shit, let me tell you just how damn bad it is. Last week. . . .

Once we tap men's frustrations, therapy often proceeds rapidly.

THE WAY THERAPISTS TREAT TRADITIONAL MEN

As much as we might like it to be true, all therapists do not value all their clients equally or treat them with equal magnanimity. To a large extent, most people like those persons who seem to like them. Likewise, most therapists prefer clients who seem to value what therapists do. More than thirty years ago, William Schofield (1964) challenged prevalent assumptions about clinician neutrality with his astute observation that therapists tend to prefer clients like themselves—that is, YAVIS clients, or young, attractive, verbal, intelligent, and successful people. Schofield's point was essential; we should not assume that therapists are free from cultural influences that affect their conduct with clients. Therapists have favorites. Do Schofield's findings pose problems for men who might become therapy clients? At first blush they don't seem to. They may in fact suggest that prospective male clients have received a degree of preferential treatment from the therapy community, which historically has been male dominated. There certainly has been abundant evidence of these advantages for men as clients.

For two decades, feminists have been influential in identifying the many ways in which psychotherapy has shortchanged women. In its simplest form, this critique holds that the psychotherapy field has harmed women by encouraging them to be overly quick to adopt the patient role, overly passive as therapy clients, and overly willing to accept male models of mentally healthy behavior for women (Brodsky & Hare-Mustin, 1980). There can be little doubt that these charges have been accurate and that psychotherapy needs to continue its efforts to adjust to women's experiences.

Yet there is another important perspective to be addressed. Of late, many men's studies experts have pointed out a curious irony. Even though the field of psychotherapy has been historically dominated by men, it has been of limited value to men because it has discouraged them from participating as clients. In brief, psychotherapy that is gender-blind (that is, conducted without awareness of gender bias) harms women through what happens in therapists' offices, but it also harms men by driving them away.

To avoid this, we must truly understand and appreciate the culture of men and masculinity and begin to entertain the idea that therapy with traditional men is a form of cross-cultural counseling. Recently, greater attention has been paid to how therapists' cultural biases have harmed ethnic and racial minorities. For example, in *Counseling the Culturally Different* (1990), Derald and David Sue strongly recommend culture-specific communicating and helping styles. They note, "Counseling and psychotherapy do not take place in a vacuum isolated from the larger social-political influences of our society. . . . It is our contention that the reasons minority-group individuals underutilize and prematurely terminate counseling/therapy lie in the biased nature of the services themselves. The services offered are frequently antagonistic or inappropriate to the life experiences of the culturally different client; they lack sensitivity and understanding" (pp. 6–7).

Admittedly, there are problems with thinking of men as a culturally different group parallel to women or ethnic and racial minorities. Unlike these groups, men have not been politically or economically oppressed. Neither has their dominant worldview been ignored by the field of psychotherapy. However, when we consider preferred interpersonal styles and processes, there is considerable utility in thinking of the cultures of psychotherapy and traditional men as different. *To some extent, psychotherapy with traditional men is always a form of cross-cultural counseling.*

There have been a number of attempts to adapt to this clash between the cultures of therapy and masculinity. Ron Levant (1990), for example, has argued that men do well when therapy has a pronounced "skills acquisition focus." Others, including psychologist Jim O'Neil (1981) and family therapists Jo Ann Allen and Sylvia Gordon (1990), have advocated psychoeducational approaches that teach men about the common problems of the male role. Interestingly, a new perspective is emerging that shifts the burden of change from the male client population to the field of psychotherapy and to the psychotherapists themselves. This perspective is consistent with the cross-cultural counseling idea that rather than demanding that the client adapt to the counselor's culture, it may be better for the counselor to adjust to and work within the client's culture.

An office directly across from the unit's group therapy room allows me to have access to a curious event, one that will make sense only many years later.

Several patients of the hospital's alcohol treatment program arrived fifteen minutes early. While awaiting their group leader, they have gotten into a raucous debate about bars and drinking patterns. One guy is pushing the idea that drinkers should frequent three bars—one for fighting, one for picking up women, and one for serious drinking. Another guy calls this ridiculous, claiming that one bar could serve all purposes. Several other group members join the debate with surprisingly impassioned opinions.

Despite the seemingly inane nature of the topic, the interactions are loud and spirited until the door at the far end of the hall opens. The group's leader approaches. As her footsteps grow louder, the group members' voices become quieter. When the leader reaches the room, she meets with complete silence. Consistent with her earlier dictates, group members have learned to end their "frivolous banter" and to get down to meaningful therapeutic work immediately. Unfortunately, no one but the group leader seems to have much to say.

In the previous chapter, I highlighted the growing problems that traditional men face. They are increasingly stressed by sweeping cultural changes, and many are reacting with confusion, rage, or some form of addictive or destructive behavior. Tragically, far too few of them are seeking help through psychotherapy.

In this chapter, I've tried to provide some explanation for traditional men's seemingly inexplicable resistance to getting the help they so desperately need. The stigma against mental illness is associated with psychotherapy in many men's minds. Plus, they see negative characterizations of psychotherapy in the media. Additionally, men struggle with restrictive ideas about masculinity—ideas that make psychotherapy anathema to their sense of pride and self-worth.

These are important ideas for therapists to grasp, because if they don't fully appreciate the causes of men's resistance, psychotherapy cannot be successful. However, there is more to this problematic impasse between traditional psychotherapy and traditional men. Just as many men have not given psychotherapy a chance, we psychotherapists have not done enough to make therapy a comfortable venue for traditional men. To accomplish this, we must understand not only their constraints but also the limiting way in which we have attempted to force restrictive therapy models onto a population that is unlikely to respond. In the next chapter I discuss key elements of psychotherapy practice that *will* allow men to participate actively and enthusiastically.

3

Core Elements

Psychotherapy can be an exhilarating process. At its best, it provides not only compassionate support but also new perspectives, new strategies, and an empowering sense of optimism for those feeling demoralized or stalemated. Not coincidentally, successful therapy makes therapists happy to go to work and makes them feel satisfied with their career choice.

Far too rarely, however, does therapy with traditional men meet this description. In the past, most therapists have accepted referrals for new male clients with resignation instead of enthusiasm. Their male clients, in turn, have often done little more than go through the motions. This, however, can change.

In Chapter One, I argued that the boundless challenges of modern life have shaken the foundations of many men's lives. In Chapter Two, I explored how men's abhorrence of psychotherapy has generated frustration and discouragement among many therapists and created a generally adversarial state of affairs between traditional men and the therapy community. This impasse strikes me as unfortunate and unnecessary. Most traditional men want to do the right thing, just as most therapists want to provide the needed help. Both groups, however, have been stymied by massive cultural differences that are reflected in their dominant worldview, language, and interpersonal style. Each group feels alienated from and suspicious of the other.

Therapists are correct, of course, to be suspicious and challenging of traditional patriarchal men. The sizable harm of the dark side of masculinity (as outlined in Chapter One) cannot be condoned and must be countered. At the same time, the therapy community sells itself short when it settles for approaches to traditional men that are only reactive, caustic, accusatory, or insensitive to their experiences. Therapists are sadly neglectful if they limit themselves to helping women and children while abandoning traditional men.

Yes, men as a group created a world that has often oppressed anyone who does not fit the description of a traditional man, including women, gays, and men who don't measure up in some way. But at an individual level, most men are victims themselves. They desperately want relief. And when they are approached correctly, they are willing to change.

In this chapter I outline basic principles of the best possible psychotherapy for traditional men. This type of therapy will excite and energize male clients, as well as their therapists. Although my model reflects some strong opinions about optimal formats and sequences of therapeutic interventions, I believe that these core elements improve all interventions—group, marital, family, and individual.

COUNTERING RESISTANCE AND BEGINNING THE THERAPY JOURNEY

Therapists not thoroughly familiar with the world of traditional men may have trouble appreciating just how difficult it is for traditional men to enter psychotherapy, and the many ways these men will try to avoid it. As I pointed out in the previous chapter, men are highly skeptical that therapy has much to offer anyone, because it seems to be a nebulous process with intangible objectives. Because of their stereotypes of therapy, they will, at some level, be apprehensive that they can become comfortable in the therapy environment. They will doubt that they have the requisite skills. They may resent the coercive pressure that compelled them to make the appointment or may be wary of how the therapist will treat them. In general, a visit to the therapist's office is a psychic equivalent to a trip to the dentist—without the assurance that anything as practical as pain relief will be accomplished.

Because they don't want to ask for help and are frequently ambivalent about change, traditional men will usually hide their emotional distress behind other symptoms or interpersonal postures. Commonly, they will have attempted to cope with their problems through flight, physical or emotional avoidance, or emotional suppression. Therefore, presenting symptoms may include alcohol or substance abuse, an unhappy marital partner, interpersonal violence, or a combination of all three. Sometimes their psychic distress will be expressed somatically. In these cases, they arrive concerned about their physical health or have come because their physician has insisted that they seek help. If the men have had difficulty "performing," whether physically, vocationally, or sexually, they may see a therapist with the narrow objective of achieving their goals in a given area (for example, improving a golf swing, selling more products, or having more sexual intercourse). At times, they will frame their distress as a lack of information and will come to the office with specific questions and a desire for concrete advice.

For these reasons, therapists face an enormous challenge when first encountering a new male client. More than simply making themselves available, therapists must take full advantage of this first chance to engage the reluctant man in therapy. They must turn the tide and shift the momentum, doing whatever is reasonable to demonstrate to the resistant traditional man that therapy has something to offer.

Therapists should not be discouraged by a traditional man's ambivalence, confusion, or lack of a well-articulated rationale for seeking help. Rarely will these men have an acceptable answer to the commonly asked question, "Just what is it that you expect to get from psychotherapy?"

Therapists, of course, will need to set appropriate limits, take appropriate steps to protect vulnerable parties, and hold men fully accountable for their behavior (such as when they are using their power to impose their will on their partner). In this first therapeutic contact, however, men can gain little from vigorous scolding, moralizing, or political lecturing. Instead, they will need a skillful explanation of the benefits of therapy and opposition to their resistance, perhaps along the following lines.

Selling Therapy

Selling a reluctant man on therapy is a complicated process demanding the highest level of therapeutic skill. No simple formula is possible. Although the therapist facing a resistant man must make many clinical decisions, the first ones may be the most basic: How hard shall I push against this man's resistance? How much of a hard sell of therapy is useful? To illustrate this decision-making process, let's return to previous case examples.

Jack, as you may recall, is a successful attorney who drops by my office for vague but potentially discernible reasons. Always demeaning of psychotherapy and mental health practitioners, he reacts with extreme defensiveness to my fairly innocuous probes. Although he leaves many hints about the disarray in his life, he nevertheless avoids any possible treatment. Here is that vignette again with an alternative ending.

JACK: Whoa, Doc, take it easy. You figuring I need some heavy-duty psychoanalyzing? [Seeming to recognize my surprise, Jack tries to take the edge off.] Hey, look. I know you head doctors are expected to sniff out personal problems, but things are terrific in my life. Sure, everybody has to take his turn swallowing crap, but I'm doing fine. God knows Linda is always bitchin' me out about some imagined crime, but I sure don't need a head shrinking right now.

GARY: Jack, look, I'm not trying to offend you or pry into your private life, but I think I owe you an honest opinion. Let me make a couple of things clear. You are a very gifted attorney. In fact, I can't imagine anyone I'd trust more with my legal needs. You've also got an enormous amount of common sense about some of the glorified psychobabble crap passing as legitimate practice. But I need to tell you that some of the smartest men I've ever known, myself included,[1] can do some of the stupidest shit imaginable! We can work ourselves to death, sacrifice, slave, and act like we are invincible or immortal. Well, forget it! You're a human being with needs! Bad things happen when people don't take care of themselves. Please give me this much credit. I've seen some of the best men I've ever known burn themselves out and end up in a pine box.

In this hard sell of psychotherapy, the therapist directly challenges the defenses and resistance of the male client. The therapist identifies the self-defeating ways in which the client denies his distress, and makes predictions about long-term implications.

The distinction between selling therapy aggressively and scolding a man for his behavior is that the second approach moralizes about how a man has hurt others with his behavior, whereas the former approach focuses on how the man is a victim himself of contemporary role pressures. Men can be confronted supportively about how they have been programmed to live a life that ultimately does them great physical, psychological, and spiritual harm. Therapists familiar with recent men's studies literature should have no problems enacting this complicated confrontation, because they will be able to see how modern men can be both the victimizers and the victimized.

A corollary soft-sell approach is also useful at times. To illustrate, let's return to Terry, the client who has come to my office for help saying that he is "emotionally abusive" but who has really come to satisfy his wife. Again, an alternative ending illustrates the approach.

1. Female therapists, of course, cannot include themselves in a broad statement about how men act. They can, however, refer to male friends who tragically and needlessly sacrifice themselves.

TERRY: Okay, Debbie, my wife, has filed for a divorce and has told me to pack my stuff. She says she's sick of my shit. I mean, she hates the way I treat her. She said there's no way she'll consider staying with me unless I get help with my emotional abuse. Look, that's the best I can do. You need to take over from here.

GARY: Terry, I'll be happy to work with you on problems that are bothering you, but I don't know how I can help with a problem that neither you nor I can see. After all, therapy is expensive and time-consuming. You say your wife feels you are neglectful of her, but you seem like a pretty decent guy to me. I guess I'm unclear where she got her ideas. In fact, it seems to me that you're doing everything you can to be a decent guy. You work hard. You're loyal to your family. In fact, I'm impressed with how well you're doing living up to some pretty burdensome expectations in your life. Hell, it wouldn't surprise me at all if things get you down from time to time. We could certainly talk about that sometime.

If significant others (even other therapists) have been giving a man an unrelenting hard sell about the need for therapy, he may do better with a soft sell. This approach recognizes the coercive forces in his life and emphasizes the therapist's respect for the man's good sense. It sides with the logic of the man's resistance (for example, that therapy is costly and time consuming and has no thorough scientific validation of effectiveness). This approach also encourages him to set his own timetable for considering change. After granting the man respect for having knowledge of his own needs, the therapist may surprise the client by attending to his psychic suffering rather than focusing on his failings and misbehavior. In this way, an embattled male client may experience enormous relief and might begin to realize that therapy actually has something to offer.

Avoiding Pitfalls

To break through a man's resistance, therapists not only need to sell the process but also need to avoid problems that commonly arise in individual, marital, and family therapy. These problems might harden a man's resistance or subvert therapy.

In many ways, the basic arrangement of individual therapy exacerbates men's difficulties in getting therapeutic help. Men are generally uncomfortable in emotionally intense, face-to-face relationships, which are the very essence of individual therapy. A man tends to experience shame when asking for help, often feeling that he is the only man with such "weakness" or "frailty." The secrecy and insulation of individual therapy may perpetuate the troubled man's painful sense that his troubles are unique. Similarly, many men are emotionally isolated from other men, even after completing individual therapy. Individual therapists can encourage men to seek new relationships outside therapy, but this doesn't always take place. Some men end up viewing their therapist as the only person who really knows them. Men tend to think in hierarchical terms, anxiously measuring themselves against other men and thinking that they are supposed to stay "one-up" with women. This can be particularly problematic in individual therapy, as a man is likely to react negatively to the "one-down" aspect of the client position.

The arrangement of marital and family therapy can also cause problems for men. Usually, the parties most interested in establishing new relationship patterns are women. Conversely, the parties most interested in maintaining the status quo are men. Therefore, unless men are helped to recognize the potential advantages of forming new relationship patterns and the adverse consequences of rigidly adhering to the old, they'll enter marital or family therapy prematurely and with a limited and regressive agenda (Brooks, 1990, 1991).

Most contemporary men come into treatment with some disadvantages vis-à-vis women, partially because men have been taught to resist seeking help. Additionally, men are relative newcomers to exploring gender roles. Many women have spent years learning about the culture's negative impact on women, but men have just begun to understand how the culture affects men. Women have often come together to compare notes and share feelings about their experiences; men rarely have done this. Women have become accustomed to self-reflection; men are relative novices.

In the following chapter, I present ideas about how having an all-male group can help circumvent these potential pitfalls. Even if the therapist is unable to adopt this option, however, certain preventive steps are useful. In individual therapy, therapists can accommodate the principles of gender-aware therapy (described more fully later in this chapter), particularly in the areas of therapist transparency and egalitarian relationships. For example, when possible, male therapists can share aspects of their own gender struggles. Female therapists can make references to the struggles of men in their own lives. Therapists can put client problems in a social context and recognize the universality of the man's struggles. To some extent, the locus of problems can be centered on the changing culture rather than exclusively on the troubled man.

The problems that arise in marital and family therapy can be averted mainly by delaying joint sessions and meeting with each marital partner separately (as described in the following section). As much as possible, a therapist should take appropriate time to engage the male client and allow him to develop some sense of the need for gender awareness and change in his relationship patterns.

Envisioning a Sequence of Change

Ideally, traditional men could benefit at any time from any therapeutic modality—individual, group, marital, or family therapy. In my experience, however, there seems to be a sequence that is best suited for men in psychotherapy.

1. First, regardless of the impetus for the initial contact, the traditional man should have a positive first experience with the mental health professional—an experience that neither shames him nor excuses his resistance but instead offers hope that therapy could be relevant to his struggles.

2. Following this initial contact, traditional men seem to benefit greatly from some exposure to the company of other men. For

reasons I outline in the following chapter, I believe this is best accomplished through intense involvement in a men's group. If a men's group is not available, therapists can encourage clients to learn about other men's experiences by attending weekend retreats or men's conferences, reading men's studies literature, or trying to form more intimate connection with male friends or family members.

3. After this "getting to know other men" phase of therapy, traditional men will be better prepared for involvement in marital or family therapy, where their personal changes can be translated into higher levels of relationship functioning.

4. Finally, some men may actually be able to consider a final phase—social activism—in which they might join efforts to change cultural institutions that restrict men's lives, or that harm women and children.

VALUING TRADITIONAL MEN

Because they have worked together for years, the two psychologists (Gary and Roberta) assume they will react almost identically to the videotaped stimulus Gary has selected for their workshop. He has chosen the movie *War of the Roses* as an example of relationship chaos resulting from extremely divergent gender perspectives. Gary screens a film segment in which Oliver Rose (the male lead played by Michael Douglas) spends minimal time with his family, instead dedicating most of his time to career advancement. After a cardiac event that he thought was life-threatening, Oliver is devastated by the indifferent response of his family. He becomes reflective and depressed. Gary is deeply moved by Oliver's pain, thinking it a vivid portrayal of a middle-aged man who has finally recognized the terrible human price he has paid for the pursuit of money and power. Roberta is left cold by the scene, thinking it yet another example of a powerful and entitled man who experiences narcissistic injury when women and children fail to meet his insatiable needs for praise and adoration. A lively discussion follows among the workshop leaders and the audience members. At the heart of the discussion is one question: How much empathy and compassion does the man deserve?

Empathy, the capacity to understand the world from the perspective of another, has long been accepted as a critical component of successful psychotherapy. One of the most established principles of psychotherapy is that clients are more likely to consider change when they feel they have been understood, appreciated, valued, and esteemed. This is especially true of therapy with traditional men, because of the many ways in which they make themselves difficult to value or understand.

Hating therapy, traditional men typically do not appear in a therapist's office until they have failed to reduce distress through a number of inappropriate, maladaptive, and often objectionable behaviors. Abusing drugs and alcohol, acting out sexually, being violent, and escaping or withdrawing emotionally are all common patterns among troubled men. Not only are these habits self-defeating but they are also unlikely to endear the men to therapists. Few therapists have warm feelings for men who evoke the diagnostic criteria for antisocial personality disorder, alcoholic, drug user, or spouse abuser.

Already angry or defensive about entering therapy, many of these men can be expected to be quite sensitive to the therapist's disapproval. If they sense it, they may exit quickly. Some men may adopt a supplicant and self-condemning stance, heaping blame and guilt on themselves while idealizing loved ones whom they have mistreated. Others may present themselves as overwhelmed, confused, or emotionally anesthetized. Regardless of the type of client presentation, the therapist faces a significant challenge. To establish therapeutic rapport, the therapist must try to find the reasons for the male client's pretherapy behavior and must highlight the client's more positive or ennobling characteristics. In brief, the capacity to value traditional men is one of the core elements of treatment.

Let's return to Gary and Roberta's dilemma. Who is right? Is the movie character, Oliver Rose, a powerful and controlling man who is experiencing a case of wounded pride and trying to manipulate others into continuing their overly solicitous attentions to his dependency needs? Or is he a desperately unhappy middle-aged man facing an existential crisis, a collapse of his fragile sense of meaning, and a realization of his loneliness and emotional emptiness?

The answer, of course, is that *both* views are accurate. It is reasonable, and even necessary, to appreciate both realities if one is to work effectively with traditional men. In a culture in which men have had the bulk of the access to political and economic power, therapists can never act in a way that condones men's victimization of others or encourages their demands for patriarchal entitlement. Yet, at the same time, psychotherapy demands that the additional reality also be recognized. Therapists must have some way to feel empathy for their traditional male clients. Although many traditional men engage in some unattractive behavior, they must be understood as persons struggling to remain loyal to a rigid and anachronistic masculine code, persons who can be valued and deemed worthy of a therapist's most dedicated efforts. Here's an example of this process that posed a special challenge for me early in my VA career.

They seemed like such a foolish bunch of right-wing flag-wavers. There were six of them, all World War II veterans, all old men who did nothing with their time anymore but meet to tell and retell war stories. Each belonged to a veterans organization and had all the requisite identifiers—silly caps, patches, pins, and patriotic bumper stickers. Their interactions struck me as almost pathetically archaic with their exaggerated military formality. Just as anachronistically, their "little women" waited patiently for them in cars that the veterans proudly parked in "disabled" parking slots. These men never missed a national holiday, as these occasions provided an excuse to dress in old uniforms and sing patriotic hymns.

According to the prevailing sentiments of the post-Vietnam era, these men are the type of superpatriots who can't wait to invoke the might of the U.S. military. Because I have had no professional responsibility to these men, I've been able to indulge my pacifist and antiwar sentiments privately. To my horror, however, I discover that the retirement of an older psychiatrist has left me with full clinical responsibility for this therapy group. This, I know, is going to be hell for us all.

As I prepare for my first group, I am calmed somewhat by my senior supervisor. Though a veteran himself, he shares many of my antiwar sentiments. Recognizing my distress, he advises that I focus less on what these men symbolize and more on them as individual men. "Just try to learn what makes them tick," he counsels. I reluctantly agree to try but fully expect some serious confrontations.

The conflict never happens. Over the next twelve weeks, as I consciously put aside my negative expectations and commit myself to a piece of scholarly field research, I become fascinated by a world I've previously never understood. Behind these almost clownish exteriors are men deeply scarred by war and its aftermath. Pedro endured eight months in a prisoner of war camp, witnessing the torture and death of his closest friends. Homer risked his life under enemy fire to collect the intestines of a dead fellow soldier whom he wanted to see buried "as a whole man." Bernard charged into an enemy bunker when he realized that his squad faced certain death. Other stories are more mundane, but each man shares the deepest allegiance to his duties as a patriotic man.

My experiences with these men certainly doesn't change my distaste for war or for the traditional process of shaping men into soldiers—into "a few good men." But it does broaden my thinking and raise my consciousness. Despite my ambivalence about many of the things these men cherish, I have come to respect, and in most cases, to care for men who have dedicated their lives to a mission larger than themselves.

SEEING MEN'S PROBLEMS IN CONTEXT: GENDER-AWARE PSYCHOTHERAPY

A talented and highly respected psychiatrist, Dr. Woodley, leads a large group of enthusiastic medical students through morning rounds on a locked-door psychiatric unit. They stop to interview Bobby, a twenty-four-year-old truck driver and rancher. He was admitted after a bar fight in which he beat up another man—one who was making moves on Carol, Bobby's girlfriend.

The psychiatrist bluntly asks Bobby, "Is it your usual habit to displace your rage onto others not directly related to your problems?" After rounds, the psychiatrist lectures the medical students on *displacement*, a mechanism of ego defense that allows responsibility for problems to be shifted onto others. He proposes individual psychotherapy to help the young man gain greater insight into the early life origins of his inability to deal with his intropunitive self.

Bobby's psychiatrist was on solid psychodynamic ground when he identified displacement as a pertinent issue. Bobby was angry at Carol and himself and had chosen to express his rage primarily at Carol's seducer. In the intrapsychic therapy that followed, Dr. Woodley may have mined a treasure of psychic material resulting from Bobby's habit of displacing his affect onto others. But this might also have been a fruitless search for a pattern that was minimally applicable. Dr. Woodley had interpreted Bobby's behavior in a cultural vacuum, that is, without making an effort to understand the dominant value system of Bobby's culture. In the absence of that effort, Dr. Woodley was susceptible to a common mistake of cross-cultural counseling— ascribing pathology to behavior that is culture-bound.

Experts in cross-cultural counseling, such as Derald and David Sue, have recently provided many illustrations of this damaging process. For example, mental health counselors who consider Japanese American clients to be repressed or overly passive have sometimes prescribed assertiveness training to change their deferential style. This intervention, an appropriate one in many cases, can be highly inappropriate in Asian cultures where subtlety and indirect communication are valued. In a similar vein, feminists have long criticized the therapy community for pathologizing women who enact their traditional gender scripts to be caring and protective of others.

Let's look more closely at the culture clash of Bobby and Dr. Woodley. Bobby, it turns out, was from a small west Texas farming community and had been raised with very traditional ideas about men and masculinity. A part-time rodeo cowboy who enjoyed beer drinking and two-step dancing, Bobby spent many Friday nights competing with other cowboys for the attention of the "sweetest young things." If drinking and dancing were the primary recreational activities, fighting was a not-too-distant third. Almost without fail, sometime during the evening, usually when the beer and "closing time" had upped the ante, one guy decided that another was moving in on a girl he had picked out for himself. There was little choice—it was better to go home alone with a broken nose or spend the night in jail than to let another guy think he could take your woman away without a fight.

Not surprisingly, this world was unfamiliar to Dr. Woodley. Like most psychologists and psychiatrists, he was raised in a middle-class to upper-middle-class environment. In fact, he was a fifth-generation physician of a New England Brahmin family with a long history of antiviolence activism. He had attended an exclusive prep school before gaining early admission into an Ivy League college. Except for a brief third grade wrestling match (he lost), he had never come close to a physical fight. His move to Texas had been a difficult one, as he was continually astonished by the crude aggression of the macho cowboys so commonly brought to him after drunken brawls.

Was Dr. Woodley completely off-base with his psychodynamic formulation of Bobby's situation? Perhaps not. Displacement of aggression may have been a problem for Bobby. But the critical point is not to make an interpretation without looking at the behavior in the context of Bobby's dominant culture—the traditionally hyper-masculine world of west Texas ranchers. His cultural point of reference (particularly in terms of violence and overt attitudes toward women) was very different from Dr. Woodley's. Bobby shouldn't be pathologized for that difference (although he *should* be held fully accountable for his behavior).

Culturally sensitive therapy adjusts its diagnostic formulations and intervention style to clients' dominant value system. When it comes to therapy for traditional men, it follows that "masculinity" should come under the microscope. A few writers about therapy for men have made this point. Both *Men in Therapy*, edited by Richard Meth and Robert Pasick (1990), and *Psychotherapy for Men*, by Robert Silverberg (1986), make explicit references to the need for men's therapy groups to make gender socialization an overt discussion topic. Psychiatrist Kenneth Solomon (1982a) notes that men benefit from "gender role psychotherapy," in which gender role issues are explicitly agreed upon as a major focus of therapy. Psychologists Glenn Good, Lucia Gilbert, and Murray Scher (1990) conceptualize gender-aware therapy with similar recommendations that gender be included as an integral aspect of counseling and that client problems be viewed within their social context. Interestingly, when this gender-aware approach to therapy is adopted, there is a corollary shift in the relationship between client and therapist. Therapists can become more transparent and collaborative in their therapeutic relationship, sometimes even becoming role models. This altered stance can be a major step in moving past the adversarial dynamic that can be so common between traditional men and their therapists.

At their hearts, these context-aware therapies urge men to see themselves in social context. That is, they learn to view themselves as products of, and sometimes victims of, their upbringing in a "gendered" culture. It is ironic that, in many ways, this process of seeing oneself in relational context is highly antithetical to the rugged individualist aspect of manhood.

According to family therapist Salvador Minuchin, the perspective that people must be understood in their "social context was developed in the second half of the twentieth century"; this approach broke with the psychodynamic thinking that "drew upon a different concept, that of man as a hero, remaining himself in spite of his circumstances" (1974, p. 4). This contextualized orientation also runs counter to the view of male development portrayed in the well-known theory of Nancy Chodorow (1978)—that is, that male development accentuates separateness and autonomy. The self-in-context perspective also contradicts the common sociocultural portrayal of "real men" as rugged individualists and conquerors of the frontier.

Simply put, traditional men like to think that they alone determine what they do and that they could not care less what others think. Men's attribution system is usually much too unforgiving in thinking "I alone am responsible for my failures." It is obviously no easy matter to convince men that their actions are heavily influenced by their surrounding environment, as this is an idea that runs counter to traditional masculinity's extreme emphasis on autonomy. Nevertheless, this challenge to men's phenomenology and attribution system can offer immense subjective relief. When men become able to see themselves not as personal failures but as products of a severe and unforgiving socialization process and as loyalists to an anachronistic masculine code, they cannot help but experience a dramatic decrease in inappropriate self-blame. This new perspective not only provides substantial comfort to many anguished men but may also generate enough energy for them to begin the corollary investigation of how socialization pressures have limited women.

ACCOMMODATING THE GOOD OL' BOY STYLE

To the naive observer, they might look like a group of farmers who have just happened upon each other over breakfast. But they are much more than that. Every morning, before plowing, tilling, or hauling, the same seven men meet at Harriet's Cafe, the only restaurant in a small town in rural Nebraska. Despite occasional minor variations, the pattern is nearly invariable—each arrives by 6:10, pours himself a cup from the waiting coffeepot, lights a cigarette, and takes his usual seat at the table. Soon they are engrossed in breakfast and their morning ritual of storytelling, teasing, joking, and sharing crop information.

On this day, Carl carries on about a recent change in state policy for volunteer fire departments. This inspires Bob to launch into a lengthy story about the former fire chief, who was as notorious for his hangovers as for his inept driving. Each man seems to have his favorite story and the laughter becomes so contagious that several have to stop eating for fear of choking. Over the remainder of the hour, Harold updates everyone on the progress of the county hog barn, Junior compliments Harriet on the "great" coffee, Cecil asks if anyone knows what has happened to the planned dam on the local river, and Phil bitches about the poor torque ratio on the new John Deere tractors. At 7:00, they push their chairs back, gripe about the bill, and head to their pickups.

Although this collection of breakfasting men may seem generally irrelevant to psychotherapists, it actually points to another core element of therapy for this population. This breakfast group, with its good ol' boy interaction style, is one variant of the most common social experience of most traditional men in America—the all-male group.

Anthropologist and early sociobiologist Lionel Tiger (1969) wrote extensively about all-male groups and introduced the controversial notion of *male bonding*. According to Tiger, men have an innate biological predisposition to establish all-male groups that perpetuate power over women. Like all sociobiologists, Tiger has had his theories subjected to criticism that has raised serious questions about the accuracy of his postulations. Despite the doubts raised about the biological basis of forming all-male groups, there has been widespread agreement that these groups have been prevalent and that male bonding is an important phenomenon.

Others, such as historian E. Anthony Rotundo (1993) and sociologist Michael Kimmel (1987), have endorsed Tiger's assertion that ritualized all-male groups have been common throughout history. Kathryn Farr (1986) conducted field research on two of these groups, ultimately reporting on dominance bonding in the "good old boy sociability group" (GOBS): "Members of GOBS groups share successful class and gender histories, and plan and engage in events that reflect dimensions of masculine play learned in boyhood. The GOBS group was found to perpetuate masculine identity and male privilege through dominance bonding, i.e., a process of collective alliance in which members affirm and reaffirm their superiority" (p. 259). Farr's work is particularly helpful, because she provides invaluable insights into what she calls the "good old boy sociability style."

Farr's observations are consistent with my own about the style most natural for men in groups.

- There are strong preferences regarding topics for group discussion. Sports, machines, and national news are highly preferred, whereas relationships, emotional states, and personal fears are almost never discussed.

- The conversational style is light, with continual banter, teasing, and joking. Invariably, because the group would not be allowed to exist in its own right (that would be an admission of emotional attachment, which seems unmanly), it is organized around some purpose other than interpersonal contact—a fraternal organization, a sports booster club, or a poker game.

- Food and drink are central, both as an excuse for the meeting and as a helpful avoidance tactic should an awkward moment arise.

- Storytelling is the most common contribution of group members, although many will chime in to give advice or offer solutions to problems.

- Although teasing is frequent, most of the interactions are mutually supportive, in what Farr calls "testimonial fashion."

- Direct personal communications or "face-to-face" confrontations are rare, as most communication is indirect. Eye contact beyond a few microseconds is rare. A tight lid is kept on expressions of anger among members, with most serious disagreement and tension deflected through humor.

- Most prominently, there is minimal or no sense of interpersonal intimacy or direct expression of affection. Group members establish thick walls or personal boundaries, never treading even remotely within another's emotional space.

- Although few ever miss the gatherings, all, if asked, would vehemently deny that a men's group even exists.

The norms of these naturalistic men's groups run completely counter to the norms of most effective psychotherapy groups. Therapy groups are likely to emphasize serious discussion of deeply meaningful personal material, open ownership of personal feelings and reactions, intense analysis of interpersonal sequences, tolerance of therapeutic silence to heighten emotional tension, intolerance of interruptions and distractions, preference for the here and now, and regular metacommunication about the group as a dynamic organism.

Because the "natural" men's group is so clearly "antitherapeutic," some might jump to the conclusion that men must completely scrap their previous group style and start from scratch. Indeed, the group therapy literature is filled with prescriptions for pretherapy training programs intended to help men overcome their deficiencies and learn proper group norms. Some group therapists give up entirely on men as fully functioning group members and suggest alternative forms that men can master, for example, skills groups or cognitive therapy groups. At their worst, these "accommodations" are demeaning and stultifying. Even at their best, they are unnecessary.

Therapists who are familiar with men's typical style in natural groups have no great difficulty adapting to the good ol' boy style (whatever the form of therapy). Rather than stubbornly digging in and demanding immediate adaptation to ideal therapy behavior, a therapist should learn to accept men where they are, "go with" the way men typically interact, and gradually shape their therapy behavior. In Chapter Four I note many effective techniques that the group leader can use to have the best of both worlds—the therapeutic norms of effective groups *and* the enthusiastic vitality of traditional men who enjoy the group setting.

EVOKING MEN'S EMOTIONAL PAIN

It is Monday, and as is often the case on Mondays, the group seems listless and "bottled up." Chuck, despite some strong signs of inner distress, won't talk about his frustration. I decide to provoke something.

"Have you guys ever had this experience I've often had? You're under a little pressure as you start to hammer a nail into the wall. On the third blow, the hammerhead slips off the nail and hits you square on the thumb. It hurts like hell!" I notice clear signs of familiar recognition among the group members. "Pissed off, you hit the nail even harder, but you only hit a glancing blow, and your thumb really takes a shot this time. Now you're furious! You remove your thumb, rear back to really cream that fucking thing!" The group members edge forward in their seats. "Your blow bends the nail and the head of the hammer goes right through the plasterboard. You throw the goddamn hammer against the wall and get the hell outta there!"

Heavily into the image and emotionally charged, Chuck stands and walks around the room, banging one fist into his other palm.

"You know, it's goddamn maddening to try, try, try, and nothing comes of it but a friggin' mess!" Glancing around the room, I can see tension in all the faces. Everyone is tense and wired—just as I hoped. Although some would use this as an opportunity to do some intense individual abreactive work with Chuck, I choose instead to stay focused on the entire group, to take full advantage of their emotional arousal, to have them express their frustration and disappointment.

It doesn't take long; everyone is ready to spill forth bitter but poignant stories. Every member has a version of how he has been trying, without much luck, to make things work out. "What's the point? No matter how much you bust your balls, it always turns to crap! What the hell do women expect? No matter what you do, they're always bitchin' at you for something else! It's just that it hurts to try and try and not be able to make anything happen. . . . It just [choking up] . . . it just makes me feel so fuckin' worthless. . . . [jumping up as the anger returns] It makes me feel like a fuckin' loser!"

Intense emotional pain is the shameful secret of traditional men. Its evocation is a core element in their therapy. Emotional pain, experienced by most men as humiliating weakness, is so terrifying that men will go to great lengths to hide from it. Rage and frustration, because they are "manly" emotions, are the primary affective states men allow themselves to experience. Christopher McLean has written that "the process of turning boys into men has, historically, been one of systematic abuse, both physical and emotional, designed to teach boys not to show most emotions, except in certain ritually prescribed situations, and if possible, not to feel them" (1996, p. 21).

Men's pain cannot remain hidden. Before significant therapeutic change can take place, therapists must understand the dimensions of men's psychic pain, develop skills to evoke its expression in therapy sessions, and be adept at showing men how to redirect the resultant energy toward more productive ends.

In Chapter One, I described the multiple variants of men's psychic pain: anger, bitterness, frustration, guilt, shame, and grief. The first step in the evocation process, of course, is to appreciate the scope and intensity of this distress. Next, the therapist must become acutely attuned to the many techniques men have for avoiding or indirectly discharging their painful feelings—for example, denial, rationalization, flight, hostile humor, and numbness.

The next step—provocation of the affect—is infinitely more complicated and perilous, because it requires a substantial shift from the usual norms of the good ol' boy group (although this stage is usually not reached, however, until the good ol' boy stage has been established). To provoke the feeling, the therapist begins to "hold a man's feet to the fire." As this may push men into very unfamiliar, and at times emotionally primitive, territory, it can only be accomplished successfully when men have basic trust and utmost confidence in the benevolent intentions of the therapist (and anyone else in the therapy room). As illustrated by my mistakenly overzealous work with Leon (in the Introduction), the therapist must move very cautiously, always remaining alert to signs of autonomic hyperarousal.[2] Because men are prone to experience rage before anything else, the therapist should establish firm ground rules against violence and arrange for a man to provide clear signals when he feels overwhelmed. Therapists must make it abundantly clear that the client, not the therapist, is ultimately in charge of the intensity of the therapy; that is, the therapist will continually ask for guidance and will back off whenever the client wishes. When in doubt, the therapist should always err on the side of caution.

The therapist must be certain to follow up with a man who has been provoked in an earlier session. A man's sudden flight, withdrawal, or silence should be carefully pursued to determine whether his emotional limits have been reached. Finally, a man needs explicit assurance that the therapist will remain available both during

2.   This is an especially sensitive issue for men who have been repeatedly exposed to high-stress situations—soldiers, policemen, firemen, and gang members—and who may have lost, to some degree, the physiological capacity to monitor their level of emotional arousal.

and between sessions, because many men fear exposure without access to emotional support.

There are many different ways of characterizing the processes of evoking men's pain. These are some that I have employed.

Digging, Prodding, and Provoking

A favorite therapy client once said my therapy style felt like someone was "digging inside him with a rusty shovel." Before the provocation stage, the therapist has accommodated traditional men's superficial emotional style, but now the therapist pushes and probes. Denials are countered by direct challenges. In groups, other members may be enlisted to challenge a man's defensiveness. To a degree, a man's irritation and annoyance are ignored, because an angry outburst may be a path to his other emotions. The therapist might say something like, "I know I'm being a jerk and pushing you pretty hard here, but I really want to be sure we're not missing something. If you are truly about to lose it, I'll back off."

Holding and Focusing

When avoidant men begin to squirm with discomfort, they need a benevolent reminder to stay focused on their pain. This may be a literal reminder to stay in their chairs or it could be a more abstract reminder to return to an earlier painful topic.

Showing and Modeling

At appropriate times, usually with an advanced client or group, it can be immensely helpful for a therapist to drop the professional facade and to reveal a raw or unvarnished emotion—rage at a recent slight, grief over the loss of a loved one, guilt over a past misdeed. Although this is most effective when done spontaneously, it must also be done judiciously with topics that the therapist can manage reasonably well. Because this process reveals that therapist has important common struggles, it can promote the therapy relationship and normalize many emotional reactions.

This tactic must be utilized most judiciously, of course. Generally it is far better to make examples highly concrete. Illustrative topics must be squarely within the realm of the man's experience, because something too "fluffy" risks trivializing the man's pain. The therapist should also be careful not to "whine," that is, complain of something that another man might see as a luxury. Finally, the therapist must not go too far in exposing his vulnerabilities, because the men should not feel they must take on responsibility for the therapist's pain.

Using Experiential Exercises

At certain times, it may be helpful to cut through men's intellectual defenses by moving them into experiential exercises. For example, the therapist can use gestalt techniques, role-playing, trust exercises, and empty chairs. These activities seem especially useful for accessing deeply buried emotions of shame and grief. I am generally uncomfortable, however, with exercises that evoke men's anger (hitting, banging, and punching), because they seem to invite eruptions of violence.

Inciting and Escalating Tension

In men's groups, the therapist may sometimes move among the men, much like a television talk show host, to incite a heightened awareness of past slights or emotional injuries. Obviously, this is a highly incendiary technique that must be used with great caution. In general, it should only be employed when the limits of male clients are well known. Although the technique provokes anger, it is primarily used to help men uncover the hurt and pain *behind or underneath* their rage. It is far too risky to incite men and send them out of the therapy room in a hyperaroused state. Therefore, the technique should always be used when there is considerable time to process the angry emotions and achieve a more composed and relaxed emotional state.

Using Therapeutic Silence

Teasing and joking make it easier for traditional men to attain a degree of comfort in close emotional quarters. In early stages of therapy, the therapist does well to join actively in this light banter. At later points, particularly when men are assiduously avoiding a critical matter, the therapist can force more confrontation of the issue by becoming silent. An unaccustomed silence from the therapist speaks loudly to traditional men—that they, not the therapist, are to take responsibility for the work that needs to be done. Almost invariably this heightens tension enough that the men have few alternatives but to "hear" the therapist and take on their new responsibility.

RECOGNIZING MASCULINE HERITAGE

Ron is stuck. As much as he tries, he is unable to get past his anger at his distant father, the man who was always too aloof, too cool, and too rejecting. Touched by Ron's distress, Chuck asks if he can share his story of his relationship with his own father. Ron eagerly accepts, and Chuck begins.

"I was about seventeen when I had this incredible encounter with my father. It was in the summer, when, as usual for me in high school, my buddies and I had spent the night drinking and drag racing till well past midnight. Sometime during the craziness, one of the guys 'blew lunch' out the back window, leaving vomit all over the side of the car. When I pulled into the driveway at nearly 3 A.M., my dad was waiting. I knew I was in deep shit—he was obviously real pissed off.

"As he came up to me, I was ready for the worst, maybe even a fight. He grabbed my left arm and seemed like he wanted to shake me. Just as I thought he'd explode, I realized he was choking up and couldn't really talk. For several seconds he tried but couldn't get anything out. Then he threw his arms around me and really lost it. He held me real tight, then started sobbing at first, then really let go with a heavy load of heaving and crying. This was unbelievable. I was totally stunned."

Chuck pauses; the memory clearly recalls many painful emotions. "As you can see, this still stirs up a few feelings for me," he says, wiping his eyes. "He told me how scared he was, how helpless he felt to straighten me out. Before I knew it, I was actually rubbing the back of his head and comforting him. From that day on, things were never the same between us. I saw him in a completely new way and never really felt so interested in defying him. Over time, I learned a lot about him and his relationship with his own father—a real hard-ass, by the way."

Over the remainder of that session, and several thereafter, group members productively share similar experiences of encounters, actual and fantasized, with their fathers.

As much as they might like to portray themselves as independent and rugged individualists, men cannot really free themselves from their families of origin or their masculine heritage. Many therapists have begun to recognize that therapeutic work with women and men is enriched by attention to the history of the women and men in their families. The concept of *transgenerational focus* refers to the notion that we are much better able to understand any particular man when we have a greater understanding of the struggles of his father, his father's father, and his father's father's father. A man's ideas about his masculine role are greatly influenced by contemporary culture, but they are also shaped by the history of men in his family and by what Murray Bowen has called the "multigenerational transmission process"—that is, patterns of interpersonal interactions transmitted across generations (Bowen, 1978).

Transgenerational work encourages active rediscovery of one's roots. Although Harriet Lerner has written principally about therapy for women, her ideas about feminist-informed Bowenian therapy apply to therapy with men. "Through both Bowen work and feminism, a woman's sense of isolation about her so-called pathology is replaced by an empathic understanding of the continuity of women's struggles through the generations and the ways in which she is both similar and different from those who came before her" (1985, p. 37).

Ann Dienhart and Judith Myers Avis have concurred with this idea that family-of-origin work is especially applicable to therapy with men because it "allows men to identify and address those patterned behaviors, often learned early in life, on which they rely to camouflage vulnerabilities, disappointments, hurts, losses, and needs" (1991, p. 41).

The therapy work of Chuck and Ron is quite similar to that envisioned by Sam Osherson, one of the leading writers on "father wounds and father hunger." Consistent with others who advocate family-of-origin work, Osherson sees men's emotional growth and healing as tied to "recognizing our fathers' actual wounds, the way they have been wounded by their lives, the complex cross-currents within our families that led to disconnection, and by exploring and testing out richer, more satisfying male identities. . . . One way of healing the wounded father is to plunge into your father's history. A man needs to find ways of empathizing with his father's pain. The women's movement has provided many daughters with a way of understanding and forgiving their mothers, but we have little corresponding sense of our fathers. We have to understand our fathers' struggle and see the broken connection between fathers and sons as part of the unfinished business of manhood" (1986, p. 178).

A transgenerational focus, though greatly aided by the study of men's connection with preceding generations of men, need not be limited to father-son work. In one of the most important recent contributions, Olga Silverstein (1994) has called for a heightened emphasis on the damage that young men experience if they are prematurely and traumatically separated from their mothers. Although Silverstein focuses primarily on needed changes in child rearing, her ideas have immense implications for therapy with men; if one extends her theory, therapists should help men not only to "find their fathers" but also to rediscover connections with their mothers. As Silverstein notes so aptly, "The real pain in men's lives stems from their estrangement from women. . . . They may be looking for their lost fathers in some ritual space, or bonding with their new-found brothers in the sweat lodge, but their feelings of loss are not going to be assuaged until that central fact of male experience is acknowledged" (p. 225).

As much as they may see themselves as unfettered and independent, traditional men benefit greatly from attention to their interconnections across generations. For this reason, transgenerational work that helps men recognize their masculine heritage is a core element of therapy with traditional men.

CHALLENGING MEN TO CHANGE

Thus far in this chapter, I've noted several core elements for therapy with traditional men. I have suggested that therapists will be more successful when they can do the following:

Be alert to all forms of therapy resistance.

Approach men with empathy and compassion.

View men's distress in context through the lens of gender experience.

Be fluent in men's relational style.

Evoke men's psychic pain.

Be sensitive to transgenerational patterns.

When these core elements are successfully incorporated into therapy, there is far greater likelihood that men will overcome their fear and distrust and experience treatment as a welcome source of comfort. Men will often experience considerable subjective relief and gain substantial self-respect as they recognize the universality of traditional men's struggles; they will come to feel, "I am not alone in this." They may reduce tension through their cathartic expression of intense negative feelings.

Although these accomplishments are quite important, however, they are not sufficient. This is the point at which my approach to men differs markedly from that of certain others. Let me elaborate.

Over the past several years, great attention has been focused on improving one's understanding of men and their ways. John Gray's *Men Are from Mars, Women Are from Venus* has become phenomenally popular by suggesting that women and men need to have a greater understanding of each other's unique interpersonal styles. Neuroanatomists have generated a considerable popular following by suggesting that women's and men's differences can be understood through more intensive study of the inherent differences in male and female brains. Sociobiologists and evolutionary psychologists have likewise become immensely popular with their suggestions that men's behavior can be understood by studying the differing adaptive challenges of women and men across their evolutionary heritages.

Each of these perspectives is welcome, because they offer intriguing avenues for a greater understanding of men's behavior. In my view, however, they are highly disappointing and even counterproductive when they call for nothing more than an improved understanding of men's behavior. It is my fervent belief that therapists cannot settle for a mere understanding of men. We must also have a complete commitment to helping men change. The subjective relief that our male clients experience through improved self-understanding and recognition of universal struggles is a critical first step, but therapy cannot stop there. Men must be challenged to reevaluate their gender role values and assumptions in an effort to bring themselves into greater harmony with a changing world.

This point of view is completely consistent with the philosophy of the women's consciousness-raising (C-R) groups of the 1960s and

1970s. In discussing C-R groups for women, psychologist Annette Brodsky stated, "In terms of contrast with therapy groups, the C-R group starts with the assumption that the environment, rather than intrapsychic dynamics, plays a major role in the difficulties of the individuals" (1973, p. 25).

Warren Farrell, one of the earliest writers about therapy with men, distinguished between a therapy group and a C-R group in this way: "A therapy group . . . can delve into *psychological* explanations as to *why* behavior occurs; it generally teaches one how to *adjust* to the societal norm. A C-R group deals predominantly with problems resulting from the attempted adjustment to sex roles. Its members encourage each other to question sex roles, rather than to depend on a leader to help them adjust" (1974, p. 195, italics his).

This final core element, then, encourages therapists to resist the temptation to settle for subjective relief. Instead, they should aim to help men change their traditional patterns. This is the point at which therapy ceases to be "adaptation based" and begins to be "transcendence based." That is, rather than seeking what Watzlawick, Beavin, and Jackson (1967) have called "first-order" change, therapy seeks "second-order" change.

The psychotherapy interventions I have described apply to a traditional man who resists therapy. These differ significantly from strategies for therapy with a "modern" or "evolving" man, such as one who enters therapy of his own volition to achieve greater self-actualization. Those who conduct therapy with these "modern" men have the luxury of openly discussing the benefits of new gender patterns and making explicit contracts toward that end.

This level of shared goal setting is not, however, likely to be possible at first with resistant traditional men. They usually enter therapy wanting to return to customary patterns—that is, to establish some sense of familiar regularity in their lives. In this state of mind, they are likely to recoil in horror at any proposed contract that seems to call for "feminization" or "emasculation." If the therapist has been skillful and the therapy has flowed smoothly, however, then the resistant male client will have had several critical experiences; he will have felt personally validated, discovered his considerable psychic pain, felt relieved and excited to form connections with other troubled men, and recognized the therapist's benevolent intentions. At this point, he may be ready to consider the next step in his gender role journey—rejecting the most rigid and harmful aspects of traditional gender roles.

———————

In this chapter, I've suggested a number of core elements that I feel are critical to successful psychotherapy with traditional men. I see them as cutting across all forms of therapy with this group and as being integral to my therapeutic model. In the next chapter I turn to the all-male therapy group, a setup I consider especially useful for traditional men.

4

Men's Groups That Work

In a particularly tense group meeting, Jesse is overcome with emotions as he recalls a traumatic Vietnam experience. He was only seventeen when his company was overrun at Ben Het. As part of a desperate attempt to save a mortally wounded buddy, he carried and dragged him three hundred yards across a "field of fire" to get him to the safety of a waiting chopper. Though hit twice himself, he made it to the chopper with his buddy on his back. Because of his own injuries, Jesse was forced to climb aboard the departing chopper and was thwarted in his frantic efforts to return for more injured comrades. As the chopper climbed to escape enemy fire, another injured troop, who had been trying to follow Jesse to safety, made a frenzied leap to get aboard. Jesse caught him by the bloody wrist and strained to pull him in. For an instant, as the chopper ascended, Jesse was able to hold him and stare into the man's terrified eyes. Then, he lost his grip and the soldier fell fifty feet to his death or certain capture. For more than twenty years, Jesse has periodically awakened in panic from nightmares where he sees the man's face and hears his screams. Jesse is wracked with guilt that he didn't jump from the chopper to try to rescue his comrade.

There's a long silence before George is able to share the feelings kindled by Jesse's story. With great difficulty, he tells the group of his intense anguish over the friends he lost in Vietnam. When the group discusses the Vietnam memorial in Washington, D.C., George admits that he doesn't have any plan to visit, for fear that he will follow through on his twenty-two-year plan to "off" himself, to commit suicide to rejoin his buddies "on the other side." He distances himself from affectionate relationships, noting that any love or pleasure is a disloyalty to Vietnam comrades who will never return. When under severe stress, he isolates himself, repeatedly watching *Platoon,* a movie that he feels helps him be close again to those he lost.

Before long, Buck, a sixty-four-year-old retired county sheriff with heart problems and severe pulmonary disease, talks of his rage and bitterness at being forced to leave his life's work on account of his health. Feeling worthless as a "civilian," he reminisces often about the camaraderie and closeness he felt with fellow officers. After hearing that one close friend has been killed recently in the line of duty, Buck castigates himself: "This wouldn't have happened if I'd been where I should have been." With a tremulous voice and wet eyes, he says, "I'd crawl five miles to get a guy out of trouble!"

What should we make of these stories? Are they only melodramatic portrayals of anachronistic, patriarchal, and aberrant male behaviors that generally result from military, paramilitary, and high-risk macho environments? Perhaps there is some truth to that, but such an analysis is not the issue here. The point of the stories is that there is an important theme in the traditional masculine code that could be helpful to therapists. This theme calls for a man to do all he can to aid a comrade in danger, to rescue a buddy, even if it means risking one's own life.

Jesse, George, and Buck are three of the most memorable clients I've encountered in more than twenty-five years of therapy with troubled men. They became central figures in a VA men's group lasting several years and characterized by deep interpersonal loyalty and affection. As distinctive as these three men have been, they are not unique. Over the years and several thousand group sessions, individual details have become blurred, but a collective impression has emerged.

I have repeatedly witnessed a process in which men in pain join together to form a healing community. Not all, of course, have shared intense military combat experiences. Many groups have united around other experiences common to men's lives—loss or rejection, fears of failing health, troubled relationships, uncontrollable rage, loneliness, or alcohol abuse. These men, and the healing groups they have created, have profoundly affected my ideas about the abilities and needs of traditional men, as well as my thinking about the most effective forms of therapeutic intervention.

Of all the vital things I have learned from my work with traditional men, nothing stands out more than one sad irony. At a very deep level, men crave close connection with other men, yet they spend their lives fearing, denying, and avoiding that very connection. Surely, one would assume, if a man is willing to go to such perilous extremes to help a friend in danger, he will be available to him at times of emotional need. Surely, a man who, in certain circumstances, would risk everything to help a buddy would not hesitate to *ask* for help at times of emotional desperation.

But this is frequently not the case, as men are peculiarly unavailable to each other at times of great need. So, is this loyalty to other men a myth? A hoax? Perhaps so, but my experience with men suggests an alternative explanation. Men truly do want to help each other, but they are seriously impeded in this endeavor by their socialization into manhood and by their continual efforts to appear manly.

In previous chapters, I've described the hallmarks of the male code and suggested how it creates numerous barriers to men's connections with one another. Men learn to be stoic—to appear cool and confident and diligently hide or repress fear and vulnerability. They are taught to take advantage of weakness in other men, even to the point of joining with other men in physical and emotional tyranny over men who appear vulnerable. Even if they wished to help other men, they would find themselves poorly prepared, because they have systematically extinguished empathy, compassion, and nurturance in themselves. Men have been so rigorously encouraged to sexualize affectionate relationships that they are horrified by intimacy with other men. Because they idealize autonomy and detachment, they quickly become uneasy in the face of overt neediness in themselves or other men.

In this chapter, I elaborate on why these restrictions in men's potential make the all-male group an ideal healing environment. I also suggest several broad objectives and a number of critical techniques for leaders of these all-male groups. In sum, I hope to pass on to therapists both my discovery of the extraordinary immediacy of the all-male group and techniques to transcend men's resistance to the connections they so desperately need.

CONFRONTING THE MALE CHORUS

In my work with Jesse, George, and Buck, I ran headlong into the problems and benefits of the male chorus, that internalized set of male voices that compels men to adhere to traditional masculine values. Earlier I described how Keith, the eighth grader coerced into an unwanted fight, experienced intense pressure to impress his male peers. With Jesse, George, and Buck, we see how these pressures can come to haunt every aspect of a man's life. Jesse and George could find no relief from their convictions that they had been disloyal to Vietnam buddies, and Buck tortured himself for failing to protect fellow law enforcement officers. Throughout his life, each of these men struggled to meet the standards of the male chorus.

The point is a critical one. Men learn to be men in front of other men. Therefore, it is in front of other men that men can *unlearn* some of the more unproductive lessons about manhood and *relearn* and *reinforce* some of the more positive lessons. An all-male group can help a man passionately reexperience past stresses and failures with the male chorus and nostalgically rediscover the more therapeutic aspects of male bonding groups. At the same time, however, this all-male group must become a place where new and different behaviors are learned; the group must teach men role flexibility instead of role constriction, tolerance instead of judgment, compassion instead of scorn, cooperation instead of competition, and intimacy instead of emotional detachment.

In my view, the therapist needs to accomplish three principal tasks: (1) stimulate affective discovery of past traumas and joys, (2) promote new behavioral patterns, and (3) strategize to meet future challenges.

Exploring Past Experiences

Most men have either repressed or consciously avoided all but the most superficial aspects of their developmental years. Yet it usually takes very little to get traditional men to begin a powerful journey of mutual discovery. Sometimes, the process can be launched serendipitously—by one man's unexpected encounter with issues that have obvious roots in childhood. For example, a man facing public embarrassment may feel ashamed in a way that he used to in the presence of his adolescent buddies. Less obvious would be rage reactions that mask shame or humiliation. Frequently, a man's aggressive reaction has been provoked by the extreme fear of public humiliation or scorn from other men that has haunted him since childhood. One man's display of intense emotion frequently provides a exceptional opportunity for a therapist to explore the issue with *all* men in the group. Here, the all-male group differs markedly from some conventional therapy groups in which the issue would be explored intensively as part of this one man's unique pathology. Instead, the therapist explores the issue as one that *all* men share.

At other times, the therapist can carefully plan for the group to reencounter the male chorus of the past. Therapists might introduce provocative questions or tasks: "What do you remember most vividly about your interactions with childhood or adolescent male peers and male authority figures? What was most joyful? What was most painful?" Therapists who prefer more experiential approaches might structure special exercises—empty chair techniques, role-plays, or nonverbal reenactments—to help men discover the previously buried or displaced affect.

Enacting New Patterns

In the all-male group, therapists can help men recognize problematic patterns as they are replicated in the here and now and try out adaptive behaviors. Some psychologically sophisticated men merely need to discover the affective roots of their distress in order to make significant progress. Most traditional men need more, however, in that they require actual practice with new behaviors.

Because skills acquisition may be a critical objective of the group, the therapist should be prepared, when indicated, to be unusually active, sometimes even serving as a teacher or role model. Once again, we see a contrast with some conventional therapies, whereby the group leader is more passive and remote.

Planning for Future Challenges

Outside the therapy group, men need tools to recognize and combat the most noxious aspects of the male chorus. I've found two types of skills most helpful: deconstructive literacy and cognitive analysis.

Deconstructive literacy is the capacity to detect the multiple ways in which culture—television, film, the popular press, and central institutions—enhances the power of the male chorus. Whenever possible, therapists should expose men to prevalent media images of "real men" and help group members learn to "read" the many messages that the media present. For example, viewing provocative scenes from the film *Full Metal Jacket* may provide many men with a vivid illustration of how toughness and emotional stoicism are shown to be hallmarks of worthy men. (The movie may also stimulate affective echoes from the men's past.) Seemingly innocuous beer commercials often carry potent traditional messages about work, violence, and male-female relationships.

Cognitive analysis is a version of standard cognitive therapy in which clients are encouraged to detect and, when necessary, alter the cognitive underpinnings of their distress. Here, therapists need to help men recognize the unnecessary "shoulds" and "musts" related to how "real men" are expected to behave. Naturally, the most dysfunctional cognitions are replaced with more realistic ones. For example, "A real man never backs down from danger" could be replaced with this message: "All men are faced with threatening situations beyond their ability. Sometimes it makes sense to do what is reasonable and to save yourself for another day—and for loved ones who need you."

If the all-male group is to be a mechanism for confronting the male chorus, a crucial issue is whether the group's captivating appeal can be used to promote larger therapeutic purposes without perpetuating narrow masculine role behaviors. The challenge is for the therapist to use the traditional allure of the male group to attract and hold men while transforming the group itself. The therapist who is keenly aware of the inner workings of men's culture will probably be best at accomplishing this most difficult challenge— taking traditional men as they are and moving comfortably within *their* world, yet using one's knowledge and therapeutic expertise to inspire the group to transcend its traditional limitations.

COUNTERING MEN'S EMOTIONAL ISOLATION FROM OTHER MEN

In many ways, George, Jesse, and Buck have given themselves the worst of both worlds. Although they cherish the value of connection to other men, they deem themselves unworthy of new connections. Similarly, Marty, the group member who considered suicide a preferable option to public shame, desperately longs for connection with other men.

Because of their emotionally isolated lives, many men find that therapy groups offer immense potential for interpersonal connectedness and recognition of common struggles. Group therapy theorist Irving Yalom (1975) has posited that a major "curative factor" of groups is their potential to develop a sense of "universality"—a sense of "we are all in the same boat." In my experience, this universality is especially salient for traditional men, many of whom see themselves as shamefully unique. For example, a troubled man often feels that he is the only one struggling to live up to his good provider role, the only one with insecurities about sexuality, and the only one feeling emotionally distant from his family. When a group member discovers that most of the other men share very similar concerns, he experiences, to borrow Yalom's words, a "disconfirmation of feelings of uniqueness . . . a powerful source of relief" (p. 7).

As I have said, the therapist's task seems threefold—to uncover memories of the past, enact new patterns, and plan for future challenges.

Exploring Past Experiences

Therapists should have little difficulty helping men rediscover the joys of male-male intimacy, because most men cherish memories of their closest childhood friends. Sometimes these memories can be evoked through films like *Stand by Me* or *Diner*. At other times, a simple exercise will accomplish the objective: "I'd like you to close your eyes and take a minute to go back into your past to remember your closest childhood buddy. Picture yourselves together. Remember what you would be doing. Try to capture the feelings and go with those images."

Grief, though more remote because of traditional men's tendency to repress painful emotions, becomes much more accessible once they have uncovered their nostalgic memories. Simple questions such as "What happened to those friendships?" and "Do you have anything like them now?" usually help men realize the pain of their losses and current loneliness.

Enacting New Patterns

In the present, therapists can identify and support all examples of interpersonal compassion and concern. Physical expressions of affection can also be encouraged, with reassurance given when men experience crippling homophobia. Internalized values and cognitions restricting male intimacy can be challenged and replaced with more realistic concepts.

Planning for Future Challenges

Outside the therapy group, men encounter a world that presents multiple challenges to any effort they make to develop even a semblance of emotional closeness or intimacy with other men. Most men feel they are far too busy or already spend plenty of time with other men. As a result, therapists will do well to help men actually plan ways to create a schedule that incorporates meaningful time with male friends. For some men, even something as simple as resumption of traditional activities—sports, lunches, or shared hobbies—will be a start. Even better are efforts to go beyond traditional activities, with careful consideration given to allowing for more personal conversation and sharing of experience. A men's group, of course, is an exceptional venue in which to generate greater connection among men. Also, men can be helped to develop new or improved rituals to mark their life transitions. For example, the severely anachronistic "stag party" can be restructured to include more personal interaction and conversation about hopes and fears. New rituals such as a "Welcome to Fatherhood" baby shower (Brooks, 1995b) can offer a chance for men to provide invaluable support to one another at a critical point in their lives.

DECENTRALIZING THE ROLE OF WOMEN IN MEN'S LIVES

True to common patterns, the isolation of Jesse, George, and Buck was most pronounced in terms of their emotional distance from other men. In contrast to this alienation, these men were thoroughly dependent on their wives. Each woman spent enormous energy attending to her husband's needs by serving as romantic partner, nurse, friend, and therapist. Not surprisingly, all three men couldn't conceive of life without these women. In Chapter One, I also described the situations of Marty and Glenn, two men who had been so dependent on their wives that they were devastated when the relationships ended in divorce.

Because men depend on women so much for "social lubrication," nurturance, and validation, the all-male therapy group can offer an especially valuable corrective emotional experience. Here, we find one of the most compelling reasons to favor a male single-sex group over the mixed-sex group. In mixed groups, men simply revert to their learned patterns of delegating nurturing functions to women—and women have a hard time resisting their socialized impulses to rescue men in distress (Aries, 1976). Without women available, however, men learn that they can become more emotionally supportive of each other than they had ever imagined.

Exploring Past Experiences

The therapist helps men explore their relationships with women, including mothers, partners, lovers, friends, professional colleagues, sisters, and daughters. Special efforts are made to uncover any conflicts about intimacy and any fears buried beneath anger and resentment. Additionally, men are gently pushed to discuss how culturewide misogyny has manifested itself in their lives.

Enacting New Patterns

The group's all-male aspect obviously prevents some here-and-now enactments of new patterns. (One might think a woman therapist could serve as a catalyst for this, but in Chapter Six I explain why I discourage women therapists from taking on this role and becoming a representative for "all" women.) In lieu of women as group members, the therapist works primarily with male group members by using group discussions as fodder for experiments outside the therapy room.

Planning for Future Challenges

To strategize for future stresses, the therapist can again use deconstructive literacy and cognitive analysis. As much as they can tolerate it, men will benefit from exposure to feminist insights (although, at first, it may not be helpful to label the ideas "feminist"). Additionally, when possible, group work can be structured to lay the groundwork for future relationship therapies—either couples counseling or marital therapy.

PROMOTING PARTICIPATIVE
SELF-DISCLOSURE

Roy, Mike, Carl, Frank, and Wayne have been meeting for several weeks. To everyone's surprise, after Carl tells an off-color joke about a whore and an impotent priest, he makes a sudden revelation.

CARL: The SOB got what he deserved . . . although I can relate to. . . . Do I really want to say this? . . . Shit, here goes. . . . I can relate to that temporary limp dick problem. Several years ago, I was with this really gorgeous broad and she was hot-to-trot. Damnable thing was I'd had about thirty beers and I'll be damned if the ol' Johnson wasn't a little slow on the uptake . . . if you get my drift. Don't get me wrong—she left a satisfied customer . . . but it was a mite disconcerting for a short spell.

This unexpected disclosure is greeted with about thirty seconds of stunned silence and restless shuffling, before Frank volunteers.

FRANK: Well, Carl, old buddy, since you broke the ice here, I guess I can say you ain't completely the Lone Ranger. . . . Damn near same thing happened to me a few months ago. . . . [He laughs nervously.] 'Bout as stiff as a piece of cooked linguini. . . . Man, was I shocked. . . . Things got better, but it never really was its usual "baton of steel" that night. . . . Worried the hell outta me.

Over the next several minutes, all the others weigh in, each acknowledging a greater degree of distress than the others until Wayne finally confesses to something very private.

WAYNE: I guess it's time I finally admitted something I thought I'd never tell any other guy. . . . The truth is, I haven't had a good erection in nearly three years!

Many men like Jesse, George, Buck, Marty, and Wayne resolutely hide their anguish. Men tend to believe that they must portray themselves as confident, secure, and untroubled. In typical interactions among traditional men, they often compete and size each other up. It follows that they are wary of personal revelations that would portray them in a disadvantaged light. Self-disclosure is anathema to traditional men. They especially avoid admitting any failure or weakness. These patterns make them reluctant to enter therapy. The therapy setup causes further obstacles. The one-on-one encounters of individual psychotherapy initially highlight differences in power and competence and may therefore be especially problematic (particularly when the therapist is also male). Viewing self-disclosure as further evidence of his inferiority in relation to the therapist, the male client may studiously avoid such openness. What may then result is what Murray Scher (1990, p. 324) has called a "jockeying for power" at the outset of therapy.

The all-male therapy group, however, can provide a powerful environment to counter these problems that are inherent in individual therapy. We know, thanks again to the work of Irving Yalom (1975), that self-disclosure is a sequential process. One person with an inclination to reveal personal information will initially make "low-level disclosures," hoping to obtain affirmation, support, and reciprocal disclosures from another. The receiver is likely to feel certain responsibilities or obligations to the discloser, usually responding to that disclosure with an appropriate comment and a similar personal revelation. As Yalom puts it, "The receiver now, as well as the original discloser, is vulnerable, and a deepening relationship usually continues, with the participants making slightly more intimate disclosures in turn until some optimal level for that relationship is reached" (p. 360).

When a man witnesses another man exposing weakness and vulnerability, he becomes much freer to acknowledge his own private fear or distress. An individual male therapist can and should model some of this openness. But there are considerable limits on the amount of self-revelation feasible or advisable in individual therapy (particularly for the woman therapist with a male client). In contrast, the all-male therapy group has major advantages in promoting self-disclosure. In fact, it is probably the optimal environment for coaxing men to reveal insecurities, disappointments, and private fears gradually and reciprocally in a gentle, shared process.

Exploring Past Experiences

Traditional men are fearful of self-disclosure because they have been taught to equate exposure and vulnerability with weakness and unmanliness. Ridicule and contempt are heaped upon the boy who cries, runs away, or, God forbid, wets himself from fear. Most men have experienced or witnessed the psychological brutalization of vulnerable boys; many have joined the bullying themselves. To prepare the group for openness and self-disclosure, it is especially useful to help them talk in general terms about men's insistence on displays of toughness and denial of self-exposure. Most of the group members will eventually acknowledge that this atmosphere terrorized many young men they knew, and some will admit that they had fears themselves. Once all participants recognize the harm that accrues through perpetuation of these shaming practices, many of them will begin to challenge the restrictions on their emotional freedom.

Enacting New Patterns

Establishing self-revelation as a group norm is a delicate operation. In general, this process requires a skilled group leader who can reflect a competent professional demeanor while simultaneously remaining comfortable with low-level personal self-disclosures that can serve as model behaviors for group members. The therapist should be attentive to and supportive of group members who reveal information, as well as mildly challenging to those men who keep their walls up, doggedly resisting even the slightest glimpse into their inner world. With the therapist's gentle encouragement, men can become more emotionally adventurous, and self-disclosure may be established as a valued group norm.

Preparing for Future Challenges

Most men realize that, regardless of how tolerant their group may be regarding self-disclosure, the outside world still expects men to be far more cautious. Therefore, some time should be spent in helping men develop a strategic plan to become more self-disclosing. This plan may include determining which situations might allow greater exposure, practicing sequences of increasing revelation, and troubleshooting situations likely to produce reactive anxiety.

ENHANCING COMMUNICATION SKILLS

Another interesting exchange occurs later in my group work with Roy, Mike, Carl, Frank, and Wayne.

ROY (highly distressed and apparently on the verge of tears): Sometimes I get so frustrated with my seizure disorder and inability to work, I think I'd rather just give up.

He starts to sob.

MIKE: Have you considered trying a temporary help agency? They sometimes have great job leads.

CARL: Oh, no you don't! Stay away from those rip-offs. Didn't I tell you guys about the time when I ran one of those things?

FRANK: Where was that, Carl? I think I might have worked for the same group. . . . Apex Contracting, wasn't it?

This brief interchange among Roy, Mike, Carl, and Frank illustrates one of the dysfunctional aspects of traditional male interpersonal communication. Traditional men have taken some pretty heavy flack for their shortcomings as communicators. From Rob Becker's smash hit play *Return of the Cave Man* to television's *Home Improvement,* we have come to accept that men may be good at making and fixing stuff but they certainly are inept as interpersonal communicators. Ron Levant (1992) captures this with his claim that the most feared words a woman can tell her male partner are "Honey, we need to talk." John Gray, with his immensely popular *Men Are from Mars, Women Are from Venus,* has come to men's defense by suggesting that men and women are just different and that each gender needs to learn to appreciate and accommodate the other.

There is a strong sentiment that most men have great difficulty as interpersonal communicators and that deficient communication skills are principal features of men's interpersonal difficulties. Warren Farrell (1987) has described a tendency for men to practice "self-listening," whereby a man "listens to a conversation not to take in or genuinely appreciate what a person is saying but only to be able to jump in and discuss his own experiences" (143–147). In this way, a man practicing self-listening seems to draw attention away from the speaker's experiences and toward his own experiences.

Deborah Tannen (1990) has argued that, because of their preference for language that emphasizes status and independence, men have difficulty with language that emphasizes connection and intimacy. She views men as far more comfortable with "report-talk" (conversation that demonstrates knowledge and skill) than with "rapport-talk" (conversation that displays similarities and matches experiences). Ron Levant (1994) finds men so lacking in the critical skills of empathic listening and nonverbal communication that he has designed skills-oriented programs to instruct men in these areas. Over the course of their lives these communication habits help traditional men fit into some "manly" environments, but they almost invariably create substantial problems for them in interpersonal relationships.

Exploring Past Experiences

Unlike the previous issue of self-disclosure, through which many young men have experienced significant emotional trauma, this issue has usually not been very problematic. Unless a woman has openly criticized a man's poor listening skills, he may be relatively unaware of his limitations in this area. In general, the most useful explorations include questions such as: "To what extent have the group members been criticized for their communication skills? How much have they noticed the popular portrayals of men as incompetent communicators?"

Enacting New Patterns

The group, as a social microcosm, is rife with here-and-now opportunities for men to experience the consequences of their communication style and, if encouraged, to experiment with alternatives. Therefore, the effective therapist is one who recognizes and tolerates men's usual style, yet is skilled at challenging them to develop new patterns. A simple illustration may be useful.

FRANK: Where was that, Carl? I think I might have worked for the same group. . . . Apex Contracting, wasn't it?

GARY: Whoa, wait a minute here. . . . I need to interrupt for a second. Guys, I think we're trying to be helpful, but we may be missing something. Can we go back to Roy's first statement? Roy, can you tell us what's going on with you? Take your time.

ROY: Well, I guess it has less to do with getting a job and more to do with feeling like a worthless piece of crap. [Raises voice.] Shit! If I can't be any more use to anyone I might as well pull the fucking plug!

Everyone became silent and seemed struck by the intensity of Roy's suffering.

GARY: Roy, that's a pretty strong feeling . . . but not unlike some I've heard come from some of the other men in here. How about it guys? What had you been saying earlier about losing your jobs?

Although men frequently want to support one another, they are constricted by limitations in their listening and communication skills. An alert therapist can be especially helpful in guiding men into more effective communication styles.

Preparing for Future Challenges

Much as is the case with self-disclosure, group members can be encouraged to develop a personal plan to improve their communication skills. Over the course of the group meetings, men should be encouraged to report their successes and failures as they begin to interact differently with significant persons in their family, work, and social environments.

INSTILLING HOPE AND EMPOWERING ONE ANOTHER

Men have an enormous capacity to inspire each other or to become encouraged by their male buddies. Anyone who has watched the antics of adolescent male skateboarders can't help but be impressed (or appalled) by the process of mutual challenge toward ever-higher levels of risk taking. Most sports fans can attest to an amazing phenomenon in which a single extraordinary play by one team member can palpably lift the morale of an entire team or in which a fatigued or injured player can ignore personal pain because of his dedication to teammates. At its worst, this social process can perpetuate harmful patterns. At its best, however, it can instill hope by offering heartening inspiration to a man in profound despair.

Let's return to Marty. I had become alarmed by the severity of his despair. He couldn't imagine a life without his former wife. But Glenn had been there. He and, to a lesser extent, other group members had firsthand knowledge of the demons haunting Marty. More important, they knew that there *was* a way out, eventual respite from the pain. A therapist can offer words of encouragement and point out irrational self-talk or faulty cognitive assumptions. Yet, at the moment of greatest despondency, little can inspire a man as much as the personal testimony of another man who has walked the same path.

For Irving Yalom (1975), this instilling of hope is another of the powerful curative factors of group therapy, because it can generate faith in the therapy process. This is especially relevant for men who enter therapy with so little inherent goodwill toward this "feminine" process. Yalom believes that group members can receive encouragement from others who are further along in the "coping-collapse continuum" (p. 6).

Exploring Past Experiences

Though traditional men have great difficulty admitting it, some have had times of despair or anguish in their lives when another man made a big difference and gave them hope. As much as possible, the therapist should help men tell these stories. Men need to hear about men who have emotionally reached out to other men. If the therapist has difficulty uncovering these stories, men can be encouraged to describe their secret fantasies and yearnings for a caring and compassionate father, brother, or male friend.

Enacting New Patterns

The capacity for men to inspire other men is integral to the metaphor of the "gender role journey" (O'Neil & Carroll, 1988). According to O'Neil and Carroll, conceptualization of men's progress along a continuum—from a stage where they resist new gender roles to their ultimate embracing of new gender roles—men benefit greatly from the support and personal testimony of other men who have successfully completed gender role journeys. We can easily see how the endorsement of enthusiastic group veterans can become a significant source of encouragement and demystification for men who otherwise would see therapy as threatening or emasculating.The implication for therapists seems clear. Whenever possible, they should point to examples of men who have successfully negotiated the painful process of making substantive gender role changes. A male leader, of course, can provide a degree of role modeling. Sometimes it may even be helpful to ask group veterans to return to make guest appearances and testimonials. Nothing speaks louder to a troubled man than another man who has faced his demons and successfully charted a new path.

Preparing for Future Challenges

To a large extent, men have the greatest likelihood of generating substantive cultural changes when they expand their therapy experiences into efforts to change the larger culture. Therefore, an important group activity is one that encourages men to consider ways to perpetuate their growth through outreach efforts to men in trouble.

Of particular value may be efforts to become involved in the lives of younger men as coaches, advisors, and mentors.

ADDRESSING SPECIAL ISSUES WITH CERTAIN TECHNIQUES

Thus far, I've described a number of broad objectives for successful group therapy with traditional men: confronting the male chorus, countering men's emotional isolation from other men, decentralizing the role of women in their lives, promoting participative self-disclosure, and instilling hope and empowerment. In the remainder of this chapter, I discuss more specific issues and techniques that can help therapists achieve these objectives.

The Group Leader's Presentation of Self

As I noted extensively in Chapter Two, traditional men hate therapy, entering the setting prepared to dislike both the process and the therapist. Also, because men are accustomed to thinking hierarchically, they may have very ambivalent feelings about the leader because of his or her inherent authority. The group leader, therefore, is in a precarious position; any extreme posture can easily provoke an overreaction. To minimize this problem, male and female therapists will have similar yet different challenges as they attempt to exorcise ghosts from men's pasts.

The male therapist who is forceful and aggressive may invoke memories of authoritarian leaders, such as football coaches, first sergeants, or certain fathers or bosses. Making such connections will inspire confidence in some but evoke anxiety and withdrawal in others. The male therapist who is intellectual and aloof may provoke reactions rooted in men's problematic interactions with medical experts or their disdain for elitist "shrinks." A reserved male therapist may cause some men to assume that they are dealing with just another indifferent bureaucrat. A sensitive and caring male therapist might be dismissed a "wuss" or sissy, a sort of displaced

preacher. And, thanks to the dominant stereotypes of all psychotherapists, any unexpected behavior might suggest to the men
that their leader is another "nutcase" who has more problems of his
own than any appreciation of real men's practical problems.

Female therapists may also remind men of problematic people
in their pasts. Any woman who firmly takes charge of therapy is susceptible to being viewed as the dictatorial schoolmarm or stereotypical "castrating bitch boss." The reserved woman therapist might
provoke disrespect or "protection," being viewed as an ineffectual
"airhead" without any true appreciation for the world of men. The
caring female therapist (depending somewhat on her age and appearance) is easily mistaken for the "seductive temptress" of male
mythology or the all-loving mother figure who is prone to smoth-
ering men.

Because of hierarchical thinking and extreme reactivity among
traditional men, therapists must find a self-presentation that walks
a middle road. Group leaders should not be seen as people who wish
to enhance themselves by demeaning group members. At the same
time, leaders must value themselves and expect appropriate respect
for the authority of the leader role.

I believe that a successful group leader is one who

Has self-confidence without appearing smug

Can take charge without appearing dictatorial

Demonstrates a commitment to therapy progress without appearing pushy or impatient

Recognizes the seriousness of men's distress without appearing
contemptuous or moralizing

Appreciates men's vulnerabilities without being overly soft or
gullible

Conveys a sense of experience without appearing jaded or bored

Refuses to tolerate men's inappropriate behaviors without appearing condemnatory or hostile

Of course, no leader can always walk this tightrope, and most will sometimes slip into an extreme stance. Fortunately, if the therapist is alert to cues in men's reactions, midcourse corrections are possible. For example, frequent arguments between leaders and members may indicate that the leader has conveyed an overly authoritarian stance and may need to "back off" and listen carefully to group members. Group members' jokes or comments about the enormity of the leader's outside responsibilities may indicate that a lack of commitment to the group has been conveyed.

The essential point here is that because traditional men are largely unfamiliar with the world of psychotherapy, they will be unusually reactive to the unspoken messages that the group leader communicates. The group leader must be keenly aware of a therapist's substantial resonance with group members.

Ground Rules

Appropriate ground rules, which are always important in group therapy, are especially critical for traditional men who lack therapy experience. I have found the following ones to be especially useful.

Voluntary Participation: Respecting Boundaries and Personal Space

Men are reared to value their personal space, resisting encroachment from others. They don't like to feel crowded. Pressure to participate or to fake enthusiasm may be counterproductive. Men may become sullen or defiant or may participate at an inauthentic or superficial level. Therefore, when possible, it may be useful to make group attendance or participation voluntary (although once a man has said he will participate, his attendance should be expected). Rather than banging heads with a resistant man, a group leader might ally with him. The leader can frame this reluctance to participate as completely understandable: "No man likes anything crammed down his throat" or "Sometimes we don't feel ready to examine our lifestyle."

It may be useful to encourage a man to attend one "trial" group session, during which he has the option of silently observing and after which he may choose to discontinue. The key issue here is that the group leader not be viewed as the agent coercing group participation. A statement such as "They may insist that you come here, but I cannot (will not) force you to participate" emphasizes the group member's power and the leader's benevolent intentions.

Consistent Attendance

Because men often resort to withdrawal or avoidance to cope with conflict and distress, consistent attendance can be problematic. Although it is useful for men to have the option of becoming or remaining a group member, they must agree to regular attendance as long as they are members. Men's tendency to avoid conflictual material is a continual issue that often makes therapy progress intermittent; there will be intense work and emotional involvement followed by "breather" sessions with escapist humor and emotional avoidance.

The critical point is that when men feel the need to "back off" or "slow down," they should do so as a group, not as isolated individuals. Slow sessions are natural and usually require little from the leader beyond an acknowledgment that group members are not in a working mood that day. In the early stages of a group, it might be useful for the leader to comment about clear cases of group avoidance. For example, the leader might say, "I notice that we haven't mentioned such-and-such topic today. Any thoughts?" In later stages of the group, when group members have more therapy skills, the leader might let group members take responsibility for dealing with the avoidance or silence.

A subissue of this need for consistent attendance is the expectation that group members commit to a "farewell session." Traditional men have great difficulty with good-byes—that is, dealing with the emotional intensity and grief of separation. Therefore, it is generally useful to agree in the first session that all group members, whenever possible, will attend a final session to say good-bye to other group members.

Disagreement Without Violence

It may seem unnecessary to make explicit rules prohibiting violence, because everyone assumes that violence is unacceptable in this context. But in traditional male culture, rules for handling interpersonal conflict can be very different than they are in the therapy environment. Within the more macho environments, public disagreement with a man's statements is often viewed as a hostile challenge. To this challenge, the response might be, "Are you calling me a liar, buddy?"

Even relatively mild, well-intentioned confrontations risk tapping the masculine code's dictate that a man must physically defend himself against threats to his honor. However, if all group members have agreed to explicit rules that endorse occasional disagreement but prohibit violence, then two purposes are served. Group members who are reluctant to fight are provided with a face-saving mechanism to escape this dictate of the macho code, and group members with problems controlling their tempers receive help with anger management.

It is frequently useful to negotiate specific strategies, whereby the leader is authorized to act decisively during times of heightened tension and near violence. For example, a group member might agree to a brief "time-out" if the leader becomes concerned that a man is becoming unduly aroused and at risk of losing control. If this agreement is made early, cooperatively, and publicly, then it will be more acceptable when implemented later.

Confidentiality

Confidentiality, of course, is an essential component of therapy work, because few would self-disclose without an assurance of privacy. This is particularly true of traditional men, who commonly have overdeveloped secret worlds and talk differently when women are not present. Rules about confidentiality come as a relief to many men, who welcome the chance to "unload" in a safe atmosphere. They may also find such rules helpful in responding to familial inquiries that they experience as "prying."

Naturally, therapy is not intended to perpetuate men's secrecy but to help them share more of their inner lives. This will not come immediately, however, so it is initially useful for men to have this shield of confidentiality. Eventually, it may be helpful to modify rigid confidentiality rules to allow for some discussion between men and their loved ones. A possible modification might be to allow for general reports of group topics (impotence, violence, substance use, and so forth) without use of names or specifics.

Communication Style

There is a freewheeling and disjointed communication style in most men's gatherings, which creates problems in the therapy process. Early in a group's existence, it is not uncommon for several men to compete for the floor or for several conversations to take place simultaneously. One man may interrupt another in midsentence with little effort to connect with the previous topic. Sometimes this problem can be surmounted if the group leader models better communication or serves as the communication "traffic cop." It may be necessary, however, to have explicit communication rules.

This is a delicate process, because the leader should maintain as much spontaneity and enthusiasm as possible without being overly intrusive. A possible positive framing of the communication rules might be, "I'm impressed with the high level of interest and enthusiasm in today's group, but I can't keep up with all that's going on. Why don't we slow down to one person talking at a time so we all can really focus on what each person is saying."

Distractions

Groups need some freedom from interruption if they are to build therapeutic intensity and consistently attend to the many subtle communications of group members. Some group leaders take a fairly extreme stance on this matter. They not only expect group members to arrive right on time but also rigidly guard comings and goings, insist that pagers be turned off, post ominous warning signs on doors, disallow everything from coffee to chewing gum, and discourage any conversation not directly related to the therapy task.

As noted in the earlier description of the good ol' boy groups, traditional men are experts at maintaining a low intensity level through a variety of distractions—joking, eating, smoking, and moving about. Because they are accustomed to endless chatter, men are especially intolerant of silence. Although it is tempting to take an aggressive stance on this matter, this may be counterproductive.

In my experience, the transition from good ol' boy group to therapy group is accomplished through gradual steps. Coffee, humor, and the occasional distractions of storytelling or advice giving all help men become accustomed to an environment that might otherwise become overwhelming. I also believe that the therapist does well initially to play the "social lubrication" role that traditional men find so alien. At a later point in a group's existence, challenges to avoidance behavior and lengthy therapeutic silence can play a crucial role in generating intensity.

Selection of Group Members

The selection of group members is one of the most critical issues determining the group's long-term outcome. Although a group might occasionally be successful without careful member selection, group success usually depends on careful attention to this issue. Given the formidable obstacle of engaging traditional men in group therapy, the leader will have a particularly tough time if he or she has not screened group members and barred extremely resistant, argumentative, or disruptive people from participating. One disruptive member can be moderated by the collaborative efforts of a committed group, but a subculture of hostile and resistant men can become impossible.

Although initial selection of group members typically falls to the group leader, that task can eventually be shared with all group members. This sharing has several advantages, in that it empowers the group, encourages veteran members to make the new member feel included, and sometimes takes advantage of information known only to other members and not to the leader (especially in inpatient situations).

Criteria

The criteria for selecting participants will always be somewhat idiosyncratic, varying according to the preferences, experiences, and skills of the specific group leader. Although there may be general consensus about the advisability of excluding grossly confused, psychotic, or demented patients, there may be agreement about little else. Over the years, I have developed the following criteria for acceptable group members.

1. The man must be actively experiencing some degree of distress. Even if this is not obvious (for example, he is not seeking individual therapeutic help or he is channeling his distress into maladaptive behavior), at some level he must be hurting. Most contemporary men eventually experience some degree of gender role strain. Those who don't, or haven't yet, are not likely to participate in therapy.

2. The man must be willing to consider changing some aspects of his lifestyle.

3. The man must be willing to take some responsibility for accomplishing the necessary changes, and he must be willing to make personal sacrifices (of money, time, and habits) to participate in therapy.

These criteria, though minimal, do eliminate men who seem to be seeking therapy primarily to escape responsibility for misdeeds, to find an audience for their complaints, or to secure financial compensation. Some might argue that these criteria are not strong enough to eliminate a large number of men labeled as having antisocial personality disorder—men for whom therapy is often seen as unworkable. Although my membership criteria will sometimes admit antisocial men, many of these men may actually do very well. In my experience, group success depends less on a member's past psychiatric diagnosis than on men's ability to tolerate the group's resocializing capacities. Too often, traditional men have been given the personality disorder diagnosis simply because they adhere to the dictates of the male code. Rather than lacking the capacity for interpersonal connection and sensitivity, they merely need a milieu in which their behavior is understood. Therefore, a group candidate should be given an opportunity to tell his story and not be screened out simply because of past negative contact with therapists. Many "hopeless psychopaths" have excelled in group environments in which their inappropriate behavior is admonished but their anger and psychic pain are recognized.

Heterogeneity Versus Homogeneity

Another problematic issue is that of heterogeneity versus homogeneity in group membership. All participants will be alike in gender, but they will vary markedly by age, ethnicity, sexual identity, social class, veteran status, and stage of the gender role journey. In general, heterogeneity is good, as it provides vitality and opportunity for growth. Extreme variations, however, may seriously tax the group's cohesiveness.

For example, men facing the multiple losses of aging and retiring may have difficulty empathizing with the "trivial" problems of adolescent males. Members of ethnic minorities cannot be expected to be comfortable with a racist atmosphere. Gay men cannot be expected to feel safe in an atmosphere of gay bashing or aggressive homophobia. Blue-collar men are sometimes deeply resentful of professional or executive men. Some Vietnam veterans are hostile toward World War II veterans or toward nonveterans, especially former peace demonstrators. Men who are barely launching their gender role journeys can be overwhelmed by the openness of men far along in the process.

I am not arguing against including diverse male populations; men desperately need to learn as much as they can about the many varieties of the masculine experience. The point here is that the leader must be attentive to the issues of heterogeneity, because extreme diversity can undermine the new group's potential.

Group Label and Description

Although the group will mainly focus on men's role issues, the group may not benefit from being billed as a "men's issues" group. Men who lack any clear appreciation of the benefits of the men's movement (or who have a strongly negative association with that movement) may be reluctant to enter a group with this designation. Once the men have begun the group, this focus can be introduced in an atmosphere more conducive to discussing men's apprehensions.

The Critical First Session

The first group session, which is important with any therapy population, is especially pivotal with traditional men. A negative first-session experience may confirm a man's worst fears and generate further therapy resistance, whereas a positive first-session experience may launch a man into an enthusiastic gender role journey. Therefore, if things are to proceed well, a new man should experience some sense of the group's potential, develop at least minimal interest in the other group members, and have his worst fears invalidated (for example, the group is not a place for exposure and ridicule of weaknesses, intense and rampant intimacy, or unbridled self-revelation).

Because so much is at stake in this initial session, the group leader may need to be more directive than is customary to ensure that the first session doesn't get off track. There are many ways to orchestrate this. Here is the method I like to use.

Introduction of Leader and Rationale for Group

As the session begins, I introduce myself and give a general rationale for the group. In this introduction, I emphasize the normality of men's experiences and deemphasize psychopathology. For example, I usually explain that it is common to have adjustment problems, particularly in such a complex and changing world.

The group is presented as a chance to explore how, despite their best intentions, men sometimes get sidetracked or locked into self-defeating patterns. If a more severe symptom (such as violence, alcohol abuse, or sexual misconduct) is the group's explicit focus, the leader can emphasize that the group will explore what it is about "manhood" that makes men susceptible to these problems.

It is often useful to note the commonalities among the group members and the group leader (if the group leader is male). I say that I am not unlike them; I also face these challenges. (A woman leader, of course, would word this differently. For example, she might say, "It pains me greatly to see my many male friends struggling with common challenges.")

The leader may want to highlight a possible "menu" of exploration topics: issues about work, health, the aging process, relationships with women, fathers, responses to criticism, and so forth. At this point, I often find it useful to validate the men, informing them that this is a special group and that I have very high expectations about what can be accomplished. I say that I have chosen the members to be in the group because I believe they can and want to improve their lives; I note that I have confidence in their potential.

Explanation of Ground Rules

Next, I explain the minimal ground rules for the group. I'm happy to take questions or explain them, but I present the rules as non-negotiable. All members must agree to abide by them.

Introduction of Group Members

Following the discussion of the ground rules, I introduce and welcome group members. Although there are advantages to an open-ended introduction format in which each group member determines his own introduction parameters, this method also has pitfalls. The main issue is that the group leader needs to establish a positive, accepting, noncompetitive, nonconfrontational, and non-pathology-based atmosphere—one that is uncommon to most men's gatherings. If left unstructured, the first session could be characterized by vicious attacks by confrontational members, domination of the discussion by group therapy veterans, or anxious silence.

Therefore, I strongly prefer a carefully controlled introduction that moves quickly to include and relax. In turn, I conduct a brief, nonthreatening interview with each man, eliciting basic information, such as age, marital status, preferred line of work, connections with family, and major stressors. I adopt a compassionate and supportive tone, taking great care to avoid any material that the man may find embarrassing or threatening. If I have had the opportunity to discuss these issues previously, as part of the screening process, I will have a major advantage in knowing how to proceed. If this is our first conversation, I will be especially careful about possible embarrassment.

I pose questions in a positive light. For example, if I suspect that a man is embarrassed by his unemployment, I won't ask, "Do you work?" or "What do you do?" Instead, I might alter the question slightly to emphasize the temporal nature of his status: "What is your preferred line of work? Are you between jobs?" To avoid the appearance of a pathology-based group, I save questions about the presenting problems for very brief and general mentions at the end of the mini-interview.

In general, the goal of the mini-interviews is to create a picture of each group member that emphasizes his strengths, his loyalty to male role dictates, and his commonality with other, similarly socialized men. Likewise, a concerted effort is made to help each man maintain his status with the others, avoiding undue exposure of weaknesses and failings so as to prevent gross inequities.

Theme Work

After guiding the group through the initial "feeling-each-other-out" phase, the leader is ready to help group members deal with their problematic issues of masculinity. In a relatively traditional group therapy format, the leader might wait for a member to introduce personal issues before having further discussion and group reaction. A leader following a more psychoeducational or consciousness-raising format might select a relevant topic and encourage group members to give opinions or personal reactions. For me, the most successful strategy is one that includes the best features of both approaches. This works in the following way.

After group introductions, if a particular topic has not already emerged, I ask group members to bring up any subject that may be on their minds—including their reactions to finding themselves in a group therapy setting or, if in an inpatient setting, their degree of satisfaction with their overall treatment. Whatever is brought forth is used as grist for a thematic discussion by the entire group. For example, if a group member expresses resentment about feeling coerced into therapy, I may initiate a discussion about power, our reactions to people with power, strategies for dealing with powerful people, and so on. A broader theme might be that of resentment and bitterness—how much is in our lives and how do we deal with it? Strongly negative comments are almost always fodder for animated and productive discussions about the frustrations in men's lives.

Capitalizing on Current Events

Traditional men frequently have very strong opinions about events in the public spotlight. Although these events typically inspire little more than arguments and intellectual analyses, they can, when processed effectively, become catalysts for exploring *personal* issues.

Public Event	Theme Issue for Men
Cowboys's victory in Super Bowl	Teamwork, pride, cooperation and love among men, competition and winning, loss and shame
Congress's vote to raise its own pay	Politics, power and powerlessness, bitterness, resentment
Pan Am plane explosion	Premature death; meaning of life; existential issues; grief, attachment to, or estrangement from family and loved ones
Allegations of Clarence Thomas's or Marv Albert's sexual exploits	Media, attitudes toward women, sexuality, fears, guilt, anxiety
President's surgery	Health and illness, self-care, male body as it ages
Massacre at Luby's Cafeteria	Rage, frustration, violence
Silence of group member	Respect for privacy needs, boundaries, the extent to which one should help others
Absence of group member	Closeness, intimacy
Member's presentation of work project	Productivity, meaning of work

In general, useful initial themes are those that focus discussion on the commonalities among the men, particularly their struggles in coping with the "world out there." Issues in the public spotlight should not be discussed as philosophical or political ramblings, as people do when calling a radio talk show, but in terms of their personal meaning. Any issue, regardless of how innocuous it may seem, can become a useful catalyst when its relevance is explored within the context of an individual man's life.

As the group matures, group members may be more comfortable addressing issues internal to the group, such as their relationships with one another. Initially however, men seem more responsive to exposing their frustrations about the world, their problems managing their anger, their distress with their impaired work capacity, or their bitterness about and distrust of women.

Building Relationships

Because of men's strict socialization to be autonomous and to distrust emotional attachment, they are initially averse to recognizing interconnections and acknowledging affection. Because relationships are the basic therapeutic elements of any group, I try to be unusually attentive to any signs of developing relationships among the group members.

Here-and-now efforts by one man to support another can be noted and complimented. Advice, and even criticism, can be framed as welcome signs of group members' growing interest in each other's welfare. Inattention to another can be framed as respect for a man's privacy. Shared experiences among group members—for example, similarities in backgrounds, problems, or reaction styles—should be noted regularly. Whenever group members mention having any contact with each other outside the group, they should be complimented for their efforts to develop interconnections and combat pressures that keep men isolated from each other. (The leader must, of course, do this while remaining alert to the problems of cliques and excessive extragroup socializing.)

Solving Problems

In some forms of psychotherapy, the therapist resists the temptation to provide answers to problems; instead, the therapist empowers clients, or group members, to discover their own answers. Irving Yalom (1975), for example, sees problem solving as an emphasis on "then and there" and an avoidance of the therapeutic intensity of the "here and now." On the other hand, behavior therapists Marvin

Goldfried and Gerald Davison (1994) have described problem solving as a key ingredient in their psychotherapy regimen. I believe that both perspectives have their merits. Although Yalom's point is important, in my view it applies more to experienced clients than to inexperienced and less psychologically sophisticated traditional men. Psycholinguist Deborah Tannen (1990) has pointed out that when men communicate, they emphasize practical aspects of situations and the provision of help as a way of expressing caring for another. When men get together in groups, they show interpersonal concern by giving advice.

To respect this feature of traditional masculinity, group leaders should be forgiving when men seem to overlook the pain of another man by offering advice and solutions. Instead of challenging this insensitivity, it may be more productive initially to accommodate the pattern, perhaps even praising the expressions of apparent concern. Eventually, when the leader has won the group's trust, a more direct message can be given: "Your efforts to solve the problem are considerate, but sometimes a man just wants other men to hear his pain." Ultimately, men need to learn that even problems that have no solution are worthy of attention, because they may create intimacy and connection through shared suffering.

Shaping New Patterns

Neither Rome nor a state-of-the-art group can be built in a day. Communication rules may curtail some of the more dysfunctional male communication patterns, but they cannot create more empathic and other-centered styles. New interpersonal patterns cannot be mandated; they must be evoked and nurtured or "shaped." Therefore, the group leader must be unusually alert to any indications of this desired behavior—a show of compassion, a gesture of support, a sign of concern—and praise the man for experimenting with nontraditional behavior.

For example, the leader may say, "I was impressed with your offer of help and support to Bob. You clearly recognized his pain."

Sometimes, in very slow groups, the leader may need to choose the best approximation of an empathic behavior, label it as a display of compassion, and applaud the group member for his concern.

Special Issues Regarding the Leader's Style

Group leaders vary markedly in terms of their most natural interpersonal style—lighthearted versus intensely serious, earthy versus cerebral, physically expressive versus reserved, and concrete versus abstract. Group leaders need to remain relatively true to their most comfortable style. Nevertheless, I think that the following stylistic issues need to be considered.

Humor

Traditional men, generally fearful of the magnitude and depth of their feelings, can be overwhelmed by grimly intense group sessions. Anyone who has experienced the sometimes brutal hazing of male adolescence can appreciate that the direct expression of appreciation and affection are especially forbidden between boys and men. Men *do* express themselves, though rarely in the direct or "sappy" style possible among women. One of the best examples of men's expressing affection is the "roast," in which men offer testimonials to their affection for another man without ever directly saying "I care for you."

Family therapists David Keith and Carl Whitaker (1984) observed that the "key" element of effective work with military men is the ability to "join the men in their homosocial fun." Earlier, I noted a similar process in the good ol' boy group.

Using humor appropriately is tricky, of course. When it is gentle and good-natured, it can relax the atmosphere. But when it is sarcastic, competitive, or tinged with criticism, it can create tension and distance, thereby perpetuating the restrictive features of men's habitual relationship patterns. At its worst, humor, such as the "harmless practical joke," can be a cruel and malicious instrument of hostile competition. Even at its best, the humorous teasing and joking common in men's groups can only go so far as substitutes for more open and direct expressions of tender emotions. Nevertheless, when appropriately introduced, humor can loosen men up and open doors to otherwise unreachable psychic terrain. Many pages could be written on this topic, but only a few suggestions are possible here.

In general, humor seems helpful when it allows men to put things in perspective, to take less seriously that which has been unnecessarily magnified. Men hung up on performance and image are well served by a group atmosphere that encourages them to poke fun at themselves. This atmosphere is best established when the leader is in a secure enough position (internally and in the group) to model that behavior, that is, to expose some of his or her personal foibles. Teasing should be kind, gentle, and reciprocal. In my experience, gentle teasing of the group leader is usually a positive sign. It may be helpful for the leader to metacommunicate about the teasing: "I've been joking with you. Is that okay?" To ensure that the humor has an appropriate flavor, the leader should guard against teasing or allowing others to tease a group member when the overall relationship is strained. Leaders should carefully monitor the group's humorous interactions to detect covert issues that may need processing.

Racist, sexist, and homophobic jokes are a cause for special concern. They may provide superficial comic relief in some situations, but they do so by introducing themes that are ultimately far more damaging to the group. Although the leader may not choose to challenge this issue immediately, he or she should not give any indication of condoning this form of humor.

In general, the bottom line is that humor should spring from an environment in which all members respect and care for each other. Teasing is directed at the *behavior* of another, not the *worth* of another. In my experience, a man is rarely offended or hurt if he understands that the other person has basic respect for him.

Language

To a great extent, people are defined by their language, grammar, vocabulary, and use of idiom. "How" people say things is sometimes more informative that "what" people say. Psychotherapists come in disproportionate numbers from a highly literate social strata, are then exposed to years of highbrow academic discourse, and are frequently rewarded for adopting abstract and convoluted language. Often, we see words as creative tools and can become intoxicated with verbal fluency. In many situations, this verbal facility serves us well, while at other times it creates unnecessary problems. For example, mental health professionals who have testified in court may have found that attorneys love to deflate overly intellectual testimony.

Too much inflated language can become problematic in the interactions between therapists and traditional men. Few things rankle blue-collar men as much as a therapist who is prone to show off verbally. On the other hand, nothing seems to generate credibility as much as a therapist's ability to get to the heart of a matter with a few simple words: "Cut the crap, Bob. What's going on with you?" or "Sorry, guys. I fucked up."

Language choice, especially profanity, must be carefully considered in light of the therapeutic context. Some therapists may never be comfortable with that form of communication. Naturally, they should not attempt to express themselves in an alien language, because this ingenuineness is not only ineffective but also patronizing and insulting. Any group rule about the use of profanity should be tempered by the realization that discouraging profanity may severely cramp many men's communication.

Touch

Men love to touch and be touched. However, of all the therapeutic double-edged swords, this may be one of the sharpest. Because thorough coverage of this topic would exhaust space limitations, it might be expedient for me to skip over this complex issue. This would be inappropriate, however, because avoidance doesn't make the topic go away, and this is a crucial topic. In my opinion, although a dictate of never touching a client (not even through a handshake, a touch on shoulder, or a pat on the back) simplifies the matter, it risks losing valuable therapeutic opportunities.

Traditional men are physical. They exalt in their capacity to interact tangibly with their environment, whether the medium is earth, wood, metal, or another person's body. Physical communications frequently have more immediacy than do more abstract and literate ones. Additionally, physical rejection is deeply rooted in early male development, when physical comforting was withheld. Gestalt therapist Edward Smith (1987) has argued that although the suppression of all physical interactions and the complete rejection of all male clients' physical overtures may often be fully necessary, this absence of contact may reinforce men's feelings of rejection and unworthiness.

What, then, should a therapist do? There certainly seems to be no simple answer, because both options—touching male clients and avoiding touch with male clients—have potential problems. Naturally, the therapist should spend considerable time weighing this issue before developing a realistic and comfortable personal policy. For me, therapeutic touch has been especially helpful in all-male groups. Whenever it can be done smoothly, I touch male clients. I always shake hands, but I also make special efforts to put my arm around a man's shoulder or embrace him during emotionally intense moments. It is not at all uncommon for men to embrace one another after a group session.

I should note a few caveats. Women therapists, of course, need to be exceedingly cautious about how their touch is interpreted (as do male therapists with openly gay men). I believe hugs should be sincere and spontaneous, never part of an empty ritual. Although traditional men can eventually become comfortable with prolonged embraces, initial contact should be brief, without stroking or rubbing. Some men feel more comfortable when the brief hug is punctuated with a few brisk back pats. Men who are at ease in the safety of the group environment may become much more tense when hugged in a one-on-one situation.

If there is tension between men, physical contact should be avoided. The common male practice of semiserious wrestling, vigorous arm punching, and shadowboxing should be discouraged, as it can easily erupt into overt violence. Finally, because touch is such a provocative issue for men, therapists should continually watch for times when nonverbal touch issues need to be dealt with verbally.

The primary point here is that men's need for touch and physical expression of positive regard has received too little emphasis by therapists. Men benefit from touch, but they rarely have enough awareness to ask for it. Therapists, for the best of reasons, have become especially cautious in this area. Caution is appropriate, but it shouldn't eliminate all consideration of therapeutic touch.

Metaphors

The traditional male psyche has been bombarded by images: the "heroic" or "mythical" male, the knight in shining armor, the male machine, and the rugged individualist of the frontier. Psychologists David Joliff and Arthur Horne (1996) have written about "metaphor work," in which men are asked to identify the dominant metaphors of their lives. Men who are otherwise closed off to introspection can easily relate to the imagery of "working like a dog," "putting your shoulder to the grindstone," and "banging your head against the wall."

Problematic Group Members

Many men adapt to the masculine script in a fashion that makes them particularly troublesome group participants. Some men "eat up" the masculine code and relate in an interpersonally aggressive, competitive, and challenging fashion. Others have "given up" and come into the group as avoidant, withdrawn, and interpersonally elusive. Both extremes are highly problematic in the challenges they present to the group. Because most traditional men are unaccustomed to the group environment and are generally unprepared to cope with these problematic types themselves, the leader needs to be alert and ready to intervene.

Dominant Men

Because some men are only comfortable when they verbally dominate their social contexts, they will behave similarly in the group environment. Although a dominating group member will unbalance the group and deprive others of therapy time, he sometimes may be subtly encouraged by more reticent men (and by an insecure leader thankful for at least a semblance of activity). The leader's challenge is complicated—to slow down the verbal domination in a manner that praises the dominator for his enthusiasm, to avoid discouraging group members who might be considering greater activity, and to minimize the appearance of a power struggle between the leader and dominator.

This situation can usually be resolved through the use of well-established group communication management strategies, such as "go arounds" or explicit conversation rules. In early groups, the leader should be careful to move somewhat briskly among group members, setting a norm for group participation. If an overt communication rule seems necessary, it could be framed as a measure to "prevent any one group member from feeling the need to carry the burden for the group." Many leaders of mythopoetic men's gatherings routinely employ the ceremonial "talking stick" as a tangible symbol of shared participation.

Hostile Men

Even when groups are set up to be voluntary, some members feel a degree of coercion to attend—and feel a matching degree of hostile resentment. If ignored, the hostility of a group member spills over to all other group members and markedly impedes the establishment of a therapeutic milieu. The leader would do well to address this matter quickly, even as soon as the member is introduced into the group. If a man's initial manner radiates hostility, he should be encouraged to put his feelings into words. If he has profoundly negative feelings and participation is optional, he might be encouraged to reconsider whether he truly wants to be a group member. If he has no choice about participation, his negative feelings should be acknowledged and validated as understandable. The leader need not feel defensive or critical of this situation. A useful position might be, "There are many reasons to resent being here, as this is time consuming and there's no guarantee it will help."

Open recognition and normalization of resistance is especially useful, because many group members may share a degree of negativity about therapy. The critical issue is that the negative feelings (for now) be directed toward their targets outside the group, not at other group members or at the group leader. In this situation, the leader can take the following stance: "As long as we're forced to be here, can we make this a positive experience for everybody?"

Competitive Men

Some men find a way to make every situation a competitive one, an arena in which to display their superiority over "less worthy" men. If not addressed, this intermember competition can create an environment that emphasizes members' facade of masculine bravado and minimizes chances of shared vulnerability.

This antitherapeutic process can be curtailed somewhat if, when the group begins, the leader emphasizes that all men are brothers, that they all share certain common problems, and that they are all incapable of fully meeting the impossible demands of the modern male role. If the leader is a man, it will be helpful for him to take the position that he himself has many challenges in meeting conflicting role pressures. He can emphasize, "We're all in this together," noting that this a struggle against the pressures of a changing world, not against each other. "Rather than trying to outdo each other, we will try to understand each other." (A woman leader might acknowledge that although she doesn't share the same role pressures, she has struggled to cope with a different set of role pressures as a woman and has great interest in learning more about the specific pressures that men face.) The leader can note that the "outside world encourages men to put up a front," but that the group's objective is to find a way to show what's behind the front. A special issue here is that the leader, especially a male one, not get caught up in traditional male competitive patterns and a power struggle. If, for example, he finds himself continually arguing with a group member, he may need to back off and analyze the interaction for subtle competitive themes.

Withdrawn and Avoidant Men

Because the group can proceed only as rapidly as its slowest member, a nonparticipating man can deaden or impede the group. To some extent, the aforementioned communication rules will help the situation, because they keep the avoidant man from completely disappearing. Increasing the intensity of his participation is a bigger problem, as too much direct pressure may intimidate him and may replicate similar interactions in his outside relational world (for example, family members who criticize him for his silence).

Instead of getting caught in the bind of pressuring versus ignoring the reluctant group member, the leader may validate the wisdom of his reticence. This man may be characterized as someone who realizes that too much exposure is risky and will guard the group against proceeding too rapidly. However, because too much of this responsibility will deprive the man of the benefits of the group, all should agree to help the man participate a bit more actively. Naturally, this works best if the reluctant man concurs with the plan.

Intellectualizers and Emotion-Phobic Men

Some men have mastered a common masculine habit of distancing themselves from emotional pain by intellectualizing and talking in a remote and abstract manner. Often, these men will spend an entire session detailing the ills of the culture, political system, or younger generation without revealing much at all of their personal distress. These group members can stimulate provocative yet affectively barren group sessions. To cope with this problem, the leader can ask the intellectualizer to move from the general to the specific. That is, instead of focusing on the larger implications of an issue, he can be encouraged to specify how it personally touches his life. Instead of a treatise on "the problems with kids today," he can be asked to talk about his own children and how they relate to him as a father. Global politics and world issues are easy for men to discuss; personal issues are where they need to be led.

Although traditional men are highly reluctant to acknowledge it, most are struggling with the substantive challenges of contemporary manhood. Many want a chance to connect with others but are severely impeded by the uncompromising male code that equates seeking help with being unmanly. Sadly, conventional psychotherapy has not yet adjusted enough to men's resistance. Currently, even in the most favorable situations, therapy appeals to only the most desperate men. In the worst situations, therapy repels traditional men. However, properly designed male therapy groups offer an ideal healing environment for traditional men and a logical early step for many in their therapy journey. It isn't always possible to expose men to a men's group. When men do attend, however, the energy and enthusiasm generated can be major catalysts for the gender-sensitive marital and family therapies described in the next chapter.

5

Marital and Family Therapy

In previous chapters, I have described the ways in which traditional gender expectations have shaped and often constrained men as individuals, marital partners, and participants in family life. Gender role strain, a problem inherent in all traditional male development, has become even worse in the past quarter century because of a number of cultural shifts, including changes in the workplace and changes among women. Although most men are experiencing considerable pressure to change, they are largely having trouble adopting more flexible and egalitarian notions of manhood. Some men enthusiastically embrace change, but many more do not. Many become entrenched and cope with their stress through various aspects of the darker side of masculinity, including dysfunctional relationship styles.

Psychotherapy, I have contended, has not yet been a significant resource for many troubled men. Most traditional men who enter therapy do so under some form of coercion or from a sense of desperation. To a large extent, conventional psychotherapy has been inaccessible to them. In Chapter Three, I presented core elements of a new psychotherapy that will engage men by placing their problems in a gender context. This perspective allows them to see that many of their troubles are inevitable problems of the social construction of gender, not just personal failings. In Chapter Four, I described how all-male therapy groups can be a critical first step in traditional men's therapy journey.

After they have immersed themselves in therapy designed to heighten their awareness of gender role strain in their lives, many traditional men will benefit from attention to their problematic relationships.[1] Because many men have entered therapy in the first place because of the pressure applied by loved ones, it is only natural that we would ultimately do what we can to help men become more effective marital partners and more fulfilled family members.

In this chapter I present three perspectives for enhancing relationship therapy with traditional men. First, I thoroughly describe the psychosocial context in which men enter the marital relationship. In other words, I describe the emotional baggage men bring with them as husbands and partners. Second, I emphasize the political dimension of marital therapy as a means of alerting prospective therapists to the multiple tactics traditional men may use to subvert change. Third, I offer some useful approaches for promoting gender awareness in marital and family therapies.

I should note that this chapter is not intended to be an all-encompassing description of all possible relationship therapies with all men. By and large, this therapy will be far less useful for couples for whom traditional roles work wonderfully. I believe these couples are rare, however. Also, this chapter is less applicable to that small minority of men who are not constrained by traditional ideas about women and marriage and who are actively pursuing or involved in nontraditional relationships. Finally, this chapter is not for those who have completely abandoned hope of forming more modern and egalitarian relationships. It is for those who want new and fulfilling heterosexual relationships, whether inside or outside of marriage.

1.   I have previously noted that I have addressed this book to psychotherapy with traditional *heterosexual* men because this male population is the one with which I have the most competence. The limitations of my experience and perspective are most dramatic in this chapter. I regret these limitations and emphasize that I have no interest in minimizing or marginalizing the experiences of gay and bisexual men, some of whom enter marital relationships (both gay and heterosexual). Although I am unable to address these issues, I continue to study them as critical to my understanding of the complete range of male experience.

In sum, this chapter is a description of how I conceptualize the next stage of the therapy journey of traditional men—the translation of heightened gender awareness and personal growth into improved marital and family relationships.

UNDERSTANDING HOW A MAN COMES TO MARRIAGE

Marital therapy with men is far more likely to be successful (and ethical) when therapists understand everything that has influenced traditional men's problems with women, as well as these men's paradoxical relationship to the marital institution itself. In Chapter One, I briefly described the complexity of men's relationships with women. I begin this chapter by revisiting that topic, adding historical, developmental, political, and gender socialization perspectives. To do this, I review some important observations about male early-life developmental issues.

Male Early Development: Psychoanalytic Perspectives

A man is created inside a woman's body, and his earliest attachments have almost always been with a woman. Nancy Chodorow has captured this beautifully:

> It is in a woman's arms and bosom that the delicately-skinned infant—shocked at birth by sudden light, dry air, noises, drafts, separateness, jostling—originally nestles. In contact with her flesh it first feels the ecstasy of suckling, of release from the anguish of hunger and the terror of isolation. Her hands clean, soothe, and pat its sensitive bottom. Her face is the first whose expression changes reciprocally with its own. Her voice introduces it to speech: it is the first voice that responds to the voice of the child, that signals the advent of succor, whose patterns of rhythm or pitch correspond to events the child

notices or body sensations it feels. She is the one who rocks or bounces it when it feels tense, who thumps it when it needs to burp. She comes when it feels anxious or bored and provides the sense of being cared for, the interesting things to look at, touch, smell, and hear, the chance to use growing powers of back-and-forth communication, without which human personality and intellect—and indeed the body itself—cannot develop [p. 33].

Unfortunately, for a young male, this has usually been a temporary state of affairs; over the next months and years, he typically discovers a bewildering conflict between autonomy and attachment. Some developmental theorists—Nancy Chodorow (1978), William Betcher and William Pollack (1993), and Sam Osherson (1986), for example—consider this conflict to be inherent in men's psychoemotional development and ultimately very damaging to men's capacity to tolerate intimate relationships.

According to this line of thought, young girls are free to connect and identify with their mothers, but young boys must be different if they are to accomplish the developmental task of defining themselves as masculine. Rather than relishing the emotional and sensual pleasures of attachment to their mothers, they are compelled to seek a more clearly defined intrapsychic and interpersonal separation. This creates markedly different gender-based developmental themes—girls focus on affection and attachment; boys focus on separation and autonomy.

The picture presented by these developmental theorists is one in which a young male's earliest encounter with a woman is replete with conflict. Drawn to yet fearful of the mother's love and nurturance, the young boy develops what William Pollack (1990, p. 317) has labeled "defensive autonomy" or "pseudo self-sufficiency." Sam Osherson (1986) posits that even minimal recognition of a desire for attachment to the mother threatens the young man's fragile sense of autonomy and generates "fears of engulfment."

What makes matters worse for the young male is fathers' frequent unavailability during this critical period.[2] In the traditional family contexts in which the father is physically or psychologically absent, it can be anticipated that a young boy will struggle with what Osherson describes as "the shame of identifying with a father perceived as rejecting, disinterested, or himself inadequate" (p. 10).

We see, then, that men's earliest experiences with women are characterized by deep emotional conflict—an immense desire for nurturance and attachment coupled with a desire for separation and autonomy. Any desire for attachment can induce shame, a situation commonly exacerbated by experiences of being shamed or rejected by male figures. Terrance Real (1997) has recently theorized that this rending of connection from "the feminine" has deleterious life-long consequences for men, including a propensity toward covert depression in its many destructive manifestations.

Restrictive Early Socialization and Hypermasculinity

Developmental researcher Eleanor Maccoby (1990) observes that the relationship between boys and girls during childhood is largely characterized by "widespread gender segregation," which is a product of boys' preference for a competitive, rough-and-tumble play style and their "insensitivity to the influence of girls" (p. 515). Although it is unclear whether this situation is created by biological or social development factors, the results are quite clear—developing males do not learn to interact with or adjust to their female peers. Boys learn to prefer the companionship of other boys and become uneasy in the presence of girls.

2. It should be noted that although there is widespread endorsement of this developmental process as problematic for males, there is considerable controversy about the degree to which it is inherent or necessary. Louise Silverstein (1993) has argued persuasively that this common pattern is fundamentally altered when the culture embraces a "new fatherhood" that eliminates sexist distinctions in parental roles, skills, and responsibilities.

Another relevant finding of developmental research is that the socialization of young males is far more vigorous and restrictive than it is for young females—again suggesting the likelihood of the intergender relationship problems men encounter in adulthood. In summarizing the research, Jim O'Neil (1982) noted that boys seem to have a more intensive socialization experience than girls and experience more pressure to conform to a vaguely defined masculine role. These developmental differences are critical. Young males who deviate from stereotypically defined masculine roles are more severely punished than sex-role-deviant girls are. Young men are severely castigated for any type of failure or indication of incompetence. Those young men who violate traditional norms risk being devalued and shamed in a way that grossly distorts emotional security and well-being.

Early male socialization is not only restrictive but also demands physical and verbal "toughness." Fathers in particular are exhaustive in their efforts to ensure that their sons will grow up to be strong and tough and, as a result, often overstimulate them from an early age. As infants, males are tossed about more and subjected to loud and tough voices, rather the soft and gentle tones that infant girls hear.

Robert Holt reviewed both animal and human research and reported on its ominous implications for men and relationships: "To take this kind of treatment the organism becomes less sensitive. Part of callousness, part of toughness is not being sensitive, not having as much pain sensitivity and not having as much general awareness of feelings" (quoted in Miedzian, 1991, p. 83).

Let's examine the implications of this intense and restrictive male socialization for male-female relationships. Obviously, one implication would be that males can be expected to display a generalized pattern of toughness, emotional insensitivity, and a consequent lack of empathy. They can be expected to resist the influence of women. In fact, some have seen this resistance as deeply embedded in American cultural traditions. In comparing European and American cultures, Rupert Wilkinson (1984) described American child rearing as focused on opportunities for natural vigor and expression. "Children should be considerate, get along with others, but not be too angelic, too artificially repressed—boys especially should show a little bit of the rascal, the hellion." (p. 29)

Echoes of this negative sentiment toward women's influence appear prominently within the mythopoetic branch of the men's movement. Many have noted that its leading spokesman, Robert Bly (1990), is preoccupied with resisting the "dangers" of feminine influence and fearing that too much of the "feminine" will rob men of essential maleness.

Resistance to women is only part of the problem, as young males are taught to distrust and reject all that is feminine and to avoid anything that smacks of femininity. The "no sissy stuff" noted by Deborah David and Robert Brannon (1976), the "anti-feminine element of the male role" noted by Jim Doyle (1995), and the "femiphobia" described by Denis O'Donovan (1988) all reflect this consistent trend in male socialization.

One of the most peculiar features of the masculine code is that even though it calls for rigid adherence to a narrow range of behaviors, it is at times oddly vague and inconsistent about what masculine behavior is supposed to look like. In fact, some have noted that "masculine" is often defined less by what it is than by what it is not. Some men's studies researchers go so far as to say "a fundamental guide for men's behavior may be a negative touchstone—anything feminine" (Thompson, Grisanti, & Pleck, 1985).

This socialization pressure for young males to reject femininity sets up serious problems for their future attitudes toward women. As "feminine" becomes a negative association for young men, women become further devalued. D. B. Lynn (1966) put it this way: "Since it is the 'girl-like' activities that provoked the punishment administered in efforts to induce sex-typed behavior in boys . . . boys should be expected to generalize and consequently develop hostility toward all females as representatives of the disliked role" (p. 466).

Matters become even worse when boys are continually surrounded by women teachers who are expected to quell the more troublesome aspects of their youthful exuberance. Nearly four decades ago, Ruth Hartley (1959) noted "the demeanor of women with whom he is forced to associate is often such that the boy feels that women just don't like boys" (p. 466).

Adolescence and Sexuality

A primary developmental challenge of male adolescence is the need to make the transition from the gender-segregated world of boyhood to a mutually rewarding intergender adult environment. Fueled by social and hormonal pressures, heterosexual male adolescents discover the other gender, which previously seemed relatively uninteresting. Unfortunately, teenage boys' lack of prior positive interactions with girls, as well as their massive miseducation about the emotional and psychological aspects of sexuality, encumbers them further in their interactions with women.

Of all our negative emotional baggage, none is more complex and conflictual than that related to sexuality. In the past two decades, a new body of literature relating to male sexuality has finally incorporated sensitivity to male gender socialization into the discourse, resulting in a rather unsettling conclusion—male sexuality is a tangled mess. Once, people thought of male-female sexual dysfunction as principally a product of "frigid" women, whose Victorian upbringing caused them to be sexually repressed. In this view, men were seen as naturally healthy and sexually focused, though perhaps in need of some technical guidance to "loosen up" their repressed partners.

Perhaps some of the finest contributions of recent men's studies literature have been those of Bernie Zilbergeld (1978, 1992), who has been one of the prominent critics of these misconceptions. A common myth in our culture deals with the supposed sex differences between men and women. According to this bit of fantasy, female sexuality is full of problems, while male sexuality is simple, straightforward, and problem-free (1978, p. 1). Throughout his writings, Zilbergeld calls for far greater attention to be paid to how men are taught to think about sexuality and encouraged to adopt a number of destructive myths (such as sex is performance, a man must orchestrate sex, and a man always wants and is always ready to have sex).

Fortunately, Zilbergeld has not been alone. A consistent issue in the men's literature has been men's hidden confusion in the area of sexuality. For example, according to Kenneth Solomon (1982b), "sexual dysfunction" is one of the six defining features of masculinity. Naturally, because full examination of the complexities of male sexuality could occupy volumes, only a few important points can be made here.

The first point to be made is that most traditional men define sex as more important and more central than do traditional women. The 1994 national research study by Robert Michael, John Gagnon, Edward Laumann, and Gina Kolata and the international research of David Buss (1994) have both provided strong empirical support for what we have generally accepted to be true. Men think about sex more, hold lower standards for a potential sexual partner (primarily, she must be physically attractive), have more sexual relationships, masturbate more, and are more likely to associate personal competence with sexual performance. In *The Centerfold Syndrome* (Brooks, 1995a), I argue that these characteristics of male sexual socialization cause men to become fixated on women's bodies, dependent on women's bodies for masculinity validation, and grossly impaired in their ability to achieve emotional intimacy with women.

Although there is widespread belief that this male sexual preoccupation is biologically based, there is more evidence that it is environmental, a function of the social construction of male sexuality (see Levant & Brooks, 1997, for a thorough review of this issue). What is critical here are the messages given to young men about sexual activity. Adolescent males receive such intense pressure to validate masculinity through sexual experiences that sex becomes separated from other aspects of social life and becomes an obsession. This venture into sexual activity is further complicated by a general lack of accurate sexual information, minimal mentoring, and a mythology that sexual ignorance is synonymous with unmanliness. Unfortunately, as young boys prepare themselves for this sexual quest, young girls are preparing themselves for quite a different experience—to attract yet control the sexual overtures of these sexually preoccupied boys. John Gagnon and B. Henderson (1975) commented upon this dilemma of differing agendas: "The young male . . . pushes for more sexual activity when dating. . . . Conversely, many young females . . . spend a good deal of time preventing sexual intimacy. Therefore, because of earlier differences in learning how to be sexual, males committed to sexuality, but less trained in affection and love, may interact with females who are committed to love but relatively untrained in sexuality" (p. 38).

Warren Farrell (1987) has noted that this situation creates "enormous sexual leverage power" for women over men, a situation that causes men to make exaggerated efforts to win women's attention and "sexual favors." Farrell sees adolescence as a time when young men are taught the "male primary fantasy"—that the most desirable women are those that meet the beauty ideal of the centerfold model. Conversely, women are taught to seek relationships with men who are successful (in terms of fame and riches). The crux of Farrell's argument is that because many young women are physically appealing (thus fulfilling the primary male fantasy) and because very few young men have achieved fame and virtually none are financially successful (thereby failing to meet the primary female fantasy), heterosexual men's first significant sexual interactions with women are marked by feelings of inadequacy and sexual powerlessness. That is, many women have power through the sexual leverage that comes with their physical appearance. Men, however, may gain comparable sexual leverage only later, when they have become successful. Consequently, Farrell argues, some young men learn to seek women's sexual attention by becoming committed to achievement. As a result, men come to crave sex, but because they view women as those who have the power to choose when sex occurs, they see sex as a "gift." When that gift is not forthcoming, men are prone to be unhappy and resentful.

We can easily see that adolescent males are set up to have significant problems around sexuality. Physiological urges and socialization pressures push them to "conquer" women, who are simultaneously programmed to control the degree of sexual activity. This situation, of course, creates psychic distress for young males (as well as for young females) and makes them resent these young women, who seem determined to prevent males from relieving sexual tension and validating masculinity.

What worsens physiological matters for adolescent males are the rather strong injunctions against the most natural source of physical relief—masturbation. Although this is the principal sexual outlet for most adolescents, most males view it as "sexual failure." Hence, we invariably hear young men refer to masturbation in such deprecatory terms as "jacking off," "beating your meat," or "spanking the monkey," rather than with positive terms such as "pleasuring oneself."

Misogyny in Patriarchal Culture

An inherent feature of patriarchal culture is a misogyny that profoundly affects men's ability to value and trust women. Men have long been socialized to view women in contradictory ways, ranging from idealization and celebration to distrust, fear, and bitterness. The history of sexist views toward women is well documented in feminist literature (Bullough, 1973) and doesn't require elaboration here. It is critical, however, that I emphasize the profound negative impact of sexism and misogyny on the lives of women, as well as on men's capacity to relate to women as desirable partners. The dilemma of male-female relations is only exacerbated when any of the aforementioned developmental sources of intergender stress is juxtaposed against a culture that offers men easy explanations for their discomfort. It has been far too easy to rationalize, "The problem is those damn women!"

UNDERSTANDING THE INSTITUTION OF MARRIAGE

Thus far, I have examined the multiple aspects of male socialization that influence men as they enter a heterosexual marital relationship. This perspective is necessary, because marital therapy works best when we fully understand all the baggage men bring with them into the therapy session. Our background exploration continues with an examination of an additional factor that must be appreciated—traditional men's most common views of the marital institution itself. That is, what does a man expect from marriage?

Jesse Bernard (1972) highlighted this expectation issue quite well when she pointed out that there are at least two marriages in every marital union—"his" marriage and "her" marriage—and that these do not always coincide. In this section, I look at "his" marriage—traditional men's most common images, fantasies, and expectations of marriage—and speculate about how these affect his behavior as a husband.

In the study of traditional men's perceptions and expectations of marriage, an intriguing paradox becomes apparent. On the one hand, marriage seems malignant, something to be avoided as long as possible. Oscar Wilde captured this sentiment with his aphorism "Marriage is a wonderful institution; every woman should be married, but no men." Men have long attacked this institution.

On the other hand, despite their dominant political position, they have not seen the need to alter it dramatically. The historical vitality of the marital institution is testament to the fact that this institution is of considerable benefit to men. Once again, Jesse Bernard (1972) has a critical perspective: "For centuries men have been told—by other men—that marriage is: no bed of roses, a necessary evil, a noose, a desperate thing, a field of battle, a curse, a school of sincere pretense. . . . [However,] contrary to the charges leveled against it, the husbands' marriage, whether they like it or not (and they do), is awfully good for them" (p. 16).

The empirical support for Bernard's assertions has been impressive. In general, husbands report being more satisfied with marriage than their wives. Married men also enjoy greater health benefits, are less likely to seek divorces, reenter marriage more quickly and more often after divorce, and die sooner after being widowed (see Brooks & Gilbert, 1995).

Although there are many complicated factors at work here, there is dramatic evidence of a pronounced ambivalence in men over the marital institution. Although they condemn it publicly, they are quite attached to it privately. To understand this paradoxical situation better, we must explore additional issues.

The "Civilizing" Value of Marriage

Among political conservatives and gender "essentialists," there is a strongly held opinion that marriage is an absolute necessity for the survival of civilization because, more than any other social force, it "civilizes" men. According to this perspective, marriage is a trade-off; women hold erotic power over men, granting sexual gratification in exchange for men's agreement to be monogamous, to marry them at all, and to be providers and protectors.

Neoconservative George Gilder is an avid proponent of this view. In *Sexual Suicide*, Gilder (1973) argued that male nature is "barbaric" and can only be civilized through marital bonds that "subordinate male sexual impulses and psychology to long-term horizons of female biology." According to Gilder, women control "the life force in our society and our lives . . . [and determine] the level of happiness, energy creativity, and solidarity in the nation" (p. 24).

Two decades after Gilder offered this perspective, evolutionary psychologist David Buss (1994) echoed these ideas. Buss sees species survival as depending on women's and men's playing out these centuries-old adaptive patterns.

Although many gender studies scholars, myself included, strongly disagree with these essentialist perspectives, we acknowledge their power in the thinking of traditional women and men. Conventional wisdom continues to be that a young man needs to marry if he ever hopes to become a solid citizen.

Marital Services

Traditional men commonly expect their wives to take care of the home (furnishing, decorating, and cleaning), the children (dressing and transporting), and the family (feeding and picking up after). Sociologist Bruce Nordstrom (1986) describes this expectation as men's idea that women will provide "marital support services." As was well chronicled by Arlie Hochschild's *The Second Shift* (1989), men's participation in domestic chores has increased minimally despite the dramatic increase in women's roles in the workplace. Joseph Pleck (1993) has found evidence that men are doing *more* domestic labor but that most traditional men continue to expect women to provide the bulk of it (just as they continue to expect theselves to be the primary breadwinners). As evidence that this situation endures, there continue to be comic portrayals of highly successful corporate or professional men who are utterly incapable of performing the simplest task in the kitchen.

Career and Symbolic Benefits

Most men rely on women to provide domestic services, and many, particularly white-collar men, also expect women to serve the symbolic role of "wife." This role calls for the woman to subjugate her activities to the advancement of her husband's career by functioning in a variety of capacities—social, clerical, and administrative. Additionally, the presence of a "wife" provides important symbolic evidence of a man's psychological maturity; it shows that he has advanced to the stage of the male life cycle commonly labeled "settling down." As phrased by Danny DeVito's character in the movie *War of the Roses*, "The world can take the measure of a man by his house, his car, his shoes, and his wife."

Emotional Benefits

Marriage is essential to most men as a necessary source of emotional security and as a remedy for emotional deficits. It provides men with social companionship. Bruce Nordstrom (1986) notes that another major benefit of marriage, according to men, is the provision of emotional security, a sense of being accepted and emotionally supported. "The marriage and the home are described by the men themselves as a base, a refuge, and a haven" (p. 37). In my work with men, I have frequently been struck by this phenomenon—single men live in a "house," "pad," or "shack," whereas married men live in a "home."

Many men also perceive marriage as a convenient way of alleviating their own deficiencies in emotional skills. Joseph Pleck (1980) has noted, "In traditional male-female relationships, men experience their emotions vicariously through women. Many men have learned to depend on women to help them express their emotions for them. At an ultimate level, many men are unable to feel emotionally alive except through relationships with women" (p. 421). Pleck views this "emotional expressiveness power" as contributing to a man's emotional dependence on a woman and as adding to his fears of losing a long-standing relationship.

In a similar vein, Jim Doyle (1995) has described how "the wife acts as a kind of socioemotional bridge between her husband and others." In this view, a man's difficulty in dealing with emotional relations with children, parents, or close friends, as well as his discomfort with certain tender emotions, causes him to expect his wife to act as "a personal emissary to convey the husband's feelings to other people" (p. 217).

Physical Benefits

Men benefit substantially from marriage in terms of improved physical health. The traditional "wife" role includes the expectation of caring for the physical well-being of family members. As a result, Jim Doyle (1995) notes, "Many wives express concern over their husband's physical health, often prompting him to take better care of himself than he would if he were single. . . . For many husbands, the first person they turn to with their aches and pains is the ever-present family nurse, who is expected to make it all better" (p. 217).

There is compelling evidence that marriage provides considerable health benefits to men, as married men have significantly lower rates of disease and morbidity. Many variables could account for this—married men's decreased risk taking, their greater sense of responsibility, and the emotional and physical comforting provided by wives. An additional factor may be related to the usual manner in which many men enter the health care system. Traditional masculine values call for men to abuse their bodies and resist most preventive health care practices. Marriage, however, may change this, as it exposes men to women's nurturing roles and gives men a face-saving excuse to care for themselves: "I'm fine, but I'll do this for the good of you and the kids."

In summary, we can see that marriage is a complex institution that offers many benefits to men. Let's turn to another factor that adds further complications—the recent changes in the marital institution.

UNDERSTANDING THE CHANGING NATURE OF MARRIAGE: POLITICAL IMPLICATIONS FOR THERAPY

To this point, I have described a rather peculiar situation. Heterosexual men enter traditional marriage with an abundance of mixed feelings toward women. This ambivalence is rooted in men's psychosocial development, early masculinity socialization, adolescent sexual experiences, and participation in a patriarchal culture. In addition, they have been encouraged to hold contradictory views toward the institution of marriage—that it is lifesaving and necessary, yet enslaving and emasculating. In the midst of this already confusing situation comes a new element—the rapidly changing political and economic environment with its potential for causing sweeping changes in the marital institution itself.

Changes in Today's Marriages

The sweeping sociocultural changes of the past four decades have been reflected both in the roles of women in larger society and in the fundamental shifts in the structure and function of traditional marriage. Most women have become far less accepting of traditional ideas of male specialness or superiority and have insisted on having the ultimate authority to define their own needs and interests. Women began to challenge the prevalent assumption that they needed paternalistic care and protection from men and called for many more sources of identity and gratification beyond those of wife and mother. Most women now expect to be viewed as independent and rational beings. Most assume full responsibility for their destinies and are far more likely to teach their daughters that they need to be ready, if necessary, to "go it alone."

Today, only about 10 percent of American families fit the traditional 1950s *Leave It to Beaver* family model of a two-parent family with children, a wage-earning husband, and a homemaker wife. More than half of women return to their jobs within one year of having a child, and 60 percent of employed men have employed spouses. The average working wife with full-time employment contributes approximately 40 percent of the family's annual income (Brooks & Gilbert, 1995). Obviously the single-career marriage is increasingly being replaced with the dual-career marriage.

Contrary to tradition, then, some partners—male and female alike—view women's employment as essential to women's self-concept and life goals and further assume that they will pursue occupational work regardless of the family's economic needs. Some men, in turn, appear less defined by the traditional "good provider" role and insist less on its concomitant privileges and entitlements. For some, a new picture of contemporary marriage is emerging, one in which women and men, having developed similar attributes and abilities, involve themselves in similar roles and activities.

But not all shifts are being made harmoniously. Although some men are making the necessary psychological transitions, many others are doggedly attached to traditional ideas of marriage, as well as age-old ideas about how women and men should behave. Many will take whatever steps seem necessary to maintain the status quo, or, in some cases, to return to more traditional relationships. For example, in the past few years, we have seen two very powerful efforts to unite men around conservative causes. Both the Million Man March and the Promise Keepers have been dedicated to uniting men and reestablishing male "leadership" in families. The great appeal of these movements seems to attest to many men's need for closer emotional ties with other men, as well as a need for spirituality. Unfortunately, these groups have also united men to pursue a reactive political agenda that, in my view, is both misguided and impossible.

Although there has been some highly visible national resistance to women's new family roles, less visible resistance has been common for many years. Feminist family therapists like Marianne Walters, Betty Carter, and Michelle Bograd have long insisted that family and marital therapists cannot be politically neutral, because these therapies have significant power implications for family members (Walters, Carter, Papp, & Silverstein, 1988; Bograd, 1991). In the following vignette I describe one of my earliest and most painful, but most useful, firsthand exposures to the political dimension of marital therapy.

Bill has called seeking a psychological evaluation. Apparently, he has already been evaluated at a local private psychiatric facility and, according to his report, has been described as a "hopeless psychopath." Not satisfied, he is seeking a second opinion.

When I first meet Bill, I am struck by his size (very large), his dress (western conservative with boots and a cowboy hat), and his manner (loud and abrasive). A self-described member of the law enforcement community, he admits to a recent "little problem" on the job. As I question him, he reveals that, for the second time, he has been charged with misconduct; he overzealously apprehended a suspect and produced numerous unexplainable injuries. Bill is generally contemptuous of the whole matter, dismissing it as "just what goes with the territory." He expects to retain his job without loss of rank or benefits after he serves his thirty-day suspension.

More problematic for Bill is the effect that the incident has had on his marriage. Mona, Bill's wife of nearly twenty years, was already uneasy with Bill's aggression. This new event seemed to galvanize her fears. When he later lost his temper and slapped her, she insisted that he leave their home. He reluctantly complied but seemed obsessed with moving back in as quickly as possible.

Mona married Bill when she was only seventeen. She was living with her family in France. Bill, who was on military assignment, persuaded her to leave her family and return with him to the United States. Over the next eighteen years, Mona functioned exclusively as homemaker and mother. Two years into the marriage, Carl was born. Within a few years, he was diagnosed with severe congenital brain damage, leaving him intellectually limited and restricted to a wheelchair. Mona focused much of her time and energy on Carl. She had virtually no outside activities and no social support system.

Over the years, Mona was greatly troubled by Bill's refusal to help with Carl and his prolonged absences from the home. When she voiced even mild dissatisfaction, however, he reacted angrily and violently. Usually, he broke furniture and pushed her around. Shortly before the separation, however, he slapped her, carried her into the bedroom, and nearly raped her before running from the house. Mona called the police and filed charges.

In therapy with Bill, I am dismayed by his indifference to his domestic violence, as well as his insistence that I contact Mona to initiate reconciliation. I eventually relent and ask her to join us in the therapy sessions. When she comes, she is very passive, soft-spoken, and reluctant to participate. Bill dominates the marital session. Toward the end, he suggests that they would make much more rapid progress if he were living in the home—this would "let us work on things on a daily basis." He also urges Mona to drop the legal charges.

This suggestion catches me by surprise, but I have been naively impressed with Bill's sudden burst of motivation. I ask Mona about this and receive a noncommittal response. Under Bill's pressure, she relents. I schedule another appointment for the following week, but the day before the appointment, Bill calls to tell me that things are going so well that they don't need any more sessions. This makes me uneasy, but I decide to see it in the best possible light.

It isn't until three years later that I am harshly confronted with the gullible and politically ignorant quality of my previous work with Mona and Bill. He calls asking for an appointment. In the session, he confesses to "getting a little too frisky with Mona." She has insisted that he move out. Once again he hopes we can set up marital therapy as soon as possible.

Fortunately, in the intervening years, I've become better educated about domestic violence and the political dimensions of therapy. I am now able to see that I sabotaged Mona's efforts to demand an end to the abuse in her marriage. Determined not to repeat my mistakes, I refuse his request.

In the next few sessions with Bill alone, I learn that Mona has used the three intervening years to find part-time work, save money, and acquire a small circle of supportive friends. Not surprisingly, Bill is offended by Mona's newfound independence. He has sought my support in an effort to suppress her new activities. Once again, he urges that I contact Mona.

I do agree to contact Mona, but this time my input is very different. I congratulate her for empowering herself and encourage her to remain steadfast in demanding a life free from threat and violence. When Bill inquires, I inform him that although I am hopeful that a reconciliation might eventually be possible, a lot of changes will be required, including his entering a group for violent men.

Men's Resistance to Change

The therapy with Bill and Mona had a major impact on my thinking about psychotherapy for traditional men. In earlier chapters, I've described the poor fit between traditional masculinity and psychotherapy, suggesting that it is useful to anticipate that traditional men will resist therapy. In Chapter Three, I noted that there are pitfalls to starting marital and family therapy prematurely, because of men's relative disadvantages as clients and their relative disinterest in seeking help. In this section, I describe problems that directly result from some traditional men's political investment in the relationship status quo. I have become convinced that psychotherapists must recognize that their interventions have political implications, because they have a crucial impact on the balance of power in a relationship.

When a traditional man is confronted by a female partner who insists that he change, the man can be expected to minimize the demand or, if necessary, try to subvert it. This should not be surprising, because no dominant group will welcome threats to its status or willingly abandon power or entitlement. Furthermore, most traditional men have strong ideological feelings that traditional marriages are "right"; they consider change to be unwise or even dangerous. Finally, most traditional men are likely to fear new marital arrangements, because, at some deep level, they already feel powerless enough.

Often, a traditional man only enters therapy after a marital partner has threatened to abandon him. In the face of possibly losing the relationship that is so central to his sense of worth, the traditional man can be expected to respond with desperate measures. In the best-case scenarios, an anxious traditional man may heed the warning signs and seriously seek to change himself and his lifestyle. In the worst-case scenarios, however, he will engage in antagonistic and adversarial efforts to disempower the partner, win the war, and return matters to their previous state. Here is a list of possible disempowering strategies that a traditional man may use (from Brooks, 1991).

I.   Coercively controlling and intimidating
      A. Physically or legally intimidating
      B. Financially intimidating and manipulating
II.   Currying favor
      A. Giving gifts and bribing
      B. Making romantic overtures and offering second honeymoons
      C. Promising to improve behavior
III. Creating confusion and manipulating others
      A. Pathologizing and demeaning the woman's demands ("It's a phase"; "It's PMS"; "It's women's lib run amok")
      B. Behaving erratically and unpredictably
      C. Enlisting collusive support of others (therapists, ministers, family, friends)
IV.   Provoking guilt and appealing to feminine nurturance
      A. Neglecting health and self-care
      B. Threatening suicide

SETTING THE STAGE FOR MARITAL THERAPY

Based on this analysis of the political dimension of marital therapy, I have developed a marital therapy treatment model that emphasizes both steps to take *before* initiating conjoint therapy and methods to use *during* conjoint treatment. First I describe what has to occur before conjoint therapy is initiated.

Creating Gender Awareness

The *therapist* must become as appreciative as possible of the gender role socialization of women and men, paying close attention to the ways in which the culture defines appropriate behavior for both genders and conveying empathy for the actions of each spouse (without condoning coercion or intimidation). For example, although it might have been easy to buy into the previous description of Bill as a "hopeless psychopath," that would have been unfair. Therapeutic rapport depended on my seeing Bill in an appropriate context. He was certainly no "SNAG" (that is, a sensitive, New Age guy), but he was a hardworking man who was loyal to many aspects of the traditional masculine code. Bill's violence, of course, is utterly unacceptable, but it is also consistent with some aspects of his socialization.

Just as Bill's behavior must be viewed in a sociocultural context, so must Mona's. Her insistence on increased empowerment must be appreciated as a realistic reaction to changing times, as women are much more involved in the workforce, marriages are far less stable, and many women's economic insecurity is a continual reality. When viewed in context, Mona's actions can be recognized as vital to her economic and psychological well-being. Bill's resistance to change can also be recognized as a predictable but unnecessary reaction to perceived threats to his role as provider, family leader, and protector.

Maintaining Therapeutic Leverage

Mona's actions represented a significant threat to the status quo. Family systems seek homeostatic balance, and actions such as Mona's typically engender "change-back" pressures. Little can be accomplished unless the therapist maintains leverage by perpetuating the homeostatic imbalance. Frequently, this leverage, a product of the woman's empowerment, can only be maintained when the physical separation continues. As I learned the hard way, my naive collusion with Bill's efforts to return home sabotaged Mona's tactical position. In fact, the simple act of prematurely seeing Bill and Mona together was misguided, in that it played into Bill's preoccupation with "winning her back" and weakened Mona's resolve.

At this point, the physical separation should be strongly endorsed by the therapist as vital to a successful therapy outcome; marital partners should be seen separately. A woman must understand that a premature reconciliation will undercut therapeutic leverage and might make future change even more difficult. She should be encouraged to remain separate from her husband and to resist her culture-bred temptation to befriend or nurture him.

Supporting the Woman

The marital work has been stimulated by the woman's newfound empowerment and push for a reformed marital relationship, but her resolve can be quite fragile. Because she will be subjected to change-back pressures from many directions, she will need extensive emotional support and guidance from the therapist.[3] Included in this guidance is extensive education about the many disempowering tactics she is likely to face and a discussion of alternative coping strategies.

If necessary, the therapist can arrange more intense support for the wife by referring her to a feminist collective or a women's sup-

---

3. I have frequently been questioned about the ethical aspects of this therapeutic step. In general, the issue seems to be, "Whose agenda are we pursuing? The therapist's or the client's?" In other words, wouldn't it be improper for the therapist to "politicize therapy" and coerce the woman into a radical posture she does not truly desire. I believe it is improper for a therapist to force a position onto a naive or unwilling client. However, the matter is far from simple, because I strongly believe that therapy cannot avoid a political stance. Therefore, although the final choice about marital reconciliation or divorce resides with the client, it is the therapist's responsibility to communicate all necessary information, including the likely consequences of a disempowered position.

port group. If the therapist follows this strategy, the husband may become upset that the therapist is "encouraging" the woman and not adequately siding with him. The therapist can best handle this dilemma by first pointing out that the woman client, not the therapist, initiated the changes. The therapist can then acknowledge that the woman's empowerment is the most reasonable and practical alternative, because any efforts by the husband to suppress her would backfire. Equally important, the therapist can offer reassurance that an enlightened response from the husband may not only salvage the relationship but ultimately benefit both partners.

Selling the Husband on Change

As we have seen, Bill was obsessed with getting Mona back and putting the entire situation behind him. Bill eagerly sought to triangulate me, to align me with his purposes. Sadly, in the first therapeutic encounter, he succeeded. By the time he returned a few years later, I had learned enough to avoid repeating my previous mistakes; I refused to participate in his efforts to subvert Mona's growth.

Yet I failed at another level, because when Bill realized that I would not repeat the subverting process, he abandoned even this minimal pretense of interest in therapy. He completely rejected my efforts to include him in my men's group. Frankly, I was somewhat relieved, because I had serious doubts that he would ever entertain change (when he immediately remarried after Mona divorced him, it validated my impression). At another level, however, I was disappointed, because I had really wanted a chance to reach him.

Here we find a critical point in the therapeutic journey of resistant traditional men. Despite my inability to sell therapy to Bill, I have found that many other men *can* be sold on a new way to live. For truly substantive therapy to take place, the therapist must be able to exploit the unsettled situation creatively. The therapist must find a way to help the desperate man move from his overly narrow "change-back" strategy to a more thorough change agenda.

A key challenge is for the therapist to demonstrate that the immediate crisis is actually an inevitable manifestation of long-standing marital issues, rather than a phase that will pass or disappear if suppressed. The therapist must counsel the husband about the shortcomings of coercion as a problem-solving strategy, particularly in light of his wife's demands for greater autonomy. The male client should learn that a more conciliatory and cooperative approach, contrary to his fears, will actually make reconciliation more likely. The husband should replace the common troublesome myth—that women secretly desire omnipotent and dominant men—with a more realistic view of heterosexual relationships in which both partners are autonomous. Additionally, the man must be encouraged to develop alternative, nonsexual, nurturing relationships and should be questioned about possible overdependence on his spouse.

Conducting Gender Role Therapy for the Husband

With luck and skill, the therapist may be able to persuade the resistant man to experiment with a brief course of therapy. The critical issue here is that the therapist approach the man from a posture that respects his dignity and wisdom yet additionally pinpoints the many ways in which his lifestyle has become dysfunctional. A men's group is ideal, but even individual therapy, when conducted in a gender-aware fashion, can accomplish the task. In essence, the man needs to "get it," that is, understand the multiple ways in which the ideology of traditional manhood impairs his ability to function as a husband (and a father, if appropriate), as well as his physical and emotional health.

Moving to Marital and Family Therapy

There is a far greater likelihood of truly transformative change when both the traditional man *and* his family system function in new ways. Later in this chapter I describe possible techniques to facilitate what my colleagues and I have described as *gender coevolution* (see Philpot, Brooks, Lusterman, & Nutt, 1997). The actual con-joint sessions come later, however. For now, the therapist's critical task is to monitor the relationship to determine when the partners are ready for conjoint treatment. In my view, three conditions should be met before conjoint marital therapy begins.

First, the woman's empowerment should be secure in both socio-economic and psychological terms—that is, she should have enough income to support herself and enough psychological strength to see the enterprise through. Second, the husband should have an ap-preciation of, and commitment to, an egalitarian relationship. Third, both parties should make a free and independent choice to pursue the therapy.[4] When reconciliation seems impractical, the therapist helps the partners dissolve the marriage and works to pro-mote more enlightened postdivorce functioning for each partner (and any children).

CONDUCTING GENDER-AWARE MARITAL THERAPY

Ron and Michelle had been reasonably happy for the first ten of their fifteen years together. Ron, age thirty-five, is a busy and career-oriented manager of a chemical plant; Michelle, age thirty-three, is unsure exactly who she is. In large part, her confusion is a source of the unhappiness that has strained their marriage and provoked her interest in calling me. She urges that I see them together as soon as possible.

In the first appointment, I am immediately aware that gloominess and despondency dominate the marital relationship. Michelle is clearly

---

4.   Once again, we face an ethical dilemma. What if the woman freely *chooses* to return to a highly traditional marital arrangement in which she has minimal socio-economic power and a subservient marital role? Although I believe that egalitarian relationships are ultimately more conducive to optimal functioning for all, I *am* willing to work with couples in this situation. Naturally, this does not apply to sit-uations in which abuse occurs.

unhappy but oddly listless and despairing. Ron has considerably more energy but is utterly baffled about what has gone wrong. Tediously, I am able to extract details of their shared history.

The second of two daughters, Michelle is her father's favorite, his "baby girl." Her father, a semiretired college professor, was always aware of Michelle as a bright and curious child but seemed more pleased with her childlike playfulness. Her mother, a registered nurse, always seemed to invest more energy into her relationship with Michelle's older sister. That sister is the mother of the only three grandchildren.

Ron is the youngest of six children born to working-class parents. He describes his family as "simple people who are very close and look after one another." He and his siblings have spent their entire lives in the same rural community.

Ron and Michelle dated each other exclusively in high school. After graduation, Ron began working his way up the job ladder in the local chemical plant. When she graduated two years later, Michelle faced a critical decision. Ron wanted to marry and have children, but Michelle wanted to go off to college. Despite heavy pressure from Ron and her mother, Michelle chose to take a scholarship at an out-of-state school.

The next year was intensely miserable for both Ron and Michelle. He had great difficulty adjusting to her absence and called her daily. Her mother vacillated between maintaining a cool distance and making guilt-inducing calls about "poor Ronny." Michelle withstood the pressure throughout the first year but finally wilted under a full-scale psychological assault from her sister, mother, and Ron. In the summer before her sophomore year, she abandoned her school plans and married Ron.

The marriage seemed to go reasonably well for the first several years. Ron found his work challenging and his salary more than adequate. Michelle took a moderately tolerable administrative assistant position at the local bank. Unfortunately, it was a dead-end job without advanced schooling. As her work began to seem repetitive and boring, Michelle became restive and frustrated.

Eventually, she slipped into long bouts of silent withdrawal with periodic flashes of anger at Ron for a range of minor sins. She hated the way he smelled when he came home from work. She was grossed out by his table manners. She disliked his work associates. She criticized him for his excessive interest in sex, as well as his clumsy and inept sexual style. She resented the regular Sunday visits to his parents' home and accused his parents of "babying" him.

Ron was hurt and perplexed by Michelle's growing querulousness. Though he privately resented Michelle's lack of appreciation for him, he worked tirelessly and unsuccessfully to please her. This seemed only to make her more unhappy. His suggestions about "starting a family" seemed to provoke an especially hostile response.

Several events pushed the marriage to the breaking point. Two years earlier, Ron had become preoccupied with a former girlfriend working at his job site. Although the relationship broke off before an affair developed, bad feelings remained. Michelle was angry; Ron was apologetic but only partially remorseful, feeling he had the right to a better deal than he was getting with Michelle.

Michelle's barely controlled restlessness broke through after a series of disquieting events. Her boss, a married man in his midfifties, came on to her, suggesting that she accompany him as a personal assistant on his frequent international trips. Michelle was infuriated by her boss's advances but even more troubled by the curiosity his offer provoked in her. World travel seemed far more exciting than the tedium of her current life.

Matters worsened when Michelle's father suffered a serious heart attack, leaving him bedridden and fearful of imminent death. When Michelle visited him at his bedside, he confessed to disappointment in himself for never having taken a stronger stand against Michelle's mother and pushed for Michelle to complete school. Michelle was devastated by this admission and angry at herself for not following through in their shared ambitions for her.

Reeling from the new developments, Michelle unexpectedly ran into Roberta, her former college roommate, who, upon completing school, had landed an exciting position with an international firm in a large metropolitan community. As they talked, Michelle became acutely aware that she had been feeling emotionally suffocated. Seeing Michelle's distress, Roberta offered her a place to stay if she ever wanted to get out and make a fresh start.

Together, these events launched Michelle into action. She confronted a stunned Ron, insisting on a marital separation so she could have time and space to think. She didn't feel ready to take Roberta's offer and had no clear sense of what she wanted, but she knew she had to get away from Ron. In the several weeks before she called me, Michelle had been living at her parents' home while Ron remained in their house.

With this background information, I am better able to understand the gloom that pervades the marital relationship. Ron and Michelle are clearly on different tracks. He professes boundless love for Michelle and a strong desire to begin having children. He is distressed and perplexed by Michelle's unhappiness, claiming that he would make any sacrifice for her. With tears in his eyes, he says, "She's the only person I've ever loved. I want to grow old with her." Michelle is notably unimpressed. If anything, Michelle becomes even more annoyed by Ron's statement. Noting the stalemate and unsure of Michelle's position, I choose to schedule separate sessions. As anticipated, the individual sessions shed new light on the marital impasse.

Because I am more unclear about Michelle, I see her first. When seen alone, she initially seems guarded and defensive, apparently anticipating criticism of her "bitchy" and erratic behavior toward Ron. Everyone (both sets of parents and their friends) loves Ron, because he is the "model" husband. Michelle is a mystery and pariah in their small-town community—what more could she possibly want?

To a degree, Michelle has incorporated this negative view of her into her self-image. At some level, she hopes that therapy might help her rediscover her love for Ron, find joy in a traditional marital role, and uncover her "maternal instincts." She wonders, "Why can't I be just like all the others and be satisfied with being the perfect wife and mother?" At the same time, however, she senses that this is wrong for her and is poised to counterattack in case I dispense more lectures on proper wifely conduct. I have no such plan; I am far more interested in determining what *she* wants.

Noting my willingness to listen and offer support, Michelle finds her voice. She insightfully describes her conflicted role in her family of origin—her father's pride and joy and her mother's and sister's competitor. As she talks, she realizes the extent of her bitterness toward Ron and her mother for undermining her college plans. She begins to connect her anxious and demoralized feelings to the limitations she feels in her job and marriage. In particular, she recognizes how Ron's love and devotion leave her feeling suffocated with anxiety and guilt.

Michelle's insights open new doors of exploration. I question her about what a wife and mother *should* be. Who are "all the others"? How did she come to learn about a woman's role, and how well do those ideas fit with her current thinking? Not surprisingly, these questions uncover many areas of conflict and dissatisfaction with traditional roles prescribed for women. Freed from the need to mouth the conventional litany about a woman's duties, Michelle admits that she has developed serious doubts about her earlier ideas and has begun to think of herself as a "budding feminist." For the remainder of the session, we explore the origins of her ideas about women's roles, her thoughts about the changing culture, and her perceptions of feminism. As we conclude, I offer a number of possible readings to help clarify her thinking.

By the time we meet again, Michelle has completed some serious evaluation of her life and long-term goals. In particular, she has begun to question Ron's "love and devotion." She has realized that Ron's claim to "do anything" only extends to a narrow range of options—not including support for her career. She remembers how he has always insisted that, because they are dependent on his income, any talk of relocation is absurd. Michelle has come to realize that Ron's love is far from unconditional; instead, it has many strings attached. She also realizes that her insecurities and fragile self-esteem have been fueled by the "bright but flighty" image with which she has been saddled. She vows to "take charge" of her life and begins inquiring about possible alternatives for her work and career. The sessions help Michelle crystallize her thinking about her life and the marriage's role in it. She feels that she is still committed to Ron but wants a dramatically altered marital relationship. It remains to be seen whether Ron will be willing and able to make those changes.

By the time I see Ron, he is a self-described "basket case." Although usually an easygoing and placid guy, he is overcome by high levels of anxiety and unpredictable crying spells. He is mystified by Michelle's behavior, wondering if perhaps she is undergoing some form of psychiatric disorder. He can make no sense of her dissatisfaction, insisting that he has always done everything possible to provide for her and make her happy. His goal is clear: "Doc, I desperately need you to help me get my old wife back."

As we discuss Ron's fears, a new wrinkle appears. Despite his career success and upper hand in the relationship, Ron has always worried about losing Michelle. He knows she is brighter than he and can, if she tries, outdo him in a number of careers. To him, his fear is only natural: "If she outperforms me and enters a field where she's surrounded by high-performing guys, what's the chance she will want to stay with me?"

Ron's admission is immensely helpful, as it points to one issue at the heart of the matter. From Ron's perspective, Michelle's ambitions present a major risk and no obvious benefit. At best, if she pursues a high-powered career, she will be even more unavailable to him as a wife and potential mother. At worst, she will meet a brighter and more successful man, ultimately abandoning him. He has one obvious piece of evidence. Over the past several months, she certainly hasn't acted lovingly toward him. Her criticism of him has been ceaseless. Ron notes, "She seems to have lost all respect for me. Everybody says I've been too nice to her and that she needs a strong man to lay down the law!"

Once again, the individual interview has revealed critical issues that are directly related to Ron's gender socialization and current views of women, men, and relationships. We explore his ideas about men and masculinity, making particular reference to marital relationships. As is already evident, he holds very traditional ideas that grossly constrain his ability to adapt to creative alternatives. I inform him of this, suggesting that although I completely understand his position, I feel that there are many more rays of hope than he has realized.

Over the next several weeks, in both group and individual therapy, I work intensively with Ron. I try to show him that attempts to suppress and control Michelle are unnecessary and counterproductive. Even if he can subvert her plans, he will find himself with a demoralized and unhappy spouse. Instead of giving her more of the "old" husband, I suggest, she needs a "new" type of husband. She needs someone who is interested in her ambitions and who compassionately supports her. "Most important," I tell Ron, "you can be that husband. That," I argue, "is your best hope to salvage the relationship."

Ron is surprised, puzzled, skeptical, but nevertheless intrigued enough to give my ideas a chance. Significantly, he agrees to meet briefly with a men's group in which he discovers many other dual-career husbands. As much as I have grandiosely hoped that my assurances will be enough, I have to acknowledge the powerful boost that Ron receives from hearing the "success" stories of other men— men who have adapted to and relished their wives' moves to independence.

In some ways, gender-sensitive marital and family therapies are like Chinese stir-fry cooking. If you are determined and patient enough to complete the exhaustive preparations, the cooking is likely to go quickly and your final product is bound to be satisfying. The extensive preparatory steps I have outlined should help the traditional man gain a greater understanding of himself and his gender role strain, to get him "up to speed" with the woman who is seeking change. This is not to say that she gains complete empathy and compassion for him before joint therapy, or he for her. The intent is to clear away some of the destructive debris that has accumulated from centuries of misogyny and rigid socialization. Michelle learns more about how gender role strain has limited her, as well as about how Ron's seemingly nonsupportive behavior is tied to his traditional male role constraints. Ron learns to appreciate the wisdom of Michelle's actions as well as new role alternatives for himself. The creation of intergender empathy and compassion, which begins prior to conjoint meetings, goes into high gear once the couple is seen together.

In the previous description of Bill and Mona, I illustrated couples therapy gone awry. The case of Michelle and Ron took a refreshingly different tack, in that Michelle remained empowered and the "change-back" forces were neutralized. This allowed me to make supportive contact with Ron and help him initiate needed changes in his own gender script.

When these steps have been accomplished, a phase of conjoint marital therapy is especially helpful. In many ways, this marital therapy is like most marital therapies, but it also involves special attention to bridging gender-based differences. This therapy (described more fully in Philpot, Brooks, Lusterman, & Nutt, 1997) features four additional therapeutic components: (1) psychoeducation, (2) gender inquiry, (3) message translation, and (4) gender coevolution.

Psychoeducation

All psychotherapies teach, but they vary in the degree to which they make their lessons an overt aspect of treatment. In this phase of gender-sensitive marital therapy, I make efforts to make the invisible more visible—that is, I move gender issues from the background to the foreground. The education can be as formal and sophisticated as the clients' situation and sophistication warrant. It can take the form of in-session digressions and examples or of more elaborate extrasession activities, such as suggested reading, videos and movies, and consciousness-raising activities.

Psychoeducation involves an effort to place each marital partner's behavior in sociocultural context, to discuss the way women and men have been taught to behave. Reality is no longer seen as an absolute but as a social construction, subject to multiple interpretations. Gender roles are shown to be interactive and mutually reinforcing. Through this process, a partner's behavior can be seen in a new and more compassionate light. Each partner is allowed to see how his or her behavior can restrict or liberate the other.

Empathy and compassion are only partial objectives. By introducing gender behaviors as arbitrary choices, not immutable biological imperatives, men and women are free to examine critically the gender socialization pressures they have been under and to reject those that do not apply. Therefore, this psychoeducational component provides women and men with a powerful motive to reevaluate traditionally narrow and increasingly outmoded gender roles.

In therapy, Michelle and Ron both benefited greatly from questioning their gender-based values and the resultant broadening of their cognitive maps. Michelle had wrestled with conflicts between her needs for self-expression and her beliefs about her wifely duties. She had bought into some destructive stereotypes about intelligent women, usually masking her abilities behind a facade of "dizziness." Ron had heavily subscribed to the idea that a man is measured by his functioning as sole provider and relationship leader. Each took important steps toward embracing new models of competent masculinity and femininity.

Gender Inquiry

Gender inquiry, an extension of the psychoeducational process, is an effort to help clients personalize general messages about gender socialization. Whereas psychoeducation increases knowledge, gender inquiry adds the affective component; clients move from discussing *them* to discussing *me* and *us*. Although all clients are raised with powerful expectations and prohibitions about the conduct considered proper for their gender, and although they continually interact with a gendered culture, their individual experiences vary according to a number of demographic variables—age, ethnicity, sexual identity, and social class.

As originally proposed by family therapist Don-David Lusterman (1989), gender inquiry is an explicit and organized effort to explicate gender role pressures. When conducted in individual therapy, the process helps the client become more self-aware and more attuned to his or her emotional reactions to gender role expectations. When conducted in conjoint therapy, as Lusterman recommends, the process is a powerful source of "empathic knowing."

Message Translation

Once the couple is in the room together, the therapist faces the task of translating their new awareness into improved relationship patterns. Many family therapists are prepared for this, having already developed a number of techniques for working effectively with couples. However, two additional perspectives should be considered—empathic interviewing and therapist translating and reframing.

The empathic interview, described more fully in Philpot, Brooks, Lusterman, and Nutt (1997), was developed by Lusterman as a skills-based intervention to enhance empathy between partners. Originally developed to apply to a range of issues, the technique is especially useful for uncovering gender-based conflicts. Because it requires a relatively high degree of psychological sensitivity, it will likely be successful only with some traditional men.

In brief, my adaptation of Lusterman's process calls for therapists to teach each partner how to interview the other; the idea is to draw out that person's central thoughts and feelings about being a man or woman. Each partner is encouraged to listen attentively to both the content and feelings of a message. Eye contact is also encouraged. The receiver of the message is then asked to paraphrase what he or she heard, until the sender concurs that the essence of the message was conveyed. During this process, the therapist should be especially active to ensure that *listening* and not *arguing* takes place.

With less psychologically sophisticated or more distressed couples, I am more likely to function as an intergender translator and reframer. In this process, much as the language interpreter occupies a central position in international negotiations, I often find it useful to serve as a communication mediator and translator of the separate languages spoken. After one partner speaks, it may be necessary for me to "decode" the message by placing it in a gender context. I will reframe the message as the partner's effort to enhance the relationship according to the logic of that person's gender world. If the receiving partner can appreciate the newly encrypted message as having some modicum of positive intent, a less reactive response is likely. The receiver may then respond positively to the sender's *intent*, even though they still need to negotiate the specifics of the problem. I illustrate from the conjoint work with Ron and Michelle.

RON: It drives me crazy that you'd throw away everything we worked for to take a few silly courses because you're bored.

MICHELLE (instantly irritated): *We?* Aren't you being a bit self-centered there? Everything we ever did was to live up to your little fantasy world. I was just along for the ride.

RON: So all the work I did was for me? Are you nuts? I busted my hump for *us* to have a better life. I never could get you to appreciate me!

GARY: Wait, please let me interrupt for a second. Ron, based on what you've told me, it seems to you that Michelle feels no gratitude for the long and hard hours you've worked. Is that correct?

RON: Yeah, that's pretty much true.

MICHELLE (interrupting): But who asked you to do that?

GARY: Michelle, hold on for a sec. Let me get this straight. Then, we'll see how this has affected you. So it's been important to you as a man to be a good provider? To make money for the good of the family? And it seems that since you've done that, Michelle should be satisfied. Michelle, can you see where he's coming from?

MICHELLE: Of course I can. For heaven's sake, I spent years as his thankful and appreciative wife.

RON: Yeah, well, what happened?

GARY: Ron, hold on just a minute. Michelle, I think Ron has gotten the idea you're taking him for granted, but I think he's missing an important point. Let's talk about your interest in school.

MICHELLE: I said it a thousand times: I need something for me. And I don't like you constantly squelching my plans.

GARY: So it seems, Michelle, that you are telling Ron something important, but he's hearing it as a rejection of his contributions. Ron, I think you're not really understanding why Michelle is pushing for her own career. I don't think she wants to reject you. It just sounds to me that she's saying she wants you to understand and support her needs and abilities.

Later in the session, I make a summary statement.

GARY: It sure sounds to me that each of you is trying to bring something to the relationship, according to what you believe you should do as men and women. It's a shame, but you're getting caught in a big shift by a changing world. Ron, you're trying to be loyal to the role of good provider, but Michelle, you are wanting Ron to play a different role—friend and supporter. Michelle, I don't think you want out, but you do seem to realize you'll be a better partner if your needs are met. Ron, you are working hard to please

Michelle and stay relevant to her life, but you're doing it in a counterproductive way. We need to see if we can come up with an arrangement that will allow growth and happiness for each of you.

Gender Coevolution

Gender coevolution is a shared cooperative process in which partners work to create a new relationship that allows both to have maximal role opportunities. Because it recognizes the reciprocal and interactive nature of gender roles, including the effect of each partner's behavior on the other's options, it features negotiating and mutual goal setting. Unlike some approaches to gender consciousness-raising that look exclusively to the outside culture, this approach situates work within the relationship context. The partner, typically an agent of socialization pressure, can also serve as a major source of psychoemotional support, with appropriate awareness. Because negotiation is vital, partners need to have similar levels of commitment to the relationship and similar amounts of empowerment to move beyond the relationship, if necessary.

In the relationship of Bill and Mona, we saw the more unsuccessful ways in which each partner attempted to shape the other's behavior. Bill sought to enforce Mona's allegiance to traditional roles, whereas Mona endeavored to introduce new options. Because they both viewed the other as antagonistic to their interests, a battle of the sexes ensued. Bill initially had power and leverage, so he was able to suppress the coevolution process. Later, when Mona acquired more power and leverage, Bill's limitations in gender consciousness (that is, an unwillingness to consider new ideas of masculinity and new relationship models) caused her to flee the marriage.

With Ron and Michelle, the coevolution process was more successful. At first, Ron responded to Michelle's push for role latitude by pressuring her further to conform—that is, to have children. When they committed to a process of gender coevolution, they developed more workable alternatives and a more harmonious environment. Michelle's move up the career ladder eased some of the financial pressure from Ron, giving him more time and energy to be supportive of her and enabling him to consider other areas of personal development for himself. Buoyed by the evidence that Ron would support her career and share household responsibilities, Michelle felt far more willing to consider having children.

Traditional men have a strong investment in traditionally defined marital relationships. When their socialization regarding women and marriage is not understood, or when their political power is not addressed, marital therapy can reinforce the most constraining aspects of marriage. However, when therapists operate with a clear appreciation of these issues, marital therapy can become a potent vehicle for gender coevolution.

The marital unit, of course, is only one part of the larger family system. The therapy journey of traditional men is enhanced by family therapy interventions. These interventions pay close attention to the interplay between male socialization and men's traditional behavior as family members.

CONDUCTING GENDER-SENSITIVE FAMILY THERAPY

Families have always been expected to function as a source of emotional support and comfort, as well as a shaper of future generations. They are where children first learn to recognize the consequences of their behavior and the way in which their presence affects others. In times past, families were also the places where children seemed to learn nearly everything else, from reading and writing to farming and sewing. As more and more of these functions shift from the family to the larger culture, and as the larger culture—from MTV to the Internet—comes to have a constant presence in our homes, it's easy to doubt that the family can continue as a viable and effective institution. Many fear that the family has become obsolete.

For some, this fear has evoked nostalgia for the past, when things seemed simpler and families seemed happier. These nostalgic yearnings have been seized on by people with regressive political agendas who wish to blame most contemporary social problems on the "moral decay of the family." Some members of the Religious Right have called for a return to "family values." The Promise Keepers, a very large group of traditional men, call for men to "take back" their leadership role in their families.

It appears to me that, by and large, people in these groups deeply appreciate the need to support American families. But they are seriously misguided and unappreciative of the very issue that family therapists have discovered over the past two decades. The *healthy* family is not defined by its structure or membership but by its ability to perform its most critical functions. This is where I most sharply diverge from the objectives of the Religious Right and the Promise Keepers. Yes, we who support families wish to empower them and help them fulfill their most lofty promises. But this cannot be achieved by seeking a return to an era when a "real man" had a "little woman" tending house, when Father knew best and Mother knew (or pretended) that he did, and when boys were made of snips and snails and puppy dogs' tails and girls were made of sugar and spice and everything nice.

Instead of trying to distort the reality of contemporary life, those interested in families need to help families cope and develop their full potential. To do this, we cannot moralize, suppress growth, or coerce women and men into outmoded social roles. Modern women and men face a period of dramatic gender role strain, in that most of the traditional gender formulas simply don't work as well as they once did. It is becoming obvious that with soaring divorce rates and the feminization of poverty, women cannot afford to attach their emotional and economic security to the vagaries of another person's behavior. Having benefited substantially from traditional gender role arrangements in many ways, men are discovering that the

benefits often come with a very high price tag—early death, estrangement from their children, loneliness, and emotional alienation.

More and more, family therapists are realizing that our past
proclamation of neutrality (that is, the stance that we are value-free
and apolitical) has been a not-so-harmless self-deception. Simply
put, when we don't help women and men recognize (and deal with)
the powerful gender messages of the larger culture, we are perpetuating and exacerbating the gender role strain that both genders face.
When we don't point out the narrow and confining aspects of traditional gender ideology, we help create a new generation of nar-
rowly socialized children. Increasingly, family psychologists are
realizing that, rather than being unwitting contributors to gender
role strain, we must become educators and translators. Unlike few
others, we can be gender brokers—agents who help families study
their gender heritage, critique contemporary culture, and develop
personal gender roles that are realistic, creative, and liberating.

Over the past three decades, family therapy has benefited from
constructive criticism offered by a number of feminist theorists.
Michelle Bograd (1991) summarizes this critique as follows:

> The feminist critiques of family therapy models and
> techniques have focused primarily on clinical and theo-
> retical biases against women clients, given the social and
> historical contexts of current family therapy practices.
> The feminist perspective on woman's place is essential
> for creating a foundation of progressive and non-sexist
> family therapy models. However, to be truly systemic, fam-
> ily therapists must also critically examine men's subjec-
> tive experiences and their interrelationships with larger
> social structures and processes. . . . Gender roles limit
> and constrict the psychological development of men and
> women, and inhibit the development of rich, mutually
> satisfying, and non-coercive intimacy. . . . Individual and

family dysfunction is related to the fulfillment of traditional gender roles [p. xiii].

We see then that the challenge to therapists goes beyond understanding women's experiences. Just as feminist theorists have
helped family therapists become more aware of women's gender role
strain, they have also laid the groundwork for family therapists to
begin accommodating corollary strains in men's lives.

In this section, I expand on the earlier marital therapy suggestions by giving ways to improve therapy with the families of traditional men. First, let me describe my work with the Hilton family,
whose members are undergoing numerous transformations.

Carolyn Hilton, forty-one, is a "military wife" of twenty-two years. She
has made the appointment for herself and two of her children—Leah,
sixteen, and Tony, fifteen. Carolyn is very concerned about Leah, because she has had repeated conflicts with school authorities over a
variety of policy issues. Carolyn is much less specific about why she
has brought Tony along. When asked about other family members,
Carolyn notes that her husband, Walt, a forty-six-year-old army col-
onel, is away on military maneuvers. She says he certainly wouldn't
have come anyhow, because he adamantly refused to participate in
family therapy several years ago. Rick, twenty, is living in another city,
having left college to pursue work in clubs as a drummer. Buffy, nine,
is in school.

In trying to obtain an expanded version of the presenting issues,
I learn that Leah is a very bright young woman, as well as a provocative and outspoken critic of almost every traditional institution. Carolyn
describes her daughter as a "radical feminist anarchist." Since she
dropped out of individual therapy with a local psychiatrist ("He was a
sexist pig, pill pusher"), Leah will only enter therapy if others also
come ("To get to the bottom of this soap opera mess").

Tony has little to say, responding mostly with nods of his head or
"Yes, sir." His reticence prompts Carolyn to interject quickly with her

motives for bringing him: "He's too quiet and shut off. He needs to learn to open up more and be more in touch with his feelings."

Tony scowls at his mother's comment. In response to my questions, he presents himself blandly as a "regular, normal, unweird" guy who plays football, studies, and participates in ROTC. He's never been in trouble except for one "public intoxication" charge a few months earlier.

For the next forty-five minutes, as I attempt to help Carolyn sharpen her concerns about her family, I have trouble getting a solid handle on the issues. Carolyn appears to be very interested in her role as mother. Aside from Walt's generous financial support, she has been a single parent for virtually the entire marriage. Walt's military assignments have kept him out of the home for most of the year, but Carolyn claimed that this ceased to be an issue many years ago. She has learned to occupy herself when he is away. She is very active with the Officers' Wives Club and began researching a book on the history of World War I army nurses. She claims to be reasonably happy, though worried about Leah and Tony. When asked about Buffy, she says little except that she is a bright and happy child whom everyone loves. Buffy has been voted fourth grade class favorite and is considering entering the Junior Miss pageant.

The session continues at the same tepid pace, before I suggest a follow-up the next week. I urge Carolyn to invite Walt and Buffy to come, as well. Only after the session do I realize that I've completely neglected to get much information about Rick; this causes me to speculate about his role as the "forgotten" family member.

The day before the next appointment, Carolyn calls, saying that Walt has been completely unwilling to come. When she mentioned to him that I'd asked her to bring Buffy, Walt became enraged, wondering why she was always dragging these kids off to headshrinkers. Deflated by his response, Carolyn says she has decided to abandon the therapy for the present time.

When Carolyn calls me next, about four months later, she seems to be on the verge of emotional collapse. She describes a chaotic situation in which nearly every family member is in some state of severe emotional distress. Leah has run off to live with Rick; while there, she has made a suicide gesture by taking a small bottle of aspirin. Tony has been kicked off the football team after a second alcohol-related arrest and a charge of driving without a license. Walt has increased his alcohol consumption to several drinks per night and has been diagnosed with a bleeding ulcer.

Reinforcing Carolyn's sense about the situation's urgency, I say that I must speak to Walt as soon as possible, and I implore her to convey this message to him. When he calls me, I describe my concerns about his family and ask him if he will come visit with me to help me figure out how to assist the family. Walt puts up a mild resistance, noting that they have "been down that road before," but he relents when I say that I will have great difficulty functioning without his help.

Walt agrees to come, but he insists on coming alone. I make a special point of soliciting his views of the current situation, validating his beliefs whenever feasible. Without appearing overly fawning, I try to praise him for his successful military career and his contributions to his family's well-being. Without directly challenging his efforts to minimize the current crises, I suggest that a joint family effort might help to quiet the distress some family members are experiencing. Reluctantly, he agrees. (Though he refuses to consider also joining my men's group, he agrees to read one of my books about the new psychology of men.)

Although family therapy begins slowly, over the next several months it takes on an intense immediacy, revealing many more issues than can be reviewed here; an abbreviated synopsis follows, instead.

In the family sessions, I learn that Rick's "omission" from family discussion was not coincidental. Rick and his father were very close for the first few years, but as Rick's interests wandered to aesthetic and "girlish" activities such as dance and music, Walt rejected him. Though a straight A student, Rick left high school in his junior year to play music in a nearby city and to room with Mark, a "close friend." Walt and Carolyn have never broached the topic of Mark, choosing to distance themselves rather than to deal with Walt's intense homophobia.

Leah also enjoyed an extremely close relationship with Rick and was devastated by his "exile" from the family. She also claims that Tony is not the simple, well-adjusted guy he pretends to be. Though Tony harshly demeans her efforts, she pleads with him to open up and admit what he once confided to her—he has considered suicide himself. Even Buffy, she insists, is heading for problems, because of her obsession with beauty, charm, and popularity. Leah has challenged her parents to talk about these issues, but they have ignored her concerns as histrionic overreactions, perhaps related to her overexposure to radical politics. To quell what they view as her constant emotional outbursts, they have sought psychiatric help and sedatives.

Eventually, Carolyn herself admits to periodic anxiety attacks and fears of the future "empty nest." She has become increasingly unfulfilled as an army wife and has taken encouragement from some of Leah's feminist books (which she has covertly read). Eventually, through Carolyn's admission of unhappiness, we are also able to uncover many previously repressed issues in Walt's life. After reading the book I recommended, Walt acknowledges periods of malaise and disinterest. He wasn't sure which came first—his denial of promotion to General or his loss of interest in his army career. He feels acutely apathetic and unappreciated. It seemed that both his family and his commanders have always taken him for granted.

In one particularly moving session, Carolyn points out that Walt hasn't been the same since a buddy's nine-year-old daughter was killed in a car wreck. Walt was almost completely unable to shake the incident. In exploring the matter, Walt and Carolyn discover the extreme investment they have made in Buffy as their last child. Walt, who was emotionally absent during Rick's childhood, has wanted to compensate by holding on tightly to his "little princess." Not surprisingly, this leads very directly to an exploration of the loss Walt has felt ever since he rejected Rick. In several intense sessions, Carolyn helps Walt confront his homophobia and finally reach out to Rick. With great difficulty, Walt makes peace with Rick. This rapprochement helps us to uncover unresolved issues with Tony, who has longed for Walt's approval.

In two years of family therapy, the Hilton family makes immense progress in negotiating difficult transitions. Walt and Carolyn acknowledge their fears of the future and consciously try to form a more rewarding couple relationship. Carolyn continues to study outstanding women in military history. Walt reevaluates his extreme emphasis on his military career and develops long-repressed interests in music and theater. He begins to overcome his homophobia and moves to reestablish his relationships with Rick and Tony. He spends considerable time with Leah, thanking her for her dedication to the family but assuring her that he and Carolyn are now more committed to reassuming their proper parental roles. Finally, Walt and Carolyn begin to "let go" of Buffy, who decides that she really prefers to be called by her given name (Gloria).

I hope that this severely abbreviated synopsis provides enough illustrative material to demonstrate the vital importance of gender sensitivity in family therapy, as well as the central role that family interventions may play in the therapeutic journey of traditional men.

Making Every Effort to Include Men

Men's resistance to therapy is well established in the literature, not only to individual therapy but also to family therapy. In the great majority of cases, women (mothers) are most likely to have initiated therapy for the family; consequently, as I noted in Chapter Two, a man sometimes resists therapy because he feels as if the woman and therapist have joined forces against him. Sometimes he has made himself so troublesome that family members have become accustomed to his absence and may even subtly discourage his presence.

This isn't always hard to do, because many traditional men see therapy as having relatively limited value anyway. At times, men resist therapy simply because they tend to dismiss its value.

Frequently, it is tempting to assume that everything possible has been done to engage a resistant traditional man. At times, it will be true that a man simply will not participate. Then, the therapist should work actively with those family members who are willing to consider therapeutic change. At other times, however, reasonably aggressive efforts may actually succeed in engaging a reluctant family member.

As illustrated by the Hilton case, it would have been easy to ignore the male family members. Walt was so convincing about his busyness and his general disinterest that all family members automatically assumed they would do therapy without him. Rick took flight to avoid family tension, while Tony hid his pain behind a wall of denial. In the face of these common male behaviors, therapists sometimes need to go the extra mile to secure a man's participation. It may help to make a special plea couched in terms such as "I need your help. You are too central to the family to ignore." Sometimes, a man resisting family therapy will agree to a private consultation, either in person or by phone, to help the therapist attain needed information. Once a man agrees to offer his opinions, and once he recognizes that his opinions are respected, a skillful therapist can usually coax him into further participation.

Connecting with the Man's Perspective

Because women are more likely to seek help and to frame problems in psychological terms, their perspectives are usually more appealing to family therapists. Frequently, by the time a man arrives at the office, the therapist has developed a fairly clear idea of the problems from the standpoint of most other family members. Therefore, the therapist must be especially careful to take a man's point of view into account before finalizing a family treatment plan. The therapist should elicit the traditional man's perspective, no matter what.

It may seem obvious or of little value. The man's primary position may be that the problems are exaggerated and need to be ignored. Even so, the therapist should publicly acknowledge this point of view as one of many valuable ones.

In the Hilton family, Carolyn actively pushed for heightened attention to family relationships, while Walt and Tony preferred to avoid these issues and focus primarily on work or competitive arenas, such as financial investing for Walt and athletics or grade-chasing for Tony. These traditional male attitudes, with their implicit demeaning of therapy and therapists, make men like Walt and Tony a significant challenge. If they are to be engaged, the therapist needs to spend effort joining with them. For example, it is possible to talk with Walt about the stresses and joys of his career and to empathize with his need to maintain an emotionally stoic front. Even his resistance to therapy can be understood as representative of his preferred coping style. In time, with this validation of his perspectives, he may be able to "hear" that he should become more tolerant of other points of view.

Going Beyond Work and Career

Consistent with traditional socialization, family definitions of typical problems for men tend to overfocus on work and career issues (just as they have historically underfocused on these issues for female members). All too often, therapists accept a man's success at his job as an indication that all is well. But career success is often negatively correlated with a man's psychological health in a number of other areas—spirituality, community involvement, sensuality, attention to physical well-being, aesthetic or artistic expression, and connection with friends. Therefore, family therapists should be prepared to attend to a wide range of arenas in which "successful" men may be underfunctioning.

Sometimes, therapists approach these issues by exploring the degree to which a marital couple allows time for "fun," that is, time to nourish their relationship. Although this is useful, it isn't enough.

Therapists should make a special effort to help families attend to the wider needs of work-obsessed men. Therapists can encourage men to take inventory of their lives, carefully examining their areas of full development, as well as those they have neglected. Many men have activities or interests that they intend to "get around to some day."

Of course, rearranging priorities can extract certain penalties—missed promotions, decreased income, or increased financial burden on others. Therapists should help families study the choices, weigh alternatives, and make collaborative decisions. Although families may opt to continue operations as usual, they will have done so by choice rather than by reflexive habit. Sometimes, however, families make unexpected choices. Family members may choose to pass up certain benefits, allowing a male breadwinner greater career latitude. A woman's career may be given special emphasis, while a man's work is deemphasized or restructured. In general, therapists can help families create role assignments that are more reflective of individual needs and no longer burdened by rigid gender traditions.

Encouraging Men to Recognize Vulnerabilities

Traditional men tend to work too hard, neglecting their needs for rest and relaxation. They ignore signs of physical and emotional malaise. As we saw with Tony Hilton (and, to a lesser extent, with Walt), a quiet male is not necessarily a well-adjusted male. Emotional stoicism is vastly overrated as a sign of mental health in male family members.

Once again, therapists should go beyond attending exclusively to problems that are readily identified and should look for problems that are quietly incubating. Therapists should be attentive to ways in which men may be neglecting physical needs, abusing their bodies, or exposing themselves to unnecessary risks. For example, therapists should ask about diet, alcohol consumption, sleep patterns, regularity of medical appointments, and style of driving.

Empowering Males as Domestic Laborers

As women become more involved in the world of work, males of all ages need to be able to function more fully in areas where they have commonly accepted relative incompetence. Most of us have heard jokes about high-powered corporate executives who regularly decide the fate of thousands but who cannot locate the baking powder or sew on a button. Most domestic labor is repetitive, tedious, and far from fulfilling. Admittedly, we now live in a service-delivery economy, in which most mundane tasks can be hired out. Nevertheless, there are certain survival skills that all human beings should master: cleaning, ironing, simple sewing, washing clothes, and basic cooking.

Lately, there has been a lot of attention given to most men's reluctance to accept their share of domestic labor—to do their duty. Although this perspective is accurate, it is only part of the story. In my view, it is a mistake to emphasize men's resistance. Instead, men should be challenged to supplement their skills and to view domestic labor as a basic ingredient of personal competence. (Women, of course, will need to allow men latitude to experiment with their own methods for accomplishing domestic tasks.)

Promoting Egalitarianism in Nurturance and Emotional Expression

Because women are more emotionally expressive, they are often encouraged to overfunction as caretakers and spokespersons for the family's emotional well-being. In the Hilton family, Leah served as the person most sensitive to the family's mood and level of distress. Although men are likely to repress or ignore their "softer" side, their emotional sensitivity and compassion can be facilitated. With effort, therapists can help women hold off from this role while empowering men to experiment with new emotional behaviors. For example, young men can gain invaluable experience in nurturing and being emotionally sensitive when they become more active in nontraditional activities, such as baby-sitting or attending to sick or elderly family members. It may be necessary for mothers to assume more disciplinarian roles, while fathers can become better at listening and connecting. Women can manage the finances, and men can take more initiative to talk on the phone with relatives, plan family get-togethers, and attend to the needs of elderly family members.

Encouraging New Models of Fatherhood

Volumes are being written on the critical importance of having new models of fatherhood. Some conservative social critics, concerned about the "moral breakdown" of families, advocate exposing children more to their fathers and to their traditional modes of family participation. But this emphasis is too simplistic and can be misplaced. Naturally children tend to benefit when there are two parents available. But the father's presence is not the only issue. Children benefit most when fathers interact with their families in vastly different ways than the children usually experience. The exclusivity of the traditional "father as breadwinner" model needs to be challenged by models of fatherhood that feature emotionally available and compassionate fathers.

Therapists can promote this shift in a number of ways. They can raise consciousness about how much fathers contribute to families beyond their incomes. In addition, therapists can help families create space for "new" fathers by renegotiating responsibilities and role assignments. Therapists can encourage men to experiment with new behaviors and to practice new parenting skills, from changing diapers to listening reflectively. Because many fathering skills are best learned at an early age, whenever feasible, all male family members should be encouraged to participate in child care.

Promoting Male-Male Intimacy

Just as fathers are being encouraged to seek higher levels of emotional intimacy, so should all male family members. Therapists should consider making greater male-male intimacy an important goal of family interventions. Special meetings can be scheduled for all male family members that, like the all-male groups described in Chapter Four, help men relate in more intimate ways. Brothers can be important resources to each other, and uncles can become closer to their nephews (an extratherapy activity). The transformation of the "good ol' boy sociability group" can also take place in the context of the extended family's male subgroups. For example, the traditional male holiday rituals of watching football endlessly and telling stories can be supplemented by more nontraditional avenues of interpersonal connection between men.

Doing Family-of-Origin Work

As noted previously, ideas about masculine heritage are passed across generations of men. The family therapist should encourage male relatives to explore how a masculine heritage was repeatedly conveyed from father to son in their family. Just as men's studies encourages the study of the personal man behind the myths of a historical figure, the male family member can be encouraged to explore how his male predecessors handled critical issues of establishing intimacy, forming connections, aging, and finding meaning in one's life. Young men can be encouraged to talk with uncles and grandfathers about issues central to manhood.

Raising Boys

Just as there has been an increased emphasis on helping young girls access instrumental and competitive skills, there must be corollary shifts for young boys. There needs to be a decreased emphasis on competition and hierarchical values, with a greater emphasis on interpersonal connection and the ability to interact cooperatively. Boys need to undertake activities that are less stereotypically male, and there should be open challenge to cultural devaluation of "feminine" activities. Subtle forms of misogyny must be recognized and countered. Interpersonal sensitivity, empathy, and compassion can receive greater emphasis as goals for young boys to attain.

For these value shifts to have the greatest chance of success, young boys should have ready access to older boys and men who model acceptance, vulnerability, and interpersonal tenderness (rather than competition, an emphasis on physical prowess, and interpersonal aggression). There will need to be major changes in our thinking about young boys and sexuality as we reshape the current model; presently, sexual activity is viewed as recreation and a validation of masculinity. Attention must be given to how the culture has celebrated and eroticized women's bodies to the point that most boys become fixated on women's breasts, legs, and buttocks.

Finally, there must be a vigorous challenge to the rampant homophobia that severely limits the potential for male-male intimacy. Boys must recognize the differences between intimacy and sexuality. Only in this way will it become more acceptable for men (whether heterosexual, gay, or bisexual) to be intimate with one another without being concerned that their friendliness will be misconstrued.

Many in our culture believe that American families have lost their way and that strong measures are needed to take us back to the good ol' days. Some men are making promises to take charge of this situation unilaterally and to reassert their leadership over the family. These are not the promises that will allow contemporary families to cope with the vast sociocultural shifts of the past three decades. Family therapists can deliver on a far more hopeful promise; by working in close harmony with our clients, we can create environments in which contemporary families provide a refuge from gender role strain and promote gender equity and opportunity for women and men.

6

Therapist Gender

Shannon, thirty-five, and David, thirty-four, are psychology interns who want to gain experience by leading my VA inpatient men's group. Consistent with my usual custom, I offer them a chance to take over my ongoing group under my supervision (through a one-way mirror). In coordinating their schedules, Shannon and David determine that it makes most sense for Shannon to lead the group for the first six weeks and for David to lead the last six.

Shannon appears even younger than her thirty-five years and is quite attractive in a traditionally feminine style. Though bright and extremely competent, she tends to downplay her accomplishments and avoid pretension. She is enthusiastic about the opportunity to lead the group but somewhat anxious because of her limited exposure to men in groups. She and her sister were raised primarily by their mother after their father abandoned the family. Although Shannon is happily married and has enjoyed generally positive relationships with men in her lifetime, she admits to a lack of familiarity with all-male environments. Because she has a strong commitment to feminist perspectives and an impatience with certain types of aggressively sexist men, she anticipates that the experience will challenge and "stretch" her.

From the first moment Shannon enters the men's group, radically new patterns and behaviors emerge. Clearly unaccustomed to an attractive woman leader, the group members seem unusually attentive to her appearance, reactive to her mood and nonverbal behavior, and openly speculative about her private life. Nearly anything Shannon does or says becomes "news" in the all-male patient community. Mysterious "insider" jokes and teasing seem rampant among the group members, both inside and outside the group sessions.

Skilled at establishing a professional posture and appropriate boundaries, Shannon identifies and gently deflects invasive questions and comments. Without any hint of reproach, she provides brief answers to questions before shifting the conversation back to discussion about the group members. She benignly ignores marginally appropriate comments. Seriously inappropriate ones receive more assertive responses. For example, Harry, a self-professed "lady-killer," is prone to comments such as "I bet your husband doesn't let you out of his sight."

Although still gentle and caring, Shannon defuses this suggestive comment with, "That's a very interesting comment, Harry. I wonder if it might give us a useful start for exploring your ideas about women and relationships."

In a short time, the men's anxiety decreases, and Shannon's physical appearance becomes a nonissue. Three weeks into her experience, however, Shannon encounters a new dilemma. Randy, a forty-year-old former golf pro struggling with alcohol dependence, seeks Shannon out between group sessions and reveals a wealth of previously secret personal material. He vows that he will never discuss certain childhood traumas in front of the group and pleads with her to provide the desperately needed chance to unload his emotional burdens. Shannon agrees to see him for four to six individual sessions but holds considerable reservations. When she explains this individual therapy arrangement to the group, several members exchange disapproving looks.

Over the next few sessions, Randy becomes silent. Tony comments on how Randy has become isolated from the others. Soon, Tony himself lapses into silence. Tom, previously rather quiet, tries to enliven matters, but his efforts meet resounding silence. "What the hell gives?" he challenges. No response is forthcoming.

Over the next week, Shannon labors to uncover the source of the group's impasse. At first, she works tirelessly and compassionately, wondering what might have suddenly begun to bother them (or what she might have done wrong). I call her out of the room and coach her to ease up and let the group resolve the problem. This produces a clumsy silence of nearly forty minutes, broken only by inane attempts at humor by Tom and other group members. Finally, Tony becomes increasingly restless, signaling that he is ready to deal with a touchy subject. Encouraged by Shannon to speak up if he has something on his mind, Tony angrily confronts Randy. He accuses Randy of turning his back on the others and beginning to act like he is superior to everyone else. Randy responds with enough defensive anger that Shannon fears a fight might break out. Resisting the temptation to intercede and soothe tempers, Shannon pushes the conflictual issue between Tony and Randy further. It isn't long before Shannon is able to help Tony realize that his anger at Randy has multiple roots.

Primarily, Tony feels hurt and rejected by Randy's emotional withdrawal following the initiation of individual therapy with Shannon. Tony confesses that he has discussed the matter with other group members. All are quick to express their anger about Randy's new cocky air. It takes much more time for Shannon to elicit the deeply buried resentment about Randy's "special" status. Even more difficult to elicit are the various self-deprecating explanations that many have constructed to account for being "overlooked." All members but Harry admit to a degree of private distress at the perception of being ignored. (Harry seems to remain privately convinced that Shannon really is sexually desirous of him and that they have an unspoken bond of mutual desire.)

GENDER AS A CRITICAL VARIABLE

In earlier chapters, I described the many ways in which the social construction of masculinity affects men as they enter (or avoid) the therapist's office. I've shown how effective therapy requires a broad understanding of traditional masculinity and a therapeutic style better adapted to its constraints. So far, I've focused primarily on the impact of gender on clients. In this chapter, I shift to a corollary issue only recently beginning to receive adequate attention— how psychotherapists themselves are affected by their interactions with a "gendered" culture (that is, a culture that continually pressures women and men to behave according to formidable role mandates). In particular, I offer ideas about the potential advantages and disadvantages that male and female therapists experience in their work with traditional men.

Therapists' Gender Values

Although knowledge has begun to accumulate about how women and men are disposed to behave as therapy clients, comparatively little attention has been given to the influence of gender socialization and gender processes on therapists. In part, this neglect is probably the result of the cherished and idealistic notion of therapy lore that competent therapists rise above their values, biases, and personal idiosyncrasies. Appropriately mature and self-aware therapists would be alert to all irrational sources of influence and possible countertransference.

In the past few decades, this revered notion has been exposed as an unrealistic and dangerous myth. Social psychologists have uncovered a range of ethnocentric biases in American psychology and have argued persuasively that all psychotherapy takes place in a cultural context. Derald Wing Sue and David Sue (1990), for example, have authored numerous articles pointing out that "counseling the culturally different" requires knowledge of client cultures *and* of one's own cultural background. Lately, as gender has begun to be recognized as a major cultural variable affecting therapists, awareness has grown that their gender values can no longer be ignored.

In reviewing the research on how gender roles affect the therapy process, psychologists Laurie Mintz and Jim O'Neil (1990) state that this line of study is "still in the early stages of development" (p. 381). Although this is unfortunately true, in the past few years, there has been a welcome increase in attention to the issue. Mintz

and O'Neil identify several areas in which male and female therapists may function differently: "The challenge facing the traditionally socialized female therapist may be accepting her legitimate
authority, while the task facing the traditionally socialized male
therapist may be to temper his socialization toward assuming
authority with that of empathy" (p. 384).

Mintz and O'Neil note a suggestive finding that some women
therapists cope with their authority discomfort by smiling exces-
sively, appearing indecisive, and laughing nervously. Female therapists may express more feelings in their interactions with clients
than do male therapists and may be generally more attuned to the
affective dimension. Additionally, they note, there has been some
empirical evidence that female therapists may form more effective
therapeutic alliances with their clients.

In her review of the issue, Dorothy Cantor (1990) notes that "in
spite of the early belief that the gender of the therapist is irrelevant
to the therapeutic process, there is concurrence in the current literature that women and men are different as therapists." Cantor
cites several of these differences. First, she finds that women therapists, much like women in the larger culture, are more likely to nurture. Also, she notes that women therapists tend to accept too much
responsibility for the welfare of their clients and tend to feel guilty
when therapy goes poorly. Male and female therapists tend to differ on the dimension of wielding power and exerting influence.
Male therapists have been found to attempt more "influence acts"
and to interrupt their clients more frequently. Female therapists
show less of a tendency to overreact or underreact to sexual material introduced in the therapy hour. To some extent, the importance
of gender may depend on the therapy approach being adopted; gender is less significant in insight-oriented therapy and more significant in supportive therapy.

The Phenomenology of Being Female

Feminist psychologist Laura Brown (1990) has reviewed both psychological and autobiographical literature and has identified several

common themes suggesting that the "phenomenology of being female" has very positive implications for women as therapists for several reasons. First, because women tend to develop identity through relationships with others, they have a greater capacity for empathic attunement with clients. Second, because Western culture treats women as outsiders or as the "other," women have developed a greater ability to observe and monitor the behavior of the dominant group. Brown argues that this situation produces "unconscious training in the skills of attending to the minutiae of someone else's expressions and movements that goes beyond empathic connection" (p. 230). Third, Brown posits that women are advantaged as therapists because they typically are facile at "empowering others." "Few women would describe what we do in this manner. . . . This power to engender power and self-sufficiency in others is called by disguised, often gendered names: 'raising children,' 'mothering,' 'the woman behind the man,' 'the good wife'" (p. 231). Fourth, because women have "the experience of living in the shadow of violence," they are especially sensitive to an issue so central to many clients' lives.

In addition to these advantages inherent in the phenomenology of female experience, according to Brown, another advantage becomes apparent when we study the qualities of effective therapists. Like most women, good therapists have a capacity for empathy and flexible ego boundaries; this means that they can create close relationships, tolerate ambiguity and powerlessness, and manage "primitive" or "young" feelings in clients. In summary, Brown feels that women therapists bring numerous attitudinal and dispositional advantages with them into the therapy office. Although I believe that Brown overlooks some downsides that surface when women work with traditional men, I find her perspectives to be especially valuable.

A FEMALE THERAPIST WITH TRADITIONAL MEN

Whenever I teach about or discuss the issues of traditional men in therapy, the question is invariably asked, "Can a woman therapist be effective with a male client? This is an important question in two respects. First, it is timely, in that women now outnumber men in therapy training programs and men are slowly becoming more likely to seek therapy. Second, the question reflects a degree of sensitivity to the potential problems inherent in cross-gender counseling. At the same time, however, this strikes me as a curious question in one respect: that the converse question has almost never been raised, although the male therapist–female client dyad was dominant for a half century of psychotherapy: "Can a male therapist work with a woman client?" But even though it may be unfair to ask a question about female therapists that has rarely been asked about male therapists, there is still something to be gained by looking at this issue.

Her Effectiveness

As was quite apparent from the case example of Shannon with the men's group, a woman therapist makes an appreciable impact on a group of men. This is utterly logical, because men have such enormous reactivity to women. Naturally, these reactions need to be addressed and must be an integral part of the therapeutic work. Because of her sex, a woman therapist will encounter many advantages and many disadvantages in her work with men.

It is my belief, however, that the therapist's gender awareness and gender sensitivity are far more critical than the therapist's gender. (It should be noted that to date most research on the impact of therapist gender on gender process has been limited to comparing the therapeutic impact of women and men therapists, without careful attention to the *gender attitudes* of these therapists. Most researchers, including Mintz and O'Neil (1990), postulate that this latter research will be far more productive.) I have found that a gender-sensitive female or male therapist will be far more successful in working with traditional men than will a non-gender-sensitive therapist of either sex. In fact, I have strong suspicions that in many situations, non-gender-sensitive therapists may actually be destructive.

Her Gender as an Overt Issue

A common issue that often arises is the extent to which the woman therapist's gender should be considered as an "up-front" or overt issue. Earlier, I noted that I have found it particularly helpful to describe myself to male clients as a fellow struggling man. Because traditional men feel embarrassment or shame about their need for therapy, a "one-down" stance can lower me from an irrationally lofty perch and help the men recognize the universality of men's problems. Men's overreliance on hierarchical thinking can be challenged productively when a male therapist consciously eschews a power position and adopts one of shared cooperation.

For many of the same reasons, I do *not* recommend this "we're all in it together" approach for women therapists. Although traditional men enter a woman therapist's office with the same degree of shame and embarrassment, they do so as participants in a misogynist culture that routinely disempowers women. Traditional men must become comfortable relating to women in authority roles. Far too often, these men attempt to deprofessionalize women therapists by trying to entice them into more comfortable roles of mother or caretaker, all-loving sister, mistress, or sweet young innocent daughter. Therefore, it is critical that women therapists do everything possible to short-circuit these efforts to undercut their status. They should insist that men treat them as their doctor or therapist and not as their "woman" doctor or therapist (or worse).

Additionally, a major goal of an all-male group (with a male leader) is the collaborative exploration of how tough the world can be for us all. A similar process could take place with a woman leader if she focuses on how a gendered culture makes life tough for both genders. However, this approach is problematic, because it risks missing a critical issue—men's ambivalence about their relationships with women. In my experience, a primary advantage of the all-male therapy group (or any therapy for men) is the opportunity it affords for discussion of this ambivalence—particularly the less socially acceptable aspects.

Certainly the female therapist could make a big issue of her gender and purposefully serve as a stimulus for men's feelings. This is highly unrealistic, however, particularly in the all-male group. In the most flagrant case, it is not reasonable to ask a female therapist to sit (figuratively or literally) in the center of the circle of men and encourage them to project their intense feelings onto her. Nor does a more subtle variant seem sensible—asking the female therapist to become the representative for all womankind, endlessly fielding such questions as "How do women feel about this?" Although it might be tempting to use this perspective to her advantage, the downside outweighs the benefits. It is much better to deflect the question, to step aside and empower the men to solve the problem, while she facilitates the process as their professional guide.

Her "Other" Status

As I noted earlier in discussing Laura Brown's work, women have typically occupied the position of "other" vis-à-vis the world of traditional men. In Chapter Three, I described men's preference for a good ol' boy style of relating to other men. Although this is far from an optimal level of interaction, it is the style many men find natural and that many women find peculiar or alien. In some ways, this stylistic mismatch is similar to the language and communication problems inherent in cross-cultural counseling, in which a central component of successful work is the therapist's capacity to understand and adapt to the characteristic patterns of the client population.

Derald Wing Sue and David Sue (1990), for example, emphasize that effective communication and counseling styles include attention to verbal as well as nonverbal aspects, such as "proxemics" (use of space), "kinesics" (bodily movements), and "paralanguage" (vocal cues).

Beth Erickson (1993) suggests that women should be able to be comfortable around men. In some ways, she believes, this might include acquiring greater familiarity with the language and values of the sports or corporate worlds. Such familiarity allows female therapists to use analogies and metaphors that men often use. For me this might come out as "He's sure bustin' your chops today" or "Why don't you cut that asshole off at the knees?"

Some women may find this shift too strained or inauthentic. Shannon, for example, had had such minimal experience with good ol' boy communication that she wisely abjured any extraordinary efforts to be "one of the boys." This is not unusual, as many groups are intensely suspicious of patronizing from outsiders. Others take a firm position: "If you aren't one of us, you can't understand us." Many Vietnam veterans have been especially outspoken on this matter.

In situations of wide discrepancies in backgrounds, I believe the best strategy is one commonly used in cross-cultural counseling. The Sues, for example, suggest that the "culturally skilled counselor" can recognize limitations and communicate a desire to help in spite of the limitations. Here, the strategy would be to highlight the difference in backgrounds and ask traditional men to provide an educational experience or guided tour of their world. For example, a woman may say, "I've never really been in an all-male environment like this. Therefore, from time to time I may ask you what you mean or why you do certain things."

This tactic has three advantages. First, it conveys curiosity and respect for a different culture. Second, it can provide important clarification of value issues. Finally, when the therapist feigns naivete, it forces male clients to focus on central value dimensions that were formerly invisible.

For example, if a group of men are talking about "kicking the ass of a guy who made a pass at another guy's date," the therapist might become curious about the assumptions implicit in this action. In explaining their actions, the men will be forced to confront the many paradoxes and inconsistencies in male socialization regarding violence.

Her Empathy for Men

At one level, having empathy for male clients is such a simple issue as to insult the reader. As much as any single variable, empathy is the key to successful therapy. Therapists must be able to empathize with their clients. In discussing men's efforts to change, Beth Erickson notes that the female therapist "needs to have a healthy respect for how formidable a task this is for men. . . . The changes this new epoch requires are far-reaching, awesome, and potentially frightening indeed" (1993, p. 26).

Empathy should not be especially difficult for female therapists. As Laura Brown (1990) notes, women tend to be more able to form connections, have empathic attunement, explore emotional depths, and be "present" with another's pain. In brief, women have usually displayed a much greater capacity to be comfortable with and responsive to men's pain when it is exposed and to sense it when it is being disguised.

But the matter of empathizing with men's pain is far from simple, as the matter has a number of troubling complications. Because men have greater access to angry emotions, they often convey distress by becoming enraged, becoming violent, and lashing out at others. Also, although *individual* men feel pain, they live in cultures in which *collective* men have great privilege, power, and influence over women. Pleas for women to "understand their men" are extremely problematic for many women, as this compassion has sometimes been used against women to cripple their needed changes and to continue male control. In discussing the "politics of men's pain," Australian educator Christopher McLean (1996, p. 12) asks, "Is it legitimate for us to even think about our own pain while women continue to experience such horrific levels of violence? Are we simply continuing an age-old pattern of male self-centeredness? Or is a denial of pain one of the building blocks of masculine oppression of women which desperately needs attention if men's behaviour is to be changed?"

In the concluding chapter of this book I address this issue more fully. For now, however, I see it as a critical but manageable issue. As I noted in Chapter Three, empathy and compassion for men are appropriate and necessary when vulnerable parties are protected from the most destructive aspects of some men's behavior. Also, although we must remain alert to the power issues in our relationship therapies, we should not see social action and psychotherapy as identical. Distrust of and antipathy for patriarchal male culture need not be translated into a reflexive antipathy for the individual male client in the office.

Nevertheless, some men and some issues will be extremely difficult for many women therapists. In particular, I have found it very troublesome to expose female psychology interns or workshop participants to case examples that graphically reveal many men's intense hostility toward women. In my experience, most traditional men resolutely hide the most extreme forms of their misogyny. Unless you listened to the lyrics of certain rap songs or the dialogue of most pornographic films, you could probably escape these horrifying and enraging sentiments. Yet when some traditional men drop their guard, the revelations can be extraordinarily painful, along these lines: "Those fucking women—if it wasn't for that split between their legs, they all should be shot!"

Amazingly, hearing this sort of outrageous sentiment generally provokes shock or abhorrence in very few men. As repugnant as these sentiments are, their expression can provide a pivotal moment in therapy with traditional men. Once such a statement has been made, it becomes possible to analyze the men's different experiences with women. Ultimately, it may become possible to uncover the hurt and shame that often lie beneath the sentiments. At other times, the sentiments can be recognized at face value but censured as rationalizations or justifications for violence toward women.

In sum, empathy is a key to working with traditional men. Most female therapists usually have no problem empathizing with most male clients. But, at times, with some men, empathy may be a great deal to request from a female therapist.

Her Sense of Responsibility

Over the next few weeks, the group makes great strides. But a week before Shannon is due to rotate out of the group leadership position, another crisis develops. Randy fails to return from a weekend pass and provides no information about his whereabouts. Group members are concerned but oddly reserved. Shannon is distraught, fearing that Randy is about to jeopardize the gains he has made in therapy. Despite her efforts to address the issue, the group members seem somewhat indifferent.

Following the session, Shannon meets with me to explore her options. Should she call his parents' home (where he planned to visit)? Is there anything she can do to prevent him from being discharged from the treatment program before he is ready to leave? We agree to wait at least another day before crystallizing a plan.

That night, Randy leaves a message at Shannon's home, saying that she should call him immediately. When she calls the number he provided, she learns that he has been drinking all weekend and still sounds intoxicated and morose. Shannon encourages him to return to the hospital, but he is negative and quarrelsome. For nearly two hours, she pleads with him, without success. She immediately calls me at home, wondering if she should take further steps. Because he has voiced no plans to harm himself or others, I urge her to do nothing further.

In group the next day, Shannon reports that Randy has contacted her (this is consistent with the group's agreement about confidentiality). Tony and Tom know this already, because he has also called them. Shannon voices great concern, but group members express more annoyance than concern. In fact, Tony is especially angry, because Randy borrowed money from him and tried to get him to go along on the "binge."

Over the course of the session, Shannon and the group members seem to be working at cross-purposes. Shannon pushes diligently to make group members more concerned about Randy's plight. They work just as diligently to convey their need for distance and autonomy. Tony is particularly outspoken. "Look, I understand you care about Randy. So do I. He's been like a brother. But what you don't realize is that I can't let myself get worked up over this. I'm pretty damn close to the edge myself. Randy let us down. We love him, but when he plays with fire, we gotta cut him loose."

For the remainder of the session, Shannon and group members explore the subject of intimacy and connection. In our follow-up supervisory meeting, she admits to being unnerved and shaken by the men's cold distance and extreme need to wall themselves off from the pain of another man.

One of the vexing aspects of functioning as an effective therapist is that some therapist attributes can be both helpful and harmful. This issue seems to manifest itself in terms of women therapists and relationship responsibility. Bepko and Krestan describe a "Goodness Code" that impels women to feel "responsible for the pleasure, happiness, comfort, and success of others in their lives" (1990, p. 99).

Beth Erickson (1993) extends these ideas into the work of women therapists, recommending that women learn to keep this "debilitating tendency" in check. Warning signs that this tendency is becoming extreme are an overcommitment to making a relationship work, oversensitivity to men's feelings, emotional exhaustion, and burnout.

For Shannon, Randy's relapse was especially problematic. Analyzing her reaction in a gender context provides rich material for therapy and supervision. To what extent was she overinvolved? Could she use the men's reactions (and male supervisor's input) to take in new ideas about intimacy and distance? Or, as Shannon thought, did the men's reactions illustrate extreme intimacy fears that were part of their core problems?

Women therapists are likely to enrich the therapy environment with their greater emphasis on interconnection and relationships. At the same time, women therapists must be alert to the dangers of overfunctioning and to the different relationship perspectives that most traditional men hold.

Her Comfort with Intimacy and Dependence

Because women are more likely to adopt what Judith Jordan (1991) refers to as a "self-in-relation" orientation, they tend to be far more comfortable with intimacy and interdependence. As noted in Chapter One, men are taught to be rugged individualists with minimal relationship entanglements. Yet, because of their emotional isolation, men are likely to feel intense intimacy desires when opportunities are presented. As we saw in the case illustration, this can become immensely threatening to many traditional men. Affection for a woman therapist provokes enormous fears of dependency; affection for other men provokes massive homophobia. As a result, traditional men are prone to engage in an odd approach-avoidance dance as they try to find a comfortable level of intimacy.

Women therapists, usually far more secure with emotional closeness, need to work especially hard to appreciate men's fears. Female therapists might do well occasionally to adopt a "go slow" posture to keep particularly conflicted men from exceeding their realistic limits (or the limits of their social context). For example, a woman therapist might work very hard to help a group of men achieve vulnerability levels that are natural for most women but quite foreign to men. Once outside the security and acceptance of her presence, however, the men might panic, anxiously rethinking how much they may have exposed or how far they may have let their defenses slip.

Her Professional Status

A new problem seems to come out of the blue. As Shannon's supervisor, I receive a call from the facility director mandating that I see her at my earliest convenience. With great solemnity and righteous indignation, the director informs me that Shannon was "discovered" in Randy's room. I ask for clarification and learn that the two were talking in his room at 9:00 one night before he fled. I say little except that I will investigate.

When Shannon and I discuss the matter, she is shocked and nearly speechless. Immediately, she reacts with embarrassment and shame, but quickly regains her composure. Sensing injustice, she asks if the administrative reaction would have been identical if David had been in the room.

Her question is both revealing and disturbing. Of course, she is right. The facility director would never have been upset by David's presence. The problem is that "a woman" went to Randy's room, provoking a strongly gendered reaction from the institution. I am disappointed to admit that I was also caught up in this, because I failed to recognize immediately the accusation's sexist nature.

Shannon was completely professional and provided critical crisis intervention counseling to Randy. Yet, because she functioned in an environment that was unaccustomed to viewing women in professional roles, her behavior was twisted to conform to more sexist ideas about women and men—that is, that there could only be one reason for a man and woman to be alone together.

This problem of professional standing is a serious one that can have both malicious and benevolent guises. In its more malicious forms, women are often expected to defend themselves against any behavior that a male client or supervisor misinterprets. In ways that men are never questioned, women are sometimes subjected to undue scrutiny of their professional appearance, conduct, or interpersonal style. In its more benevolent forms, this dynamic manifests itself as patriarchal protectiveness. Without consulting the female professionals themselves, administrators will sometimes make policies for their protection. In addition, "gentlemen" group members will demand that all men treat the "lady doctor" respectfully and use appropriate language, thereby signaling men to adopt a certain disingenuous social role that impedes therapeutic progress.

I'm not suggesting that women exercise questionable judgment, expose themselves to physical danger, or behave in a seductive manner. When working with traditional men, however, women therapists must be alert to a range of subtle and not-so-subtle actions that will restrict their professional functioning. Unfortunately, they must be prepared to insist that their standing as professionals be respected.

A MALE THERAPIST WITH TRADITIONAL MEN

By the time David assumes group leadership, he has developed a chip on his shoulder. For weeks, he's heard nothing but praise for Shannon's therapy skills and is eager to demonstrate his own considerable talents. Although he prefers to conceptualize client problems from a cognitive-behavioral perspective, he tends to be fairly quiet, reactive, and analytical in his leadership style. Group sessions quickly take on a very different tone, as group members seem puzzled by David's silence. When they make overtures, he remains relatively unresponsive. Questions about his background or experiences are coolly rebuffed as inappropriate. Gradually, as men introduce problematic issues, David becomes more involved. Frequently, he challenges the active member to identify the mistaken assumptions or faulty thinking lying behind his actions. When group members suggest interpretations, David corrects them. Soon, the group becomes far more cautious, except Billy, a graduate student especially skillful with David's interpretive style.

In the second week, the group rebels. When David confronts Tom about his "failure to take therapeutic responsibility," Tom challenges David, "What the hell do you know about living in the streets? Have you ever gone three days without eating? You don't know shit!" Angrily, Tom storms out of the room.

In supervision, David is unhappy and resentful. As I question him, I learn that he has felt ignored and dismissed. He claims that it was unfair for Shannon to lead the group first. He feels that she had the "prime time" to work with the group and that his therapy style has been undercut by her history with the group. As we explore the legitimate and irrational aspects of David's concerns, he begins to unwind and recognize the many dimensions to his reactions.

His graduate program was torn by gender conflict. Some male faculty members met feminist perspectives with bitterness. Rancorous arguments erupted about the "feminization of psychology," gender quotas, and the quality of the research on gender differences in therapist skills. As a result, David realizes, he became determined to function effectively in his therapy groups (although his long-term goal was to be an administrator of a mental health center).

As we talk about his background, David also acknowledges that he has always been an intense competitor with both his brothers and his fellow graduate students. He takes great pride in his accomplishments, although he feels he rarely gets the recognition he deserves. When we discuss his feelings about the group, David reports satisfaction with some of them but great impatience with how the "winos and psychopaths" interfere with progress. Recognizing myself in David, I describe my similar experiences and frustrations. I reassure him about his talents and therapeutic skills. I endorse his view that therapeutic gains are difficult with this population and encourage him to place less pressure on himself. "Ease up," I say. "Just get to know these guys and, if you feel comfortable, let them get to know you."

Although initially tentative, David does become comfortable with revealing parts of himself to the group. The atmosphere shifts dramatically as David taps painful memories of his struggles to impress male authority figures and establish a comfortable place in his male community. He effectively uses his firsthand knowledge of men's reactions to women in power, helping the group locate their anxiety and insecurities. Once he relaxes, David calls on his many years of participation with all-male groups to become a skilled group facilitator—at times joking and teasing, at other times pushing men into new patterns of interaction.

Just as the description of Shannon's work illustrates that female therapists can work very effectively with traditional men, so does the description of David's work. This is consistent with my comments in earlier chapters, in which I highlighted the many benefits of the all-male group environment. However, in light of the evolving research on how therapy differs according to therapist gender, certain comments seem warranted.

An earlier section discussed the advantages that accrue to women because of their socialization and phenomenology. It is therefore reasonable to raise the corollary question: Can men work effectively as therapists for traditional men?

To address this issue, we must return to an observation that Mintz and O'Neil (1990) made about the shortcomings of existing research on therapist sex differences. Most research has looked principally at therapists' gender and not at their gender attitudes and values. This is critical because men who become therapists are in many ways quite different from most traditional men. As has been long recognized, male psychotherapists are far more likely than typical traditional men to be caring, nurturing, and empathizing. Certainly, traditional socialization and gender role construction predispose men toward certain countertherapeutic values, but most male therapists have ample access to a range of "androgynous" behaviors.

But there's more to male therapists' potential advantages than just their relative freedom from some of the behavioral limitations of many men. Male therapists may also have certain specific advantages in working with traditional men. Because they are men, they can facilitate therapy through kinship, credibility, empathy, and the potential to serve as a catalyst for transformative experiences.

Kinship

A male therapist will make therapy difficult for traditional men if he refuses to recognize his kinship with fellow men, demeans "aberrant" men as qualitatively different from himself, and thinks of his male clients only as "them." I have already advised that a woman not make her gender an overt topic in therapy. On the other hand, I believe that many distinct advantages result when a male therapist takes a "we're all part of the same struggle" approach. As illustrated by David, a transparent and self-disclosing male therapist can be a powerful catalyst for intimacy and a crucial role model for new behaviors.

Credibility

To the extent that a group sees itself as unique or oppressed, it is likely to welcome a therapist into its inner circle. Ethnicity experts Tyler, Sussewell, and Williams-McCoy (1985) discuss an "ethnic validity" model of psychotherapy that describes the advantages of various therapeutic pairings. In particular, they note that when both client and therapist are part of a "non-culture-defining group," considerable benefits ensue from the shared sense of experience and identity.

Although it may be a bit of a stretch, to some degree this situation holds for traditional men in psychotherapy. Although male status confers certain privileges, many traditional men view themselves as oppressed and threatened by a rapidly changing culture. In the therapist's office, they see themselves as especially vulnerable. As a result, many traditional men respond very well to a male therapist who accentuates that he shares their dilemmas. (Naturally, the purpose of this posture is to promote a therapist-client connection, not to encourage men to unite reactively as "victims" of women's empowerment.)

Empathy

Women's "other" status may make them more empathic than men. Yet male therapists who intensively reflect on their personal gender role journeys have unique access to a source of empathic connection with male clients. A male therapist knows firsthand about the emotional aspects of being a son, father, worker, male lover, or buddy. At worst, this empathy could make the therapist vulnerable to male collusion or to a backlash against women or the larger culture. At best, however, it gives him the rich opportunity to experience the deepest therapeutic connection with another man.

The group progressed very well until encountering a significant slump as the Christmas holidays approached. When David had announced he would be away for the week of Christmas, all group members accepted the news without complaint. Yet by the third week of December group morale was at rock bottom. Troubled and concerned, though unaware of the degree of holiday despondency, David urged the group members to help him understand their lethargy. There was a minimal response at first, but eventually one group member admitted that holidays were always a "bummer" for him. Others joined in. Each was hopelessly estranged from his family and was experiencing deep pain and remorse he had difficulty putting into words.

Disturbed and perhaps feeling a little guilty, David swung into action. Enthusiastically he reintroduced cognitive models for coping with distress. "Isn't distress," he asked, "only what you allow it to be? Rather than morosely suffering about Christmas past, wouldn't it be more realistic and rational to start new traditions? Rather than focus on the half-empty glass, shouldn't we focus on the positive aspects of our current situation?"

David may as well have been speaking in an ancient Celtic dialect as everyone stared straight ahead. Finally, Tom, with a bemused grin, turned to David and said, "Doc, you've come a long way, but on this one you don't have a clue."

This really pissed David off. He felt he had provided these men with first-class cognitive interventions, but they were sarcastic and unappreciative. I questioned David closely about his reactions, particularly his emotional reactions to the men's holiday depression. David initially balked but soon admitted that the men's pain had made him anxious. He realized that he had desperately wanted to help the men distance themselves from their despair. Additionally, he had bought into the men's idea that without women Christmas sucks because men simply cannot nurture one another.

Inspired by our discussion, David went back to the group with a new perspective. Rather than trying to help the men deny their unhappiness, he urged them to go with it, to learn as much as they could from it. In doing so, he urged them to examine how they had chosen to suffer separately and wall themselves off from one another. Over the next several painful sessions, the group members uncovered many anguished memories, but also became closer than ever before. When the holidays passed, each admitted that the period had been horrible but that they also learned something important about how men care for one another.

As Laura Brown (1990) noted, women therapists sometimes are more ready than men therapists to allow clients to experience painful and primitive emotional states without a compulsion to fix the problems. I have repeatedly emphasized the narrow range of interpersonal behavior alternatives available to traditional men: rational problem solving, hierarchical competition, emotional distance, stoicism, and homophobia. Likewise, I have stressed how traditional men rely on women to provide emotional support, masculinity validation, and socioemotional communication, and to "hold" their emotional anguish.

Men cannot learn to broaden their emotional repertoires and lessen dependence on women unless at some point in their lives they learn to do this without a woman being present. It's inescapable that the true impact of functioning without a woman cannot be experienced with a woman present. Men in an all-male setting have a unique opportunity to manifest transformative experiences such as nurturing, communicating compassionately, and tending to one another's affective needs.

Obviously, for this to take place a very special male therapist is needed. This man must have thoroughly explored his own gender constraints, including any history of overdependence on women. He must have examined and overcome the homophobia rampant in traditional male socialization. He must have a deep commitment to the potential that men, without relying on women's guidance, support, or encouragement, can develop male-male relationships characterized by empathy, compassion, and affection.

GENDER AND THERAPY SUPERVISION

Earlier in this chapter, I argued that gender socialization and the social construction of femininity and masculinity affect therapists as well as therapy clients. Additionally, I offered some food for thought about the differential issues that confront male and female therapists in their work with traditional men. Before leaving this topic, I want to make one more point. Gender issues are not limited to client interactions with the environment or with therapists.

Over the past twenty years, research has shown that psychotherapy and supervision are isomorphic processes. Howard Liddle, Douglas Breunlin, and Richard Schwartz (1988), leading theorists on psychotherapy supervision, have suggested that the processes occurring between supervisor and therapist may be functionally quite similar to those occurring between therapist and clients, and even between or among clients.

Louise calls to make an appointment for herself and her husband, Lloyd. Because Marsha, my psychology intern, has sought a marital therapy case, I arrange for her to see the couple while I provide live supervision behind a one-way mirror.

Louise, forty-one, and Lloyd, forty-three, have been married for eighteen years. Both are employed. Louise has done the bulk of parenting for their daughters, Alice (who is seventeen) and Tricia (who is fifteen). The presenting problem is Louise's extreme unhappiness with Lloyd's passivity and lack of participation in family activities. As Marsha attempts to get a better feel for the problems, she learns that

Louise feels emotionally isolated and lonely. Louise reports that their marital lives have fallen into an unbearable routine. Every night when they both return home from work, Louise prepares dinner while Lloyd takes a nap. They eat dinner, and Lloyd goes to his study where he works on his computer for a few hours before going to bed.

After twenty minutes of attending to Louise's concerns, Marsha turns to Lloyd for his perspectives. To her amazement, Lloyd says nothing. Instead, he raises his shoulders and turns his palms up as if to say, "Beats me." Marsha waits several more awkward moments before saying, "Lloyd, I wonder if you could give me some idea of how all this matches your experience."

Lloyd replies simply, "Sounds about right to me."

Marsha waits for the amplification that she assumes will follow, but nothing comes.

Rattled and a bit irritated, Marsha responds, "Surely you have something to say about this."

"Not really," Lloyd replies. "That's about it."

Marsha shuffles in her chair and then makes eye contact with Louise, who is giving her a "See what I mean?" expression.

Over the next twenty minutes, Marsha and Louise alternate in their efforts to cajole Lloyd to speak up. Louise catalogues her many years of dissatisfaction with Lloyd, while Lloyd slumps in his chair. Exasperated, Marsha says to Louise, "I can certainly see why you're going nuts. You clearly are getting no help. Lloyd, I wonder how you expect anything good to come of this with your passive attitude!"

I call into the room and ask Marsha if we can have a minute to consult. When she comes back to the consultation area, she is steamed. I ask her about it, and she acknowledges her irritation. I say it looks like she and Louise are ganging up on Lloyd. She becomes tense and asks, "So, you think it's Louise's fault?"

"Well, it must be annoying as hell to have someone harping at you all the time," I say.

"Not nearly as hard as busting your tail trying to make a relationship work and getting criticized for it," snaps Marsha.

Because there are multiple levels of interaction (between supervisor and therapist, between therapist and clients, and possibly between clients), supervisors should be especially aware of gender-based impasses in supervisory relationships. Problems between clients and therapists that do not receive sensitive and gender-aware supervisory input will be exacerbated by new levels of collusion and triangulation.

In the previous vignette, gender may have been one factor influencing how Marsha (a female therapist) and I (a male supervisor) responded to the therapeutic issues presented by a troubled couple. Marsha may feel compassionate toward emotionally burdened women and reactive toward withholding or emotionally withdrawn men; perhaps this is why she sided with Louise in her efforts to provoke a response from Lloyd. I feel compassionate toward withdrawn men and reactive toward assertive women; thus, I sided with Lloyd's resistance to influence. This isomorphic pattern must be recognized for what it is and processed thoroughly so that therapy can proceed. (Suggestions for this appear in the following chapter.)

In the future, it should become possible to document the advantages and disadvantages of various supervisor-therapist pairings for specific types of clients and client problems. Training experts have just begun offering ideas. Some say that supervisors should become unusually aware of how gender socialization promotes nurturing and caretaking skills in female therapists and promotes leadership and executive skills in male therapists. Until we reach a point at which all therapists have equal access to all required skills, it may be useful to give special consideration to man-woman supervisory teams or pairings that might promote broad repertoires of skills and sensitivities.

Psychotherapy with men is greatly enhanced when therapists understand the many stresses of traditional masculinity. Therapists themselves are subject to socialization pressures and continually interact with a gendered culture. Both male and female therapists bring potential resources and shortcomings into their work with this population. When the subtle influences of gender are understood and accommodated, psychotherapy interventions are most effective and liberating.

In the final chapter, I broaden discussion beyond the relatively small percentage of men in therapists' offices to look at the wider culture and ways to help make it a better environment for all of us.

7

Gender Role Strain in
Therapy and Beyond

In his 1981 book, *The Myth of Masculinity*, Joseph Pleck introduced a theoretical model with enormous implications for the way we think about men and masculinity. Pleck offered the "gender role strain" paradigm to replace the "gender identity" paradigm that dominated previous thinking about gender.

In brief, the gender identity paradigm posits that men have a powerful psychological need for a clear and fixed gender identity. This model provides the theoretical underpinnings of "essentialist" views of masculinity—ideas that all men have an unchanging, inherent masculine essence. Essentialist thinkers believe that genetic makeup, hormones, brain wiring, or evolutionary heritage are responsible for creating fundamentally different male and female essences. They consider gender conflict to be inevitable and advise against "messing with Mother Nature."

Conversely, the "gender role strain" paradigm posits that gender roles are social constructions that are internally inconsistent and generally harmful to both genders. Because they are socially constructed, gender roles can be changed when necessary, producing more flexible and adaptive behaviors for women and men.

BENEFITS OF THE GENDER ROLE STRAIN PARADIGM

Adopting the gender role strain paradigm leads to several very important alterations in therapists' approach to traditional men seeking therapy.

Model of Nonadversarial Relationships

Therapists will find the gender role strain paradigm more compatible with their overall therapeutic objectives because it offers a model of nonadversarial relationships between women and men. As noted previously, many traditional men enter therapy seeking a return to conventional relationship arrangements. From this perspective, women (and therapists) who seek change are the "enemies" and must be quieted for a man to maintain his traditional patterns. In other words, "Things would be just fine if unhappy women and troublemaking therapists would only leave me alone."

From the gender role strain perspective, however, the traditional man's position is naive and problematic. Cultural pressures are causing major problems not only for many women but also for *men*. The issue is not one of women versus men but of women and men together trying to find new relationship models so that they can adapt to a demanding and rapidly changing culture.

Less Threatening View of Change

Inherent in the gender role identity model is the belief that the well-being of individuals and the culture depends on women's and men's remaining true to their "essential" and immutable definitions of femininity and masculinity. Therapists who suggest change, therefore, could be viewed as radical troublemakers.

The gender role strain perspective, however, reveals the folly of this argument. Traditional gender roles are shown to be not only socially proscribed, internally inconsistent, and changeable across time and situations but also inherently stressful to women and men.

When therapists make this perspective clear, the matter changes markedly. The truly dangerous courses are those in which women and men either remain ignorant of the powerful constraining influence of traditional gender roles or recognize them and demand devout allegiance to them. Therapists can help women and men to instead recognize exploration, awareness, and collaborative negotiation as inescapable routes to emotional health.

Invitation to Gender Role Exploration

A most crucial implication of the gender role strain paradigm is that it calls for a more differentiated and more ambitious therapy. For decades, mental health graduate programs trained students to work with "people," with minimal attention to gender, age, race, ethnicity, social class, or sexual orientation. Most therapists learned to practice a "one-size-fits-all" psychotherapy. We now know that we don't work with generic "people" but with men and women who differ according to their race, ethnicity, age, and sexual orientation. With the increased appreciation of gender role strain's debilitating effects, simplistic models of generic therapy appear naive and anachronistic.

Feminist critics were the first to bring needed attention to gender, as they insisted that effective and ethical therapies must attend to the special issues that women face. Of late, this perspective has broadened to include calls for greater attention to both women's issues and men's issues.

Psychiatrist Kenneth Solomon has advocated gender role therapy for men, in which gender role issues would be an explicitly agreed-upon focus of therapy. The primary goal of this therapy would be to move the client toward "psychological and behavioral androgyny." For Solomon, successful therapy with a man not only addresses presenting problems but also helps prevent future ones by allowing him to integrate "the positive aspects of both masculine and feminine roles." In this way, he can "flexibly call upon a wide behavioral, affective, and cognitive repertoire to respond as any situation demands" (1982a, p. 250).

Carol Philpot (1991) describes "gender-sensitive psychotherapy" that addresses the special needs of women and men and the growth limitations imposed by stereotypical expectations. "Gender-fair" psychotherapy, as articulated by Roberta Nutt (1991), prescribes that therapists acquire a knowledge of gender socialization issues and promote nonstereotypical roles for women and men.

Glenn Good, Lucia Gilbert, and Murray Scher (1990) propose gender-aware therapy as a "synthesis of feminist therapy and knowledge about gender" (p. 376). Gender-aware therapy includes a recognition of gender as an integral aspect of counseling, a consideration of problems within their societal contexts, active efforts to change gender injustices, the construction of collaborative therapeutic relationships, and respect for clients' freedom to define personal gender roles.

Feminist therapy, gender role therapy, gender-sensitive therapy, gender-fair therapy, and gender-aware therapy share a common component in that they call for therapy to extend well beyond an automatic adaptation to traditional gender roles. Although clients may choose to continue living according to narrow role definitions, they should make their decisions after therapists have educated them about gender socialization, gender role strain, and the possible benefits of new role definitions.

Early in my training, an especially feisty supervisor stated his definition of himself as a therapist. "My job," he said, "is to comfort the afflicted and afflict the comfortable." I've never known if that thought was his own, but it has stayed with me ever since. In fact, in some very critical ways, this idea may be central to my approach to therapy with traditional men, because it suggests to me that gender-aware therapists should try to warn clients about the perils of adhering rigidly to narrow traditional gender roles. Let me illustrate how this might take place.

Neil is the picture of satisfaction. This is difficult for me to grasp because a mere three weeks before, he pleaded for an emergency appointment, claiming, "My life is in shambles." When I saw him, I agreed that his life was a mess.

A tenured medical school professor with multiple grants, publications, and professional awards, he is a model of academic success. Unfortunately, it has been years since he has been able to fall sleep without several drinks. Holly, his wife of twenty-four years, has threatened divorce because of the way he has neglected her and their three teenage children. Neil isn't exactly happy with the marriage either, thinking Holly is far more interested in the children and in her own career than in him. He admitted that he has lost all sense of "who I am," has virtually no friends, and hasn't done anything "fun" in more than ten years. His days have been rigidly organized around teaching, researching, compulsively exercising, and evening drinking. He acknowledged that he wondered about therapy, but never saw a way to fit it into his schedule and wasn't sure it had much to offer him (because he has already read most of the books and knows many of the psychology professors well). When he first came to see me, however, he claimed he was ready to do "whatever it takes."

Three weeks into therapy, everything looks much rosier to Neil. In the first ten minutes of our session, he proudly announces that he has "cut back" on his drinking, shifted one teaching assignment, and begun planning a Disneyland trip for the entire family. I nod approval of his changes and wait. Nothing. He is through. Mission accomplished.

Neil fills the next thirty minutes with anecdotes and gripes about the declining state of medical education. When I fail to "dismiss" him from the session, he becomes restless. I observe, "Neil, it seems you're thinking matters are pretty much taken care of."

"Aren't they?" he responds.

"Well, perhaps they are. But I'm worried. Over the past several years, I've talked with a lot of men like you—bank presidents, university professors, physicians, attorneys, and lots of other very successful guys. A lot of them, also like you, are leading very stressful and very deadening lives. I worry about you and your next twenty to thirty years. You yourself admitted that the joy and passion were gone from your life. What are we going to do to pay attention to that?"

Neil claimed to be satisfied and ready to resume his life with some minor cosmetic changes. He certainly was more comfortable than he had been in some time. However, because he seemed to be paying only minimal attention to his potentially self-destructive male role, I felt that I needed to "afflict" him. That is, before "blessing" his departure from therapy, I felt that I should make some effort to point out how his lifestyle, like that of many other successful traditional men, carried the seeds of future problems.

Shifts in the Therapist Role

Ellen Piel Cook (1990) has reviewed gender research and found that women and men live in "different worlds." These differences are manifested in numerous ways—types of stressors encountered, use of social support, problem definition, problem attribution, dominant reactive emotions, willingness to seek professional help, and behavior in the therapy office. As noted previously, men often try to deflect, deny, or suppress their distress. Sometimes, these coping mechanisms are effective, but frequently they generate problems of substance abuse, workaholism, compulsive sexual behavior, high-risk thrill-seeking behavior, or irresponsible social conduct. These behaviors can cause an "afflicted" traditional man to appear in a therapist's office.

This is where the gender role strain paradigm and the affliction aphorism seem especially applicable. Although the troubled traditional man desperately wants to be comforted, he almost always wants the comfort to come without serious disruption of his dominant worldview. That is, he would like to be assisted in performing more effectively as a traditional man.

Although I *am* interested in providing a degree of immediate relief and comfort to a man, I am not interested in providing short-term relief by ignoring gender role strain and, at some level, allowing long-term suffering to occur. Therefore, in one very important way, I am interested in "afflicting" traditional men; I want to confront their gender role strain by challenging their dominant and highly dysfunctional definitions of masculinity.

To accomplish this, therapists must become highly knowledgeable of gender issues and, at times, be proactive. In addition to having conventional diagnostic and therapeutic skills, therapists should be able to enrich their professional functioning by recognizing the role that gender plays in client problems. Additionally, they should be able to detect *future* problems, even when clients are feeling reasonably comfortable.

After this proactive work occurs, the therapist-client relationship undergoes subtle changes. In some important ways, the sharp and unbreachable dividing line between "pathological" client and "healthy" therapist grows less distinct; in essence, the therapist working with a traditional man becomes an educator, teaching him about the pernicious effects of masculine socialization on *all* men. In this process, the therapist will need to be comfortable with a more egalitarian therapist-client relationship, more self-revelation, and an appreciable degree of role modeling. In some very profound ways, the therapist needs to be deeply appreciative of the stresses of role strain and compassionate to a man's efforts to counter it.

Because the gender role strain paradigm and the gender-aware therapies it engenders demand new styles and behaviors, I'd like to focus some special attention on the process of becoming a gender-aware therapist.

THE ROAD TO BECOMING A GENDER-AWARE THERAPIST

Because gender values are so central to our lives, we cannot address them without having a range of complex theoretical, professional, and personal reactions. For this reason, the process of becoming a gender-aware therapist involves both cognitive tasks of knowledge acquisition and affective tasks of personal exploration and growth.

Educating and Training Gender-Sensitive Therapists

Knowledge acquisition, of course, typically falls in the domain of educational institutions. More than a decade ago, Lucia Gilbert (1987) reviewed the state of graduate education regarding gender issues and recommended far greater attention to gender issues, especially to many aspects of male socialization. Most surveys of graduate training programs indicate an upsurge in attention to women's issues but a corresponding lack of attention to men's socialization issues and the intersection of women's issues and men's issues. When "men's issues classes are offered, they are more commonly attended by women students" (p. 554).

Clearly, graduate training needs to pay greater attention to the breadth of gender issues and men's issues. Additionally, advanced professionals should consider men's studies as a central component of their ongoing continuing education. A growing number of appropriate men's studies books have begun to appear, as have continuing education workshops. I hope that the material presented in this book will also contribute appreciably to the knowledge base about traditional men and psychotherapy.

Exploring Reactions to Gender Issues

Any exploration of central values is likely to provoke strong reactions, regardless of the intent to maintain scholarly and scientific objectivity. Derald and David Sue (1990) recognize this combination of cognitive and affective challenges when they describe the characteristics of the "culturally skilled counselor." Among these characteristics are (1) awareness and sensitivity to one's own cultural heritage, (2) awareness of biases, (3) comfort with value differences, (4) sensitivity to the occasional need for referral, and (5) awareness of one's own value blind spots in terms of attitudes, beliefs, and feelings. Clearly, the process of becoming more culturally diverse has many affective components.

During the annual American Psychological Association conference, a fascinating yet complicated issue emerged. Several male psychology graduate students (Habben & Petiprin, 1997) sponsored a panel and interactive discussion to air their feelings about the teaching of gender issues in graduate training. These male students, although outspokenly supportive of women's empowerment, acknowledged a range of troubled and conflicted feelings. They felt that some of their faculty and peers simply did not like men or anything about traditional masculinity. Some believed that they were targets of disdain whenever they voiced opinions opposing those of feminist faculty and students. Some felt that male bashing, if not condoned, was at least tolerated.

This matter has numerous problematic aspects. Clearly, the study of gender issues is not a dry academic exercise, as efforts to achieve a sense of personal integration and interpersonal harmony require a person to pass through many troublesome phases. Women are likely to be angry about the abuses of misogynistic and patriarchal culture. Men, even supportive ones, are subject to feeling hurt or defensive about that anger. Additionally, many men feel that there are some positive aspects to traditional masculinity and that not all men should be demeaned.

For me, that symposium and other similar experiences illustrated that gender issues must be taught in a variety of formats (Brooks, 1992, 1994). Scholarship must be supplemented by discussion and supportive interaction.

Jim O'Neil and Marianne Roberts Carroll (1988) have made an especially important contribution to this issue by offering the metaphor of the "gender role journey." This term describes the process of incorporating gender information into one's personal and professional ideology. In its most basic form, the gender role journey is a series of affective and attitudinal stages encountered as people move from "acceptance of traditional gender roles" through ambivalence, anger, and activism until they achieve "celebration and integration" of new gender roles.

In addition to recognizing the multiple emotions that spring from gender studies, this metaphor suggests that a structured workshop format would be helpful to allow people to explore their emotional reactions. This format would promote collaborative discussion of the most effective courses of action.

Other mental health professionals have suggested similar experiential activities for therapists. Psychiatrist Stephen Bergman and psychologist Janet Surrey (1992) have proposed "Woman-Man Relationship" workshops to help explore problematic ideas about traditional gender roles and to "identify prototypical impasses and work toward creating mutuality in male-female relationships."

Although it was described in Chapter Five as a component of gender-sensitive couples therapy, Philpot, Brooks, Lusterman, and Nutt's (1997) "gender inquiry" exercise could be extended to therapists who want a greater understanding of their personal heritage regarding gender relations.

In my own experience, I've had notable success with a gender-aware psychotherapy exercise. I developed this activity to raise therapists' awareness about the multiple ways in which gender affects therapy. For a particular client, the therapist should speculate about

1. Meaningful messages the client has received about appropriate conduct as a man or woman

2. The way those messages have affected the client's coping style and have led to the development of the specific symptom

3. The interplay between the client's socialization and his or her manner of participating in therapy

4. The impact of personal gender socialization on the *therapist's* conduct in the therapy room

5. The degree to which the therapist-client interaction contradicts or replicates stereotypical patterns in the broader culture

6. The degree to which the therapy takes place in a larger context (for example, church, school, prison, the military, and so

forth) that promotes a certain way for the client to interpret his or her gender role

ACTION OUTSIDE THE THERAPY ROOM

Up to this point, I've described the implications of the gender role strain paradigm in terms of the need for therapists to conduct gender-aware therapy once they have become more attuned to their own gender-based values and helping styles. Another significant implication of the gender role strain paradigm can be described by returning to the "affliction" aphorism.

As noted, gender-aware therapists not only need to comfort men who have been constrained and harmed by rigid role expectations but also need to help their male clients broaden role definitions, generating greater adaptability and flexibility so as to prevent certain future problems. Additionally, I think gender-aware therapists would do well to consider themselves possible agents of broader sociocultural change. In some ways, sexist cultural institutions are too comfortable with traditional expectations of women and men and need to be "afflicted" by an appropriate agenda of social activism and change. What follows is a brief overview of potential actions beyond therapy.

Challenging National Institutions

A major contribution of the feminist perspective in mental health has been its opposition to the sexist social system, its refusal to shape therapy clients in limited traditional gender roles, and its emphasis on social activism to reform the social system itself. Similarly, social activism may also have an important place in men's gender role journeys. Social activism may be one activity that facilitates a traditional man's progress in his gender role journey and may ultimately promote gender role transcendence.

Aside from the personal benefits of social activism, there are benefits that can only be produced when the sexist social institutions are altered. In this vein, therapists can supplement therapy by encouraging male clients to take part in men's retreats or other aspects of the growing men's movement. One of the most enduring men's organizations has been the National Organization of Men Against Sexism (NOMAS), which holds an annual "Men and Masculinity" conference and sponsors a number of antirape, antiviolence, and antipornography programs.

The Media

Because of its significant role in shaping public opinion, the national media are a logical place to start. As we know from public reactions to televised events such as *Roots*, the Super Bowl, and the O. J. Simpson trial, television has phenomenal power and immediacy. Media research has discovered that the average American child watches between seven and eight thousand hours of television *commercials* between the ages of three and eighteen (Davis, 1990). Those hours continually reinforce children's views of how the world works and how women and men are supposed to conduct themselves. Recent content analysis research has revealed that although there has been some change over the past two decades, television advertising continues to portray men and women in the traditional fashion. For example, women are now more likely to be seen as having an occupation, but they still are not as likely to be portrayed as "experts." (The voices of commercial narrators are still male more than 90 percent of the time.)

The Sports Establishment

The sports industry is another national institution that is extremely influential with men of all ages. By any reasonable standard, the American sports industry is badly out of control; it has been allowed to run amok in socializing and influencing American men. Once, sports and athletics were considered useful activities to help boys learn group cooperation, attempt personal challenges, improve physical endurance, and overcome adversity. Lately, however, sports have gone far beyond the modest role of teaching young men about life; for many men they have become life itself.

How many times have we heard fanatical coaches and rabid athletics boosters claim that football teaches young men the most important lessons in life: always strive to be number one, never let your guard down, and never let the other guy see you sweat? In general, life becomes a giant athletic event with one ultimate goal—outperforming other men and winning life's most valuable commodity. What is that commodity? The "thrill" of a victory that brings financial success, peer respect, and women trophies.

Sports don't have to be run this way. Parents and fans can regain control of them. Athletics can once again provide an arena in which people can improve physical abilities without becoming obsessed with results and victory or being humiliated by the agony of defeat. Women, as well as men, can participate and be on center stage. Men, as well as women, can cheer, encourage, and support women performers.

Redefining Fathering

Psychologist Louise Silverstein (1996) has been one of the leading advocates for a redefinition of fathering. She asserts that such a redefinition is "central to both the reconstruction of masculinity and the achievement of equality for women within western, industrialized society" (p. 3).

This redefinition of fathering has probably been one of the most celebrated features of the men's movement, as there seems to a wave of support for fathers' greater involvement with their children. Men are now much more likely to participate in childbirth classes and the delivery of their children, to lighten work responsibilities so as to participate more in their children's lives. Many fathers are demanding more legal rights after divorce. A highly popular mythopoetic men's movement calls for the spiritual discovery of continuity between generations of fathers and sons. A central message seems to be that the historically absent or "peripheral" father should become more present in the lives of his children.

Joseph Pleck (1993) has asserted that if workplaces develop more "family supportive" policies, men can develop new family roles. He has claimed, for example, that although men have been reluctant to use formal paternity leave benefits, they have been quite likely to use "informal" leave and to negotiate the demands of their jobs to meet family needs in other ways.

Although I am a great supporter of this push to include fathers, I recognize that formal policies alone are not enough. Despite new policies, corporate culture maintains an unspoken belief that men who take family leave are "unmanly" (Alexander, 1990). According to Pleck (1993), many people still hold the belief that house-husbands are, to a certain degree, less manly than working men. Corporate culture is not the only repository for fears of creeping "wimpishness"; many traditional men are highly insecure about the implications of adjusting to new male role models. No antidote to these irrational fears is more effective than the testimony of men who have made such changes. Also, researchers such as Carolyn Cowan (1988) have identified a growing body of empirical evidence supporting the idea that greater involvement in fathering is psychologically beneficial for men. Men who actively embrace fatherhood develop more aspects of themselves, relate more satisfactorily with their families, and report greater satisfaction with their lives.

It's time now for men to begin reaching out to other men through a range of men's movement activities and to help other men realize the benefits of fathering in new ways. New models of fathering, more accessible than ever, provide hope for transforming the traditional ways in which men experience gender roles, as well as helping society move closer to gender equity.

Transforming Boy Culture

Earlier, I suggested that men's groups allow men to learn new behaviors in an environment similar to the "boy culture" in which they learned many traditional values. Although a men's group is particularly effective with male patients who were traumatized by boy culture, we should not lose sight of the need to reshape that culture itself.

Boy culture is what historian E. Anthony Rotundo (1993) has referred to as a breeding ground that prepares boys for manhood. In his analysis of this culture, Rotundo traces the historical development of boy culture to the 1800s, when boys were largely freed from the necessity of work in the family and were allowed to explore the streets, backyards, and vacant lots of the cities or the orchards and fields of rural America without adult supervision. Through these activities, boys developed separate, cohesive, and independent peer groups in which certain values—mastery, loyalty, and self-control—were emphasized. Although these ideas are now considered virtuous, other values with more problematic aspects were also taught. Boy culture emphasized physical prowess, courage and suppression of weakness, emotional and physical stoicism, daring, and loyalty to allies. Embedded within these activities was a high level of aggression and violence. Older boys routinely bullied younger ones, territorial battles were fought along racial or ethnic lines, and animals were sadistically killed and tortured. Fierce independence from authority was valued, frequently to the point of vandalism and antisocial activities.

Frank Pittman's "male chorus," noted in Chapter One, seems closely related to the idea of boy culture. According to Pittman, the male chorus is composed of "all the guy's comrades and rivals, all his buddies and bosses, his male ancestors, and his male cultural heroes, his male models of masculinity, and above all, his father" (1990, p. 42). Pittman sees the male chorus as invisible, omnipresent, and inescapable as a constant internal critic of the manliness of a male's actions.

Another critic of contemporary boy culture is Myriam Miedzian (1991), who has argued that boys in contemporary culture are encouraged to be "obsessionally competitive," rather than simply assertive and competent.

The implications of this are clear. There need to be major efforts to transform many aspects of traditional boy culture. Particularly vital in this activity will be those women and men who appreciate new models of masculinity and who can provide behavioral alternatives for young men.

A FINAL WORD

Most people agree with the adage "If it ain't broke, don't fix it." Many also believe that the traditional codes of masculinity have functioned very well and should not be changed. But the gender role strain paradigm reveals the falseness of this complacent assumption. Just as psychotherapists should be proficient at providing comfort to afflicted men, they should also recognize the problems inherent in rigid traditional masculinity. They must develop ways to expose men to the benefits of a gender role journey. Furthermore, we all benefit when therapists embark on the task of broad social change to promote new models of masculinity.

Change, of course, produces anxiety, particularly when significant loss is anticipated. A critical point here is that this reconstruction of masculinity, while producing the loss of men's patriarchal privileges, will create many more benefits. Self-destructive behaviors are often the result of an overly narrow view of masculinity or of an attachment to outdated gender role mandates. By enthusiastically embracing a new and broader conception of masculinity, men will experience far greater role flexibility, as reflected in decreased violence, improved self-care, wider definitions of personal worth beyond their work roles, and richer, more varied relationships with women, their children, and other men.

The many traditional men described in this book are a relatively small subset of the hundreds I've had the privilege of encountering over the past twenty-five years. I certainly wouldn't claim that the encounters were always satisfactory or completely successful. All in all, however, I think many of them were. And thanks to the lessons I have learned, I think I am now a far better therapist for traditional men. In this book, I've tried to convey the essentials of these lessons and my reflections on them.

I strongly believe that almost all traditional men want to do the right thing, even though it's getting harder for them to comprehend just what that is. Most of these men experience a significant degree of gender role strain, but few are able to cope with this smoothly. In fact, many cope with it so poorly that they find themselves somewhere they never imagined they would be—in a psychotherapist's office.

Unfortunately, many therapists are frequently no more comfortable with this situation than the traditional men themselves. Conventional training has not prepared therapists well enough for work with men who seem to hate therapy and nearly everything it represents.

In this book, I've outlined a model of psychotherapeutic intervention that I believe will be more appealing to traditional men and more gratifying to therapists. I hope this is helpful, because the next decade will bring us to a critical cultural crossroads. We will either embrace the bountiful opportunities made possible by women's new empowerment or we will recoil into regression and political backlash. Sadly, many groups have exploited this unsettled situation to promote agendas that needlessly polarize women and men and call for reactionary shifts to traditional relationships and to "good old days" that never really existed. In this turbulent environment, compassionate, thoughtful, and gender-aware psychotherapists offer unique hope for challenging men to reach out to each other, interact sensitively with women, challenge regressive institutions, and mentor the next generation of men.

We therapists must be continually alert to the destructive potential of the darkest aspects of traditional masculinity. Yet we can also hold utmost confidence in the potential of those men who desperately want a better deal for themselves, their culture, and their loved ones. Therapists are uniquely positioned to be leaders in the painful but ultimately exhilarating process of helping traditional men discover realistic and compassionate masculinities.

References

Ackerman, N. W. (1967). The emergence of family diagnosis and treatment: A personal view. *Psychotherapy, 4*, 125–129.

Alexander, S. (1990). Fears for careers curb paternity leaves. *Wall Street Journal,* pp. B1, B4.

Allen, J. A., & Gordon, S. (1990). Creating a framework for change. In R. L. Meth & R. S. Pasick (Eds.), *Men in therapy: The challenge of change* (pp. 131–151). New York: Guilford Press.

Are men really that bad? (1994, Feb. 14). *Time, 14*(3), 52–59.

Aries, E. (1976). Interaction patterns and themes of male, female, and mixed groups. *Small Group Behavior, 7*, 7–18.

Balswick, J. O. (1988). *The inexpressive male.* San Francisco: New Lexington Press.

Barnett, R. C., & Baruch, G. K. (1987). Social roles, gender, and psychological distress. In R. C. Barnett, L. Biener, & G. K. Baruch (Eds.), *Gender and stress* (pp. 122–143). New York: Free Press.

Bell, D. H. (1982). *Being a man: The paradox of masculinity.* Orlando, FL: Lewis.

Bennett, W. J. (1995). *The book of virtues.* Morristown, NJ: Silver, Burdett & Ginn.

Bepko, C., & Krestan, J. (1990). *Too good for her own good: Breaking free from the burden of female responsibility.* New York: HarperCollins.

Berglund, M. (1984). Suicide in alcoholism. *Archives of General Psychiatry, 41,* 888–891.

Bergman, S. J., & Surrey, J. (1992). *The woman-man relationship: Impasses and possibilities* (Working Paper No. 55). Wellesley, MA: Stone Center for Developmental Services and Studies, Wellesley College.

Bernard, J. (1972). *The future of marriage.* New York: World.

Bernard, J. (1981). The good provider role: Its rise and fall. *American Psychologist, 36*, 1–12.

Bernstein, J. (1987). The male group. In L. Mahdi, S. Foster, & M. Little (Eds.), *Betwixt and between* (pp. 135–145). LaSalle, IL: Open Court Press.

Betcher, R. W., & Pollack, W. S. (1993). *In a time of fallen heroes: The re-creation of masculinity.* New York: Atheneum.

Bly, R. (1990). *Iron John: A book about men.* Reading, MA: Addison-Wesley.

Bograd, M. (Ed.). (1991). *Feminist approaches for men in family therapy.* Binghamton, NY: Haworth Press.

Bork, R. H. (1996). *Slouching towards Gomorrah.* New York: Vintage Books.

Bowen, M. (1978). *Family therapy in clinical practice.* New York: Aronson.

Brehm, S. (1985). *Intimate relationships.* New York: Random House.

Brod, H. (1989). Work clothes and leisure suits: The class basis and bias of the men's movement. In M. S. Kimmel & M. A. Messner (Eds.), *Men's lives* (pp. 276–287). Old Tappan, NJ: Macmillan.

Brodsky, A. M. (1973). The consciousness-raising group as a model for therapy for women. *Psychotherapy: Theory, Research, and Practice, 10*, 24–29.

Brodsky, A. M., & Hare-Mustin, R. (1980). *Women and psychotherapy.* New York: Guilford Press.

Brooks, G. R. (1990). Psychotherapy with traditional role oriented males. In P. A. Keller & L. G. Ritt (Eds.), *Innovations in clinical practice: A sourcebook* (pp. 61–74). Sarasota, FL: Professional Resource Exchange.

Brooks, G. R. (1991). Traditional men in marital and family therapy. In M. Bograd (Ed.), *Feminist approaches for men in family therapy.* Binghamton, NY: Haworth Press.

Brooks, G. R. (1992). Educating, training, and mentoring a generation of gender-sensitive psychotherapists. *Men's Studies Review, 9*, 2–4.

Brooks, G. R. (1994). Teaching gender: Mistakes, resistances, and political conundrums. *Psychotherapy Bulletin, 28*, 15–18.

Brooks, G. R. (1995a). *The centerfold syndrome: How men can overcome objectification and achieve intimacy with women.* San Francisco: Jossey-Bass.

Brooks, G. R. (1995b). Rituals and celebrations in men's lives. *Society for the Psychological Study of Men and Masculinity Bulletin, 1*(1), 6.

Brooks, G. R., & Gilbert, L. A. (1995). Men in families: Old constraints, new possibilities. In R. F. Levant & W. S. Pollack (Eds.), *A new psychology of men* (pp. 252–279). New York: Basic Books.

Brooks, G. R., & Silverstein, L. B. (1995). Understanding the dark side of masculinity: An integrative systems model. In R. F. Levant & W. S. Pollack (Eds.), *A new psychology of men* (pp. 280–336). New York: Basic Books.

Broverman, I., Broverman, D., Clarkson, F., Rosencrantz, P., & Vogel, S. (1970). Sex role stereotypes and clinical judgments of mental health. *Journal of Consulting and Clinical Psychology, 34,* 1–7.

Brown, L. S. (1990). What female therapists have in common. In D. W. Cantor (Ed.), *Women as therapists* (pp. 227–242). New York: Springer.

Bullough, V. (1973). *The subordinate sex: A history of attitudes toward women.* Athens: University of Georgia Press.

Buss, D. M. (1994). *The evolution of desire: Strategies of human mating.* New York: Basic Books.

Cantor, D. W. (Ed.). (1990). *Women as therapists.* New York: Springer.

Chesler, P. (1972). *Women and madness.* Garden City, NY: Doubleday.

Chodorow, N. (1978). *The reproduction of mothering.* Berkeley: University of California Press.

Cook, E. P. (1990). Gender and psychological distress. *Journal of Counseling and Development, 68,* 371–375.

Cowan, C. (1988). Becoming a father: A time of change, an opportunity for development. In P. Bronstein & C. Cowan (Eds.), *Fatherhood today: Men's changing role in the family* (pp. 13–35). New York: Wiley.

Crose, R. (1997). *Why women live longer than men.* San Francisco: Jossey-Bass.

David, D. S., & Brannon, R. (1976). *The forty-nine percent majority: The male sex role.* Reading, MA: Addison-Wesley.

Davis, D. M. (1990). Portrayals of women in prime-time network television: Some demographic characteristics. *Sex Roles, 23,* 325–332.

Dienhart, A., & Avis, J. M. (1991). Men in therapy: Exploring feminist-informed alternatives. In M. Bograd (Ed.), *Feminist approaches for men in family therapy* (pp. 25–49). New York: Haworth.

Dosser, D., Balswick, J. O., & Halverson, C. (1986). Male inexpressiveness and relationships. *Journal of Social and Personal Relationships, 3,* 241–258.

Doyle, J. A. (1995). *The male experience* (3rd ed.). Dubuque, IA: W. C. Brown.

Erickson, B. (1993). *Helping men change: The role of the female therapist.* Thousand Oaks, CA: Sage.

Faludi, S. (1991). *Backlash: The undeclared war against American women.* New York: Crown.

Farr, K. A. (1986). Dominance bonding through the good old boys socializing group. *Sex Roles, 18,* 259–277.

Farrell, W. T. (1974). *The liberated man.* New York: Bantam Books.

Farrell, W. T. (1987). *Why men are the way they are.* New York: McGraw-Hill.

Farrell, W. T. (1993). *The myth of male power.* New York: Simon & Schuster.

Fasteau, M. F. (1974). *The male machine.* New York: Dell.

Feirstein, B. (1982). *Real men don't eat quiche*. New York: Pocket Books.

Francke, L. B. (1997). *Ground zero: The gender wars in the military*. New York: Simon & Schuster.

Gagnon, J., & Henderson, B. (1975). *Human sexuality: An age of ambiguity*. Boston: Educational Associates.

Gilbert, L. A. (1985). *Men in dual-career families: Current realities and future prospects*. Hillsdale, NJ: Erlbaum.

Gilbert, L. A. (1987). Educating about gender and sexuality issues in graduate training: Introduction. *Professional Psychology: Research and Practice, 18,* 554.

Gilbert, L. A. (1993). *Two careers/one family: The promise of gender equality*. Thousand Oaks, CA: Sage.

Gilbert, L. A., & Scher, M. (1987). The power of an unconscious belief: Male entitlement and sexual intimacy with clients. *Professional Practice of Psychology, 8,* 94–108.

Gilder, G. (1973). *Sexual suicide*. New York: Bantam Books.

Gilligan, C. (1982). *In a different voice*. Cambridge, MA: Harvard University Press.

Gilmore, D. D. (1990). *Manhood in the making: Cultural concepts of masculinity*. New Haven, CT: Yale University Press.

Goldberg, S. (1973). *The inevitability of patriarchy*. New York: Morrow.

Goldfried, M. R., and Davison, G. C. (1994). *Clinical behavior therapy*. New York: Wiley.

Good, G., Gilbert, L. A., & Scher, M. (1990). Gender aware therapy: A synthesis of feminist therapy and knowledge about gender. *Journal of Counseling and Development, 68,* 376–380.

Grant, B. F., Harford, T. C., Hasin, D. S., Chou, P., & Pickering, R. (1992). DSM-III-R and the proposed DSM-IV alcohol use disorders, United States, 1988: A nosological comparison. *Alcoholism: Clinical and Experimental Research, 16,* 215–221.

Gray, J. (1992). *Men are from Mars, women are from Venus*. New York: HarperCollins.

Gross, A. (1978). The male role and heterosexual behavior. *Journal of Social Issues, 34,* 87–107.

Habben, C., & Petiprin, G. (1997, Aug. 16). *Conversation hour: The new psychology of men and the graduate school experience*. Paper presented at the annual convention of the American Psychological Association, Chicago, IL.

Harris, L., Blum, R. W., & Resnick, M. (1991). Teen females in Minnesota: A portrait of quiet disturbance. In C. Gilligan, A. G. Rogers, & D. L. Tolman (Eds.), *Women, girls, and psychotherapy* (pp. 119–135). Binghamton, NY: Harrington Park Press.

Harrison, J., Chin, J., & Ficcarrotto, T. (1989). Warning: Masculinity may be hazardous to your health. In M. S. Kimmel & M. A. Messner (Eds.), *Men's lives* (pp. 296–309). Old Tappan, NJ: Macmillan.

Hartley, R. L. (1959). Sex-role pressures in the socialization of the male child. *Psychological Reports, 5*, 459–468.

Harway, M., & Hansen, M. (1993). An overview of domestic violence. In M. Hansen & M. Harway (Eds.), *Battering and family therapy: A feminist perspective* (pp. 1–12). Thousand Oaks, CA: Sage.

Heilman, R. (1973). *Early recognition of alcoholism and other drug dependence.* Center City, MN: Hazelden.

Hite, S. (1987). *Women and love: A cultural revolution in progress.* New York: Knopf.

Hochschild, A. (1989). *The second shift.* New York: Viking Penguin.

Joliff, D. L., & Horne, A. M. (1996). Group counseling for middle class men. In M. Andronico (Ed.), *Men in groups: Insights, interventions, and psychoeducational work* (pp. 51–68). Washington, DC: American Psychological Association Press.

Jordan, J., Kaplan, S., Miller, J., Stiver, I., & Surrey, J. (1991). *Women's growth in connection.* New York: Guilford Press.

Keith, D., & Whitaker, C. (1984). Military families and family therapy. In F. Kaslow & R. I. Ridenour (Eds.), *The military family* (pp. 145–166). New York: Guilford Press.

Kelley, K., & Hall, A. (Eds.). (1992). Mental health counseling for men [Special issue]. *Journal of Mental Health Counseling, 14.*

Kimmel, M. S. (1987). The contemporary "crisis" of masculinity in historical perspective. In H. Brod (Ed.), *The making of masculinities: The new men's studies* (pp. 121–153). Boston: Allen & Unwin.

Kimmel, M. S. (1994). Masculinity as homophobia. In H. Brod & M. Kaufman (Eds.), *Theorizing masculinities* (pp. 119–141). Newbury Park, CA: Sage.

Komorovsky, M. (1940). *The unemployed man and his family.* New York: Dryden Press.

Komorovsky, M. (1976). *Dilemma of masculinity.* New York: Norton.

Lamb, M. (1987). The emergent American father. In M. Lamb (Ed.), *The father's role, cross-cultural perspectives* (pp. 3–25). Hillsdale, NJ: Erlbaum.

Lerner, H. G. (1985). Dianna and Lillie: Can a feminist still like Murray Bowen? *Family Therapy Networker, 9*, 36–39.

Levant, R. F. (1990). Psychoeducational services designed for men: A psychoeducational approach. *Psychotherapy, 27*, 309–315.

Levant, R. F. (1992). Toward the reconstruction of masculinity. *Journal of Family Psychology, 5,* 379–402.

Levant, R. F. (1994). *Masculinity reconstructed: Changing the rules of manhood—at work, in relationships, and in family life.* New York: NAL/Dutton.

Levant, R. F. (1995). Toward the reconstruction of masculinity. In R. F. Levant & W. S. Pollack (Eds.), *A new psychology of men* (pp. 229–251). New York: Basic Books.

Levant, R. F., & Brooks, G. R. (Eds.). (1997). *Men and sex: New psychological perspectives.* New York: Wiley.

LeVay, S. (1993). *The sexual brain.* Cambridge, MA: MIT Press.

Liddle, H. A., Breunlin, D. C., & Schwartz, R. C. (1988). *Handbook of family therapy training and supervision.* New York: Guilford Press.

Liebow, E. (1980). Men and jobs. In E. H. Pleck & J. H. Pleck (Eds.), *The American man* (pp. 365–376). Englewood Cliffs, NJ: Prentice Hall.

Lips, H. M. (1989). Gender role socialization: Lessons in femininity. In J. Freeman (Ed.), *Women: A feminist perspective.* Mountain View, CA: Mayfield.

Lisak, D. (1997). Male gender socialization and the perpetration of sexual abuse. In R. F. Levant & G. R. Brooks (Eds.), *Men and sex: New psychological perspectives* (pp. 156–180). New York: Wiley.

Long, D. (1987). Working with men who batter. In M. Scher, M. Stevens, G. Good, & G. Eichenfield (Eds.), *Handbook of counseling and psychotherapy with men* (pp. 305–320). Thousand Oaks, CA: Sage.

Lusterman, D.-D. (1989). Empathic interviewing. *Men and women relating: The carrot or the stick?* Symposium presented at the Annual Conference of the American Association of Marriage and Family Therapy, San Francisco.

Lynn, D. B. (1966). The process of learning parental and sex-role identification. *Journal of Marriage and the Family, 28,* 466–470.

Maccoby, E. E. (1990). Gender and relationships: A developmental account. *American Psychologist, 45,* 513–520.

Majors, R., & Billson, J. M. (1992). *Cool pose: The dilemmas of black manhood in America.* San Francisco: New Lexington Press.

Marin, P. (1991, July 8). Born to lose: The prejudice against men. *Nation,* pp. 46–51.

McGill, M. E. (1985). *The McGill report on male intimacy.* Austin, TX: Holt, Rinehart and Winston.

McLean, C. The politics of men's pain. (1996). In C. McLean, M. Carey, & C. White (Eds.), *Men's ways of being* (pp. 11–28). Boulder, CO: Westview Press.

Messner, M. (1992). *Power at play: Sports and the problem of masculinity.* Boston: Beacon Press.

Meth, R. L., & Pasick, R. S. (Eds.). (1990). *Men in therapy: The challenge of change.* New York: Guilford Press.

Michael, R., Gagnon, J., Laumann, E., & Kolata, G. (1994). *Sex in America: A definitive survey.* Boston: Little, Brown.

Miedzian, M. (1991). *Boys will be boys: Breaking the link between masculinity and violence.* New York: Doubleday.

Mintz, L. B., & O'Neil, J. M. (1990). Gender roles, sex, and the process of psychotherapy: Many questions and a few answers. *Journal of Counseling and Development, 68,* 381–387.

Minuchin, S. (1974). *Families and family therapy.* Cambridge, MA: Harvard University Press.

Myers, M. F. (1989). *Men and divorce.* New York: Guilford Press.

Nardi, P. M. (Ed.). (1992). *Men's friendships.* Thousand Oaks, CA: Sage.

Nordstrom, B. (1986). Why men get married: More and less traditional men compared. In R. A. Lewis & R. E. Salt (Eds.), *Men in families* (pp. 31–53). Thousand Oaks, CA: Sage.

Norwood, R. (1985). *Women who love too much: When you keep wishing and hoping he'll change.* Los Angeles: Tarcher.

Nutt, R. (1991). Ethical principles for gender-fair family therapy. *Family Psychologist, 7,* 32–33.

O'Donovan, D. (1988). Femiphobia: Unseen enemy of intellectual freedom. *Men's Studies Review, 5,* 14–16.

Okin, S. M. (1989). *Justice, gender, and the family.* New York: Basic Books.

O'Leary, V. E., & Donahue, J. M. (1978). Latitudes of masculinity: Reactions to sex-role deviance in men. *Journal of Social Issues, 34,* 17–28.

O'Neil, J. M. (1981). Male sex role conflicts, sexism, and masculinity: Psychological implications for men, women, and counseling psychology. *The Counseling Psychologist, 9,* 61–80.

O'Neil, J. M. (1982). Gender-role conflict and strain in men's lives. In K. Solomon & N. B. Levy (Eds.), *Men in transition: Theory and therapy* (pp. 5–44). New York: Plenum.

O'Neil, J. M., & Carroll, M. R. (1988). A gender role workshop focused on sexism, gender role conflict, and the gender role journey. *Journal of Counseling and Development, 67,* 193–197.

O'Neil, J. M., Good, G. E., & Holmes, S. (1995). Fifteen years of theory and research on men's gender role conflict: New paradigms for empirical research. In R. F. Levant & W. S. Pollack (Eds.), *A new psychology of men* (pp. 164–206). New York: Basic Books.

Osherson, S. (1986). *Finding our fathers: The unfinished business of manhood.* New York: Free Press.

Philpot, C. L. (1991). Gender-sensitive couples therapy. *Journal of Family Psychotherapy, 2,* 19–40.

Philpot, C. L., Brooks, G. R., Lusterman, D.-D., & Nutt, R. (1997). *Bridging separate gender worlds.* Washington, DC: American Psychological Association Press.

Pittman, F. (1990). The masculine mystique. *Family Therapy Networker, 14*(3), 40–52.

Pittman, F. (1993). *Man enough: Fathers, sons, and the search for masculinity.* New York: Perigree.

Pleck, E., & Pleck, J. H. (Eds.). (1980). *The American man.* Englewood Cliffs, NJ: Prentice Hall.

Pleck, J. H. (1980). Men's power with women, other men, and society: A men's movement analysis. In E. Pleck & J. H. Pleck (Eds.), *The American man* (pp. 417–433). Englewood Cliffs, NJ: Prentice Hall.

Pleck, J. H. (1981). *The myth of masculinity.* Cambridge, MA: MIT Press.

Pleck, J. H. (1987a). American fathering in historical perspective. In M. S. Kimmel (Ed.), *Changing men: New directions in research on men and masculinity* (pp. 83–97). Thousand Oaks, CA: Sage.

Pleck, J. H. (1987b). The contemporary man. In M. Scher, M. Stevens, G. Good, & G. Eichenfield (Eds.), *Handbook of counseling and psychotherapy with men* (pp. 16–27). Thousand Oaks, CA: Sage.

Pleck, J. H. (1993). Are "family-supportive" employer policies relevant to men? In J. C. Hood (Ed.), *Work, family, and masculinities.* Thousand Oaks, CA: Sage.

Pollack, W. S. (1990). Men's development and psychotherapy: A psychoanalytic perspective. *Psychotherapy, 27,* 316–321.

Real, T. (1997). *I don't want to talk about it: Overcoming the secret legacy of male depression.* New York: Scribner.

Robertson, N. (1988). *Getting better: Inside Alcoholics Anonymous.* New York: Morrow.

Robinson, E. A. (1952). Richard Corey. In F. O. Matthiessen (Ed.), *The Oxford book of American verse* (pp. 469–470). New York: Oxford University Press.

Rotundo, E. A. (1993). *American manhood: Transformations in masculinity from the revolution to the modern era.* New York: Basic Books.

Rubin, L. B. (1976). *Worlds of pain: Life in the working-class family.* New York: Basic Books.

Sabo, D., & Runfola, R. (1980). *Jock: Sports and male identity.* Englewood Cliffs, NJ: Prentice Hall.

Sanchez-Hucles, J. V. (1997). Impact of the environment on families: Urbanicity's unique opportunities and challenges. In M. Harway (Ed.), *Treating the changing family* (pp. 191–218). New York: Wiley.

Sanday, P. R. (1990). *Fraternity gang rape: Sex, brotherhood, and privilege on campus*. New York: New York University Press.

Scher, M. (1990). Effect of gender-role incongruities on men's experience as clients in psychotherapy. *Psychotherapy, 27,* 322–326.

Schofield, W. (1964). *Psychotherapy: The purchase of friendship.* Englewood Cliffs, NJ: Prentice Hall.

Sennett, R., & Cobb, J. (1973). *The hidden injuries of class.* New York: Vintage Books.

Silverberg, R. (1986). *Psychotherapy for men: Transcending the masculine mystique.* Springfield, IL: Thomas.

Silverstein, L. B. (1993). Primate research, family politics, and social policy: Transforming "cads" into "dads." *Journal of Family Psychology, 7,* 267–282.

Silverstein, L. B. (1996). Fathering is a feminist issue. *Psychology of Women Quarterly, 20,* 3–37.

Silverstein, O. (1994). *The courage to raise good men.* New York: Viking Penguin.

Smith, E. (1987). Body-focused psychotherapy with men. In M. Scher, M. Stevens, G. Good, & G. Eichenfield (Eds.), *Handbook of counseling and psychotherapy with men* (pp. 109–118). Thousand Oaks, CA: Sage.

Solomon, K. (1982a). Individual psychotherapy and changing masculine roles: Dimensions of gender-role psychotherapy. In K. Solomon & N. B. Levy (Eds.), *Men in transition: Theory and therapy* (pp. 247–273). New York: Plenum.

Solomon, K. (1982b). The masculine gender role: Description. In K. Solomon & N. B. Levy (Eds.), *Men in transition: Theory and therapy* (pp. 45–76). New York: Plenum.

Stephenson, J. (1991). *Men are not cost-effective.* Napa, CA: Deimer, Smith.

Straus, M. A., & Gelles, R. J. (1990). How violent are American families? Estimates from the National Family Violence Resurvey and other studies. In M. A. Strauss & R. J. Gelles (Eds.), *Physical violence in American families* (pp. 95–132). New Brunswick, NJ: Transaction.

Sue, D. W., & Sue, D. (1990). *Counseling the culturally different: Theory and practice.* New York: Wiley.

Tannen, D. (1990). *You just don't understand: Women and men in conversation.* New York: Morrow.

Task Force on Sex-Bias and Sex-Role Stereotyping in Psychotherapeutic Practice. (1978). Guidelines for psychotherapy with women. *American Psychologist, 33,* 122–123.

Thompson, E. H., Jr., Grisanti, C., & Pleck, J. (1985). Attitudes toward the male role and their correlates. *Sex Roles, 13,* 413–427.

Thompson, E. H., Jr., & Pleck, J. H. (1987). The structure of male role norms. In M. S. Kimmel (Ed.), *Changing men: New directions in research on men and masculinity* (pp. 25–36). Thousand Oaks, CA: Sage.

Tiger, L. (1969). *Men in groups.* New York: Random House.

Tolson, A. (1977). *The limits of masculinity.* London: Tavistock.

Tschann, J. (1988). Self-disclosure in adult friendship: Gender and marital status differences. *Journal of Social and Personal Relationships, 5,* 65–81.

Tyler, F. B., Sussewell, D. R., & Williams-McCoy, J. (1985). Ethnic validity in psychotherapy. *Psychotherapy, 22,* 311–320.

U.S. Bureau of Labor Statistics. (1991). *Labor force statistics derived from the current population survey: A databook.* Washington, DC: U.S. Government Printing Office.

Vessey, J. T., & Howard, K. I. (1993). Who seeks psychotherapy? *Psychotherapy, 30,* 546–553.

Walters, M., Carter, B., Papp, P., & Silverstein, O. (1988). *The invisible web: Gender patterns in family relationships.* New York: Guilford Press.

Ward, S. K., Chapman, K., Cohn, E., & Williams, K. (1991). Acquaintance rape and the college social scene. *Family Relations, 40,* 65–71.

Watzlawick, P., Beavin, J. H., & Jackson, D. D. (1967). *Pragmatics of human communication.* New York: Norton.

Wilkinson, R. (1984). *American tough: The tough-guy tradition and American character.* Westport, CT: Greenwood Press.

Williams, J. (1977). *The psychology of women: Behavior in a biosocial context.* New York: Norton.

Wolfe, T. (1988). *Bonfire of the vanities.* New York: Bantam Books.

Wood, J. T. (1994). *Gendered lives: Communication, gender, and culture.* Belmont, CA: International Thomson.

Wright, P. (1982). Men's friendships, women's friendships, and the alleged inferiority of the latter. *Sex Roles, 8,* 1–20.

Wright, P. H., & Keple, T. W. (1981). Friends and parents of a sample of high school juniors: A exploratory study of relationship intensity and interpersonal rewards. *Journal of Marriage and the Family, 43,* 559–570.

Yalom, I. (1975). *The theory and practice of group psychotherapy.* New York: Basic Books.

Zilbergeld, B. (1978). *Male sexuality.* New York: Bantam.

Zilbergeld, B. (1992). *The new male sexuality: The truth about men, sex, and pleasure.* New York: Bantam Books.

The Author

Gary R. Brooks received his Ph.D. from the University of Texas at Austin in 1976. He currently is chief of psychology service at the Central Texas Veterans' Health Care System in Temple, Texas. He is an associate professor in psychiatry and behavioral sciences with the Texas A&M University Health Sciences Center, adjunct faculty member at Baylor University, and instructor of men's studies with Texas Women's University. He has been president of the Division of Family Psychology of the American Psychological Association, president of the Society for the Psychological Study of Men and Masculinity, and an executive board member of the National Organization of Men Against Sexism (NOMAS). He has written more than thirty articles and book chapters and has authored or coauthored three other books: *The Centerfold Syndrome: How Men Can Overcome Objectification and Achieve Intimacy with Women; Men and Sex: New Psychological Perspectives;* and *Bridging Separate Gender Worlds*. He has traveled nationally to present continuing education workshops on psychotherapy for men. He received the 1996 Distinguished Practitioner Award of the APA Division of Men and Masculinity and the 1997 Texas Distinguished Psychologist Award.

Index